THE SCIENCE OF E

The Economic Teaching of Leon MacLaren

To Christopher
I do hope you
enjoy

Raymond 2013.

THE SCIENCE OF ECONOMICS

The Economic Teaching of Leon MacLaren

RAYMOND MAKEWELL Ed.

For nothing is so productive of elevation of mind as to be able to examine methodically and truly every object which is presented to thee in life, and always to look at things so as to see at the same time what kind of universe this is, and what kind of use everything performs in it, and what value everything has with reference to the whole, and what with reference to man, who is a citizen of the highest city.

Marcus Aurelius

SHEPHEARD-WALWYN (PUBLISHERS) LTD
IN ASSOCIATION WITH
THE SCHOOL OF ECONOMIC SCIENCE, LONDON

First published in 2013 by
Shepheard-Walwyn (Publishers) Ltd
107 Parkway House, Sheen Lane
London SW14 8LS
in association with
The School of Economic Science
11 Mandeville Place
London W1U 3AJ

www.shepheard-walwyn.co.uk and
www.ethicaleconomics.org.uk

British Library Cataloguing in Publication Data
A catalogue record of this book
is available from the British Library

ISBN: 978-0-85683-291-8

Typeset by Alacrity,
Winscombe, Somerset
Printed and bound in the United Kingdom
by Short Run Press Ltd, Exeter

Contents

Acknowledgements

THIS BOOK builds on the work of many people over a long period of time, most of them unknown to me; their work I acknowledge with gratitude. Thanks are due first to Peter Green who was instrumental in the preparation of the original course and who has given invaluable advice on the early drafts of this book. My thanks go also to Clare Goldschmidt who converted the source material into a usable electronic format, to Naomi Smith and Brian Hodgkinson for reviewing the final draft, and Hugh Hanson and Peter Fennell for their assistance with the diagrams, to Anna McClelland who has edited, corrected and refined the text as it has developed, and to Anthony Werner for his advice as publisher. In addition, I should like to thank the Henry George Foundation of Australia for their financial support.

Foreword

JUST OVER seventy-five years ago Leon MacLaren joined with his father and others to found the School of Economic Science in London. The School's purpose was to study natural laws governing relations between men in society and that was why they called economics a science. So far as they were concerned a science is a study of laws that already exist in nature; economics is a human study; and therefore its heart is the study of human nature and its interaction with the natural universe. The essence of their approach was that laws are discovered from the nature of things and are not the product of human will, although there is human scope for adaptation and elaboration – and error.

They drew this vision of economics from the writings of Henry George but declined to be enslaved to his doctrines. Convinced that truth and justice were valid and essential guides in their study, they kept their teachings under constant review and developed an understanding of economic laws, and courses for teaching them, which have profound relevance to the modern world.

When the School was founded in 1937 Britain and the world were struggling to emerge from the worst economic depression in human experience. Poverty was widespread and with it came disease, crime, shattered morale and frustrated lives. Yet still some were able to amass large fortunes while the great majority of people struggled to establish and maintain the most basic living standards. Some corporations and privileged individuals prospered while ordinary people found their wages reduced to a bare minimum amid cut-throat competition from their fellows for every available job. John Maynard Keynes offered an answer with his *General Theory of Employment, Interest and Money* but it actually took a world war to change the situation.

In the ensuing seventy five years the wheel has turned full circle. After the horror of a world war followed by sixty years of relative peace, the world economy is transformed, but still faces the same difficulties. Britain, America, Europe and their trading partners once again struggle to emerge from the deepest recession since the 1930s and that affects the whole global economy. Once again people, especially young people, struggle to find employment; living standards are compromised; morale is low; and John Maynard Keynes' solution of government intervention and subvention is still seen as the answer even though it is obvious that governments cannot afford it. People everywhere cry out for a new understanding of economics while economists, politicians and business moguls insist on re-establishing the old model as quickly as possible. If there is a difference, it is that the economy is now global, the world population is more than twice what it was then, and the disparities, nationally and internationally, between rich and poor are even greater than they were in the 1930s.

So what do truth and justice have to say about this? The first thing is that there is no excuse for it. There is, in truth, no excuse for poverty and justice requires that human beings find the means to eliminate poverty wherever it appears. There are two factors involved. The first is individual human beings. Where people *will* not work and produce wealth for themselves and others, poverty is inevitable. That is, or should be, a matter of personal choice. But the second factor is equally important and compelling and not a matter of individual choice: where economic systems deny people access to all that they need to work and produce wealth for themselves, poverty is equally inevitable and injustice its inseparable companion.

Leon MacLaren set out to discover and expound principles of economics founded in justice in response to the needs of his time, but also to the needs of human beings in all times, including ours. The result was the courses of which this book is a distillation. He was able to expound key principles of economics which, if observed and applied now, can offer a brighter, more secure and more civilised future for the human race living in harmony with each other and the natural world.

The first principle is the simple observation that man is a land animal. From this observation flows the realisation that economics is primarily about the interaction between humanity and the land from which all material wealth is ultimately derived. Therefore the con- ditions under which individuals and businesses have access to land are crucial to economic outcomes. Allow ready access to land and, with corresponding access to necessary capital, people can produce all that they need. Restrict access and those who can command access obtain a huge economic advantage over everyone else. The fundamental economic problem becomes that of allowing ready access to everyone who will make use of it while providing sufficient security of tenure once access is obtained.

The second principle is simple justice – to render to everyone their due. This includes the economic opportunity to create wealth for themselves and their families and the right to the full fruits of their labour. With this comes the observation that economic disparities are caused when people are denied the full fruits of their labour, allowing some to accumulate wealth at the expense of others.

The third principle is that human beings are gregarious and naturally work together to create and share wealth and improve their collective lives. It has long been observed that human beings are much more economically productive when they work together. This offers the prospect of prosperous communities of prosperous individuals which are the just outcome of economic arrangements in harmony with the laws of human nature.

A fourth principle might be called the principle of development. It is based on the unfashionable observation that both the universe and human society are natural hierarchies accommodating level upon level of ability, scope and refinement. The working out of this principle in relation to society and its economic arrangements, as well as to humanity, is perhaps the single most distinctive and important contribution that Leon MacLaren makes to economic thought.

All this is laced with the conviction that all human beings have immense potential to fulfil and that their happiness and well-being turns on the freedom and capacity to fulfil that potential. Economic arrangements can facilitate or hinder human development, but they cannot prevent it except when they deprive people to the extent of condemning them to ignorance and starvation.

Simple principles such as these provide the basis for reviewing and assessing the problems of modern economics. Money and banking, markets and international trade, public revenue and taxation, human development, the role of governments, environmental impacts, can all be assessed and re-assessed in the light of simple principles that point to the potential for human beings, even in their present and expected unprecedented numbers, to live harmoniously with each other and the Earth in freedom, mutual respect and peace.

This book distils Leon MacLaren's thought as he set it out in a series of written courses in the late 1960s with the help of others, most notably Peter Green who was then Principal of the School of Economic Science. It has been brought up to date to demonstrate its continuing relevance and importance. The principles set out here address the social and economic aspects of the human problems of living together in harmony and peace. Leon MacLaren spent much of his life and energy addressing the other aspect, that of the choices individuals make about realising their own potential. Ultimately they are two sides of the same coin. Economics and philosophy stand together to point out ways to human fulfilment. This too is a message for the present time. If there is an urgent need to re-assess our understanding of economics, there is an equally urgent need to re-assess our understanding of ourselves. Leon MacLaren's work and thought can help with both.

IAN MASON
Principal
School of Economic Science
August 2012

Introduction

Who Was Leon MacLaren?

LEON MACLAREN was born on 24 September 1910 in Glasgow and christened Leonardo da Vinci MacLaren. In the course of his eighty-three years, through the courses he developed and taught at the School of Economic Science in London, MacLaren has influenced and continues to influence thousands of people around the world. And yet, he rarely spoke about himself and scant details are available of his personal life.

His father was Andrew MacLaren,[1] a true polymath whose talents, wit and oratorical gift laid the foundation for his son's development in many directions. Convinced that the principles of Henry George offered the way out of the misery and poverty which he had seen around him in Glasgow as he grew up, Andrew began almost before he was out of his teens to campaign fiercely for land and tax reform. In 1922 Andrew MacLaren was elected as a Labour Member of Parliament.

From his father Leon MacLaren inherited a profound knowledge of music and the arts as well as a deep understanding of the laws of nature. One day he asked his mother about the great book which his father frequently consulted when preparing his speeches. So it was that he first came to read Henry George's best-known work, *Progress and Poverty*.

When he was sixteen, sitting by a lake, he had an experience which set the direction for the rest of his life. In his words:

> It became very clear to me that there was such a thing as truth and there was such a thing as justice, and that they could be found and, being found, could be taught. It seemed to me that that was the most valuable thing that one could pursue. So I resolved to pursue this when I was twenty-one.[2]

1 See John Stewart, *Standing for Justice: A Biography of Andrew MacLaren MP*.
2 Brian Hodgkinson, *In Search of Truth*.

1

True to his resolution, in 1931 amidst the turmoil of the severe economic depression, MacLaren joined with a dozen or so young enthusiasts for the movement to promote land value taxation and they began to give free lectures on economic justice. As the lectures progressed it became apparent that the terms used in Economics lacked clarity and consistency and led to confusion. He decided as a result to set up a school to enquire into truth and justice, though as yet he had little idea what form such a school should take, apart from a notion that it should be Socratic in method.

Begun in 1937 with the help of his father, the Henry George School of Economics initially met in a Parliamentary committee room. A year later the first public evening classes were offered. By 1939 some three hundred people were studying the economics material he had written.

To support himself MacLaren studied law and in 1938 he was called to the Bar at the Inner Temple. The following year he was nominated to stand for Parliament against no less a person than Winston Churchill. Perhaps happily for the future of the School, when war was declared the election was cancelled.

As war began some members of the School joined the armed forces and for a time no classes were held. He himself was exempted from military service on medical grounds and undertook civil duties. The Blitz in 1940 prevented any reopening but soon afterwards evenings were booked in a restaurant and the classes widely advertised. MacLaren described how students bravely walked to and from the meetings along streets lit only by the flames of burning buildings.

Despite the hazards of wartime, serious work continued in order to understand Economics and develop the teaching material. It was decided to offer a correspondence course. The course they developed analysed in depth the theories of the classical economists, among them Locke, the French physiocrats, Adam Smith and Ricardo, and debunked the 19th century wage fund theory and the doctrine of Malthus. The School's aim was to eliminate misconceived economic ideas generally prevalent in society, such as the idea that capital employs labour (implying that employment and output rest primarily on the availability of capital); and that natural resources, or land, are scarce, severely limiting the production and distribution of wealth.

The School taught by contrast that land and labour are the primary factors of production, that were these both free to cooperate fully there would be no scarcity, and that capital defined accurately as 'wealth employed to produce more wealth' is the product and servant of labour.

This approach also highlighted shortcomings in the teaching of Henry George. In 1942 the name Henry George was dropped and the School became 'The School of Economic Science', the word 'science' signalling the belief in the existence of natural laws of Economics and a method of direct observation free from personal opinion and vested interest.

During the last years of the war finances were strained to the limit and student numbers fell. MacLaren responded by writing a textbook, *Nature of Society*, presenting a concise account of the distinctive principles of Economics developed by the School to date. First it offers a systematic account of the principles relating to rent, wages, capital, credit, money and taxation. The book gives a central place to the relation of the individual to the community, the very purpose of the latter being to allow full scope to the inherent qualities of every man and woman. Freely available, marginal land and fair taxation release the creative talents of those who work.

The book also takes a major step in presenting a correction of the view that interest is a natural return on capital, showing instead that it is simply a charge made for a loan of money:

> Clearly, the power of the lender to command interest has nothing to do with the use to which the loan is put. Whether the borrower uses it to build a factory or acquire a dwelling house, whether he spends it on tools of his trade or gambling on horses, will make no difference... The coupling of interest with capital has been an unfortunate error prolific in its progeny of falsehoods. It arises from confusing the power to exact payment for loans with the use to which some of the loans are put... It gives to the idea of a loan a quality it should not possess, a suggestion of productiveness and of social benefit, obscuring the indebtedness and dependence which the loan so plainly advertises.[3]

Marking a definite break with Georgist doctrines, this view implies that capital as wealth used in the production of further wealth, is not a factor of production in itself, but is merely stored-up labour and land. The elaboration of the understanding of capitalism and in particular of the limited liability company which follows, thoroughly undermines the generally accepted view of capitalist economies.

Although much of the *Nature of Society* was based on course material which MacLaren had himself written, as it approached completion he found himself unable to write a conclusion.

3 Leon MacLaren, *Nature of Society and Other Essays*, page 45.

3

At this crucial moment he chanced to meet Peter Goffin, author of a book called *The Realm of Art*, a wide-ranging survey of ideas about the nature of humanity, society, art, science, religion, evolution, creativity and free will. It also discussed aspects of philosophy: reality, mind and matter, knowledge, and most importantly for the way in which the School was to develop, consciousness. The book was full of quotations from many eastern and western sources. Several of this great pot-pourri of ideas accorded particularly with MacLaren's search at that time: the emphasis on Man's potential for growth and creativity; the concept of human nature being rooted in love and harmony; the evaluation of eastern ideas; or simply the centrality of consciousness.

The impetus given by this encounter was the inspiration needed to write the final chapter of the book. Entitled 'The Law of Human Progress', it began with the following sentence: 'The purpose of being born is to live and of living, to live more abundantly.' The concluding sentences pointed in the direction of future philosophical enquiry, which may have surprised students of Economics, but was to enrich greatly the life of the School and in so doing to deepen the study of Economics:

> Though a society is at war with itself, the retrogression may be arrested and the conditions of progress restored if the members of the community will use their natural powers to understand their predicament, to discover in what elemental respects they are denying their own nature. There has been of late a welcome flowering of philosophical thought, drawing its inspiration largely from those old eastern civilizations which gained such deep understanding in the subjective mode, and, if this prospers, it may enrich and balance the intensely objective knowledge of the natural sciences.[4]

A successful series of lectures on Philosophy given by Peter Goffin at MacLaren's invitation made it clear that from the level of natural law the School must now inevitably move on to investigate human nature itself, asking questions about mind, spirit and existence: from the study of Man in society to the study of Man himself. In August 1944 the constitution of the School was amended to reflect this development. The new primary objective became:

> To promote the study of the natural laws governing the relations between men in society and all other matters ancillary thereto.[5]

4 *Ibid*, page 169.
5 Brian Hodgkinson, *In Search of Truth*.

4

In accordance with the School's principle of 'learn and teach', as understanding developed so the courses evolved and increased until by the 1960s the Economics curriculum consisted of nine terms of ten weeks each. Rather than seeing Economics as an isolated field of enquiry, the course had become a study of human beings and their economic customs and practices. It included a view of the whole of society, justice, ethics, politics and history, as well as the production and distribution of wealth, expanding the students' viewpoint and revealing the underlying law and harmony in human affairs.

Leon MacLaren died on 24 June 1994 in his eighty-fourth year. The School he founded continues to flourish and to expand its fields of study.

Leon MacLaren's Economics

This book is based on the last Economics course in the preparation of which Mr MacLaren was directly concerned. It was delivered over three years of three terms each, commencing in 1966. The Introduction to this course begins:

> Our subject is Economics. Through this study we shall aim to discover the natural laws which govern the relations between men in society, and the laws, customs and practices by which communities are governed.
>
> We shall see that this is a vast and noble subject. There is nothing petty about Economics. If it begins to appear petty then we have lost our way in a fog of detail and it is time to step back and widen our view.
>
> In the course of our studies we shall need to consider trade, money, taxes, interest, rating and so on. But let us never forget that these should be the servants of society and not its masters. Economics is primarily about men and women and communities – not interest rates, foreign exchange and limited liability companies.
>
> We must also realise that, without understanding, theories are useless in Economics: they can lead us a terrible dance. How then are we to work? We must learn to rely on observation and reason. When we have begun to see for ourselves and to get back to original causes, then we can use theories to help us to formulate the economic laws.
>
> Now observation should be simple for us, for Economics is a study of Mankind. This being so, the evidence we need is all around us. Why then is the understanding of Economics so elusive? Why does it attract so much mystique and so much controversy? We shall discover this for ourselves all too soon. Since childhood we have been subjected to other people's ideas, theories and prejudices. First from our parents, then school teachers, professors, friends and those with whom we work.

Even more have we been exposed to the claims, dogmas and prejudices of politicians and the media. In self-defence we have built up our own body of opinions – probably without realising it. Now, as we try to look afresh at the world around us, we shall find these opinions rushing in to colour what we see. A very special effort is required to set all this aside and to see objectively. This is the only way to study Economics, but if we can master this art we shall find it boundlessly rewarding.

MacLaren's definition of Economics is to be found in the first paragraph above, and in the objectives of the school he founded. These he expressed as 'The study of the natural laws which govern the relationships between men in society', to which he appended in his book 'principally as these relate to the creation and distribution of wealth'.

He noted also that 'The purpose of society is that, by cooperation men may grow in skill, happiness and knowledge, thus leading to prosperity in every sense.' These, he suggests, are the foundations for the study of economics: ignorance, poverty and misery – embodying injustice – the alternative. MacLaren put it simply in a lecture in 1951, 'Some men work to maintain others who labour not. That is unjust.'[6]

The definition quoted above is the beginning of a number of significant departures from modern academic Economics. Its focus is to uncover root causes rather than to explore statistical inferences, and the reference point is not men and women as consumers but as noble, free and independent beings.

The 1966 course refers frequently to 'master-men', a concept that has gone almost completely out of mind and requires some explanation. In the English tradition, a master-man was one who fully supported himself and his dependents by his own means, having achieved a recognised degree of skill or experience in his trade or profession.[7] Such a man would in today's terms operate his own business and not be beholden to another for a job. The position implies personal pride, dignity, strength of character and integrity. A master-man enjoyed an independence and freedom not enjoyed by those whom he employed. The term does not imply any hierarchy of professional work.

The alternative to supporting oneself as a master is to be an employee, which, although the term is unfashionable today, is to be a servant.[8] The vast majority of the population today are servants

6 Leon MacLaren, *Justice*.
7 To the extent that to be offered support from the state, such as free education, would be regarded as an indignity.
8 Although dictionaries distinguish a 'master' from a 'journeyman' or one who is learning the trade or profession.

even if they have responsibility for others in the organisations they serve.

English-speaking peoples, he pointed out, pride themselves on their freedom and the civil law enforces this. But anyone who can lose their livelihood at short notice is hardly free. Economic policies that merely encourage employment and support the poor diminish the prospect of individuals finding a fulfilling life.

To discover the conditions which allow every individual to find a fulfilling life is, he considered, the true goal of Economics.

This Book

The 1966 Economics course was prepared for a London audience. The subject matter of the course was illuminated with examples which would have been familiar to that audience.

This book aims to present the principles and themes of that course to a contemporary audience throughout the English-speaking world, where the forces of language, law, religion, government, customs, and public institutions are all essentially the same. As will become evident, these forces play a major part in our economic life. To accommodate this wider audience, examples and statistics have been drawn from all these countries, but the structure and text here broadly follow the original material. There is inevitably some repetition as the subject matter is considered from different perspectives.

Section 1 deals with first principles, and provides the basis for all subsequent discussion. It considers the foundations from which we can begin to view economic activity and the natural laws that govern the creation and distribution of wealth (Chapters 1 to 3).

Chapter 4 introduces the additional forces operating on top of these foundations in the capitalist economic system. Chapters 5 to 7 return to first principles, dealing with the factors that make exchange possible. These include value, price, credit and money. Understanding what these are and how they operate has engaged philosophers and economists for millennia. Leon MacLaren's approach is to start afresh, beginning with observation of how the factors come into play. The result is a clarity that is wanting in much economic thought. Some of the examples have been modified but the thrust of the text follows the course material.

Throughout Section 1 historical and contemporary examples are used to illustrate first principles. In Section 2 (Chapters 8 to 14) the situation is reversed and first principles are used to explain the major phenomena of the capitalist system, particularly as they manifest in the English-speaking world. These include money, banking and inflation; how production is organised; international trade and finance; economic cycles; and taxation. A description of the historical development of some of these systems is given to show how the forms, as they appear today, have evolved.

Much has changed over the fifty years since the course was prepared, and modifications have been required to bring this section into the 21st century. At that time it was generally accepted that economic cycles had been eliminated, the banking system operated in a manner closer to its traditional roots, and currencies were fixed against the American dollar (and in turn against gold). International trade and specialisation have advanced rapidly. I have extrapolated from the course material to deal with these changes as I envisage MacLaren would have responded. This applies especially to the chapter on banking. The history of the concept of limited liability in Chapter 11 has been adapted from a later version of the course to fill an obvious gap.

A further change is that the volume of statistical information available has increased enormously, especially data covering long periods of time. This information makes many of the original arguments more compelling.

Section 3 starts to consider broader issues. Chapter 15 examines land tenure in Anglo-Saxon times and the duties associated with occupation of land, and traces how these duties have gradually been eroded over time, until today we accept absolute ownership of land without any concomitant duties. This leads in Chapter 16 to a consideration of private property: the differences between private property in what is produced, and private property in what is given by nature.

Chapter 17 looks at the natural roles of government: law and justice. Following Justinian's definition, justice is served by each person carrying out his or her duties. These duties have first to be discovered. In the civil sphere we find that they are recognised and are largely followed. But in the economic sphere this is not the case.

Chapter 18 moves on to consider the economic duties, both of individuals and of the whole community.

Section 4 (Chapters 19 and 20) considers society as a whole, examining the forces that govern and direct it at different levels with differing degrees of power and influence. Here Economics is given a place within nations, nations within cultures, cultures within civilisations, and civilisations within Mankind as a whole.

SECTION I

First Principles

The principles that guide us, in public and in private, as they are not of our devising, but moulded into the nature and the essence of things, will endure with the sun and the moon — long, very long after Whig and Tory, Stuart and Brunswick, and all such miserable bubbles and playthings of the hour, are vanished from existence and from memory.[1]

EDMUND BURKE
(as quoted in the *Nature of Society*)

---

1 Draft letter to Bishop of Chester, 1771, *Correspondence*, 1 pp332-3. Note: Whig, Tory, Stuart and Brunswick were the political parties of the time.

CHAPTER I

Preliminaries

HUMAN BEINGS live in the natural world, transforming it to create what they want and the conditions in which they want to live. For practical purposes the natural world is the dry surface of the earth, the transformation is production (work) and the result wealth (the product of work).

These then are the primary factors – human beings, land and work – underlying all Economics, the study of which transcends any particular economic or political system.

The intent here is to keep the picture very large, to include all generations, past, present and future. We inherit the wealth of our forebears and bequeath to our children the product of this generation.

We are social creatures and live in communities. The community by its existence provides for an individual's development and support. A community requires a location on the dry surface of the planet. The proximity of the community as a whole to any place where people work dictates how much support the community provides towards an individual's productive efforts on that site. The variations in productiveness can be vast.

In this chapter the comparative advantage one site has over another is expressed in terms of money, but whenever wealth is mentioned, we are referring to goods and services produced, not money.

Throughout this book production includes both goods and services.

1.1 Humanity

To discover the natural laws we must examine the nature of the different factors in our study. Let us start with men and women. All men and women have needs: the basic needs for existence and the secondary needs for a full life.

Basic Needs

The basic requirements for human life are air, water, food, warmth, shelter and the capacity to have children.[1]

The fundamental needs arise from human nature and are major factors in shaping society. As society evolves the needs become refined. Air may be scented, water brewed with tea or coffee or distilled into whisky. Food may be blended with herbs and spices; clothes become subject to taste and fashion. Shelter may also be large, ornate and spacious or small, simple and cosy. The responses to fundamental needs are adapted in different ways according to times and places.

Secondary Needs

To fulfil only these basic needs would provide a bleak and unsatisfying existence. From our nature arise also the needs for mental, emotional and spiritual development through education, entertainment, sport, philosophy, religion and all the arts and sciences.

People work to meet both basic and secondary needs for themselves and their dependants. Parents who do not work hard to care for their children are considered unnatural; men and women exert themselves for their hobbies and sports; many artists work hard to produce paintings they cannot sell; and poets compose sonnets no one wants to hear.

All individuals have talents in greater or lesser degree, but only through development and use can talents be realised. A fine baritone voice is of no use if its possessor does not sing, and if he stops singing his voice will deteriorate. A concert pianist must practise every day, lawyers and doctors cannot afford to neglect their vocations for very long. Talents must be used constantly if they are to flower fully, and this involves work.

When people work they do not only consider the reward. Indeed if someone is engaged on work for which they are naturally suited and which uses their creative powers, the difficulty can often be to stop them working.

It is in human nature to work.[2] When we see a young child copy the grown-ups there can be no doubt that to work is natural. Only by

1 Whilst having children may be a lifestyle choice for individuals or couples, it is necessary from the larger point of view of the planet, the human race and the nation.
2 One writer put it: 'Man does not merely like to work, his happiness is absolutely dependent on it. He needs an outlet for his energies; he needs to join with other men for mutual stimulation in productive companionship. These are overpowering needs, and a man faces virtual destruction if they cannot be met. He may find this or that substitute, this or that ▶

12

work are people able to develop their full potential. And by the fruits of their work they are also able to satisfy their desires, more or less fully, as the case may be. The incentive to work appears to come from within, for both their appetites and their powers give quality and drive to what men and women do. In short, it seems that everyone works to live, and that living has a different meaning for each. Perhaps the strong compulsion to work within us all is nothing less than a manifestation of the will to live.

If, however, people are forced into work which is not to their liking, and are prevented from pursuing work which uses their natural talents and aptitudes, their will to work may be weakened. Equally, to be able to enjoy the fruits of another's labour with no effort of one's own may also weaken the will to work.

The study of Economics cannot be limited to the present time and place; its sphere of study is no less than the whole human race. The attainments of each generation would be impossible without the heritage and tradition that have been built up in the past. The discoveries of one generation become accepted as commonplace in the next and are the platform for further progress. As in an individual, so in society: learning and skill are built up slowly and used to meet the necessities of the day.

Modern life and Economics are determined by the work of the whole human race. Today there is a permanently occupied colony in outer space (the International Space Station). It is easy to see this as the achievement of the present generation. But is it? So much has been provided by past generations: the study of aero-dynamics originating with the sailing boat; the study of metallurgy and the production of other materials from the Iron Age; the study of astronomy from the times when it was used to foretell the future to the current measurement of distances by radio telescopes; the study of mathematics from the time of Pythagoras and the ancient Egyptians. The list is endless – it is clearly not the work of one generation.

Civilisations and cultures may come and go but their influence carries forward. Discoveries have been accumulated over countless generations.

---

2 *contd*:

palliative; but not for long. To be without work – which is not the same as being without employment – is slow death, just like being without food, only slower. The human stage, therefore, is set for the creation of wealth, inasmuch as wealth presupposes Man's work, and work is what Man needs for his happiness even more than he needs wealth.' E.F. Schumacher in *The Liberation of Work*.

Great historical changes are closely related to the work of mankind. For instance, the changes from hunting to pastoral and agricultural communities; from nomadic to settled; from agrarian to industrial; from handwork to mechanical power. Within these eras are great cycles in which human achievement, energy and prosperity rise and fall – a vast movement of constant change that encompasses and over-shadows all.

1.2 The World in Which We Live

Human life depends on air, water, sunshine, food, clothing, shelter. These all arise from the great cycles in nature which are in turn governed by cycles in the solar system, and from the orbits of the earth around the sun upon which the seasons depend.

Our water comes from the cycles that convert sea-water to vapour in clouds, clouds to rain, leading to the formation of rivers from which we extract water for drinking, hygiene and irrigation.

Food comes from the life about us – generally from freshly killed or harvested animal or plant life. Animals depend on plants, which in turn find nourishment in the soil. The soil depends on moisture, sunshine, humus, bacteria and other life forms. All depend on the cycles of night and day, the fluctuations of the tides and the seasons bringing rain and sun to enable life and growth.

Humanity is an inseparable part of the whole universe on which it is utterly dependent for the means of life.

Our habitat is land, the dry surface of the earth. Land is essential for our very existence. Without land no house can be built. The sailor must return to dry land to maintain the ship. Even the astronaut and miner must return to the dry surface of the earth. Every one of us must have land on which to work; a farmer needs several hectares to provide a living, a factory worker only a few square metres, a clerk still less.[3] Children need land for their schools and for exercise and play. Land is needed for entertainment, sport and even for study. Whatever the activity, it cannot take place without some measure of land.

Roads, railways, buildings and all that they contain, machinery, cars, power stations, base stations for mobile phones, the entire man-made world, all occupy land and originate from work on land. There are no

---

3 Especially in terms of ground space where office workers are accommodated in multi-storey buildings.

exceptions. Coal mined from the depths of the earth must pass through the pithead; oil drilled from under the sea must be piped to dry land and stored there until required. All the above may be shown diagrammatically. Diagram 1 shows the whole fundamental framework of this study. The detail will be filled in gradually, but it will always be relative to this, for the framework is dictated by the unchanging nature of Man and the universe.

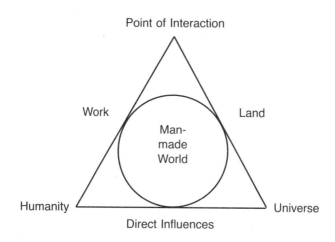

Diagram 1 – The Factors of Production

1.3 The Point of Interaction

The third point on this triangle is labelled the 'point of interaction'. It has been suggested that the man-made world arises from work on land by the whole human race using the materials made available in the universe. But the form of the man-made world depends upon the conditions under which work and land are joined.

The full significance of this third point will be developed later. For the moment a simple analogy may serve to illustrate it. Imagine a coffee shop in the financial centre of almost any major city at lunchtime on a business day. Then imagine the same coffee shop at the weekend. Clearly the trading results would not be the same even though the same land and effort are applied. The varying factor is the conditions where work and land are joined, the point of interaction.

To take another example: until 1989 the city of Berlin was divided into two quite divorced communities very different from one another.

There was little difference in the land on which each was situated – they had been one entity a few years before. The people on each side had the same background, often they were from the same families. They were all capable of the same work. But the conditions where the work took place had changed markedly.

Similarly Athens and Sparta,[4] two Greek city states, were from the same historical period and close geographically, but the Athenians and the Spartans led utterly different lives and left behind them a very different heritage. They were the same race, at the same time, working on similar land. The differences were in the political systems, which changed the conditions where work and land met – at the point of interaction.

These illustrations may give some sense of the third point in the diagram. At the point of interaction is felt the influence of the laws and customs of the community and of its opinions and beliefs, which may advance or hinder its natural purpose. Conditions of slavery hindered the natural direction of the community, as did racism in Nazi Germany, apartheid in South Africa, or the extreme taxation in France before the Revolution of 1789.

The system of land tenure affects the conditions in which land and labour meet. People cannot make anything without land, and once they have made something, it cannot be stored without land. If anyone is to keep what they produce, they must have control of the land on which it is produced and stored.

If someone takes a 99-year lease of land and builds a house on it, at the end of 99 years their successor loses the land and loses the house. A shopkeeper turned out at the end of a lease will lose his customers. A farmer may be prevented from farming, and thus denied the benefit of crops sown and improvements made, by the power of a landowner to terminate a lease.[5]

To receive rent for land requires a title to the land and the title has to be recognised by law or custom. Clearly the laws and customs relating to land tenure affect the conditions in which land and labour meet. They have an effect on the man-made world, working to the advantage or disadvantage of the community.

4 Rivals for hundreds of years until the Roman occupation of Greece in 146BC.
5 99-year leases tend to be more common in the United Kingdom than in other parts of the English-speaking world. Many countries have legistlation to provide some protection for the tenant when the lease expires.

1.4 Man in Society

Man is naturally gregarious and turns to others for company and for protection against common danger. The community also brings the advantages of both combined labour and specialisation. If one man had to be his own huntsman, farmer, builder, joiner, tailor and cook his standard of living would be very low indeed. No wonder Robinson Crusoe was so pleased to meet Man Friday!

We first meet specialisation within the family, where traditionally the man was the breadwinner while the wife cared for the home and children. But for the breadwinner specialisation is almost endless. A bricklayer may spend the entire working day laying perhaps hundreds of bricks. In return the whole family benefit from the labour of others, obtaining food, enjoying a roof over their heads and clothes on their backs. They can turn on the water tap, switch on the light, ride on the buses and trains, have the children educated, receive medical attention when needed, turn on the television and get the latest news from the Internet. Think for a moment of the specialisation involved to provide all this.

Can the sole purpose of specialisation be to provide a high standard of living, often at the cost of giving men and women repetitive jobs in mass production? Is it not more important that specialisation should enable people to use their particular talents to the full? In this way individuals will grow toward their full potential whilst the community reaps the benefit of their particular gifts. One of the primary functions of a community is to set its members free from the strictures of necessity, to give them scope to be themselves and to follow occupations of their own choice in which they may grow to full stature in sensibility, skill, understanding and achievement.

Consideration of communities must not be limited by personal experience. There have been countless communities through the ages. There are many communities in the world today each more or less dependent upon the others. Each has its own possibilities, its own problems. Each plays a unique role in establishing the conditions at the point of interaction where work and land are joined. Consider the adverse effects of slavery, or colour bar, of religious or political persecution, of harsh taxation or an inequitable system of land tenure. If instead, these conditions are based on a knowledge of what is natural and lawful, then the community will truly serve its members and allow them to fulfil their potential. But insofar as the conditions are based on fallacious ideas or selfishness, to that extent will the community fail in its true purpose and its members suffer accordingly.

Chapter 17 will look more closely at the man-made laws, customs and practices by which communities are governed.

1.5 Production

Production may be usefully represented as a cycle, as in Diagram 2. The cycle of production starts with natural resources and ends with consumption of the product. The diagram shows the principal steps in the cycle. The value of this diagram is that it integrates the various aspects of production rather than breaking them down into component parts.

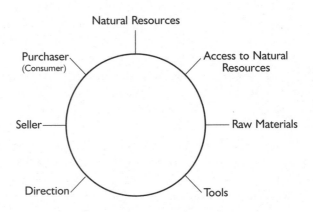

Diagram 2 – The Cycle of Production

To begin at the beginning: so far as mankind is concerned, the universe is given; it is there. **Natural resources** are part of the universe. But the transformation from nature to a resource requires work: work to gain knowledge, work to turn this knowledge to use, and work to acquire the necessary skills. As knowledge and skills increase so natural resources grow. Even today it is clear that only a tiny part of the powers of nature is available to man. Examples of natural resources include:

- Farming – the result of discovering how to till the soil. In the Paleolithic Age there was no cultivation and the fertility of the soil was not a natural resource;

- Uranium – which has always been available below the surface of the earth, was not a natural resource until the knowledge of how to extract and use it became available. This knowledge was gained by work in the form of research and study;[6]
- Iron – was not known as a natural resource before the Iron Age;
- Electricity – was known for many years but became available as a natural resource only during the 20th century.

Minerals are in the ground and once the knowledge and skill to mine them exist, work is necessary to explore and prospect, climb mountains, clear jungles, bore trial holes and sink shafts, to gain **access to natural resources.**

Raw materials are the natural resources of the universe brought to people to work upon. The difference between natural resources and raw materials is one of movement, and the motivating force is human labour. Coal in a coal seam is a natural resource. Coal at the steel works is a raw material.

People need **tools** in order to use their skills to the best advantage. A bricklayer is of no use without a trowel nor a pianist without a piano. A metal worker needs a lathe, a motor to drive it and a workshop to house it. These are all tools. A well-equipped factory, a lorry, a goods train, a brick kiln, a cooling tower, a power station, an office block, a telephone, and a computer are all tools when used for production.[7]

Production entails a change of form of raw materials using tools. This requires **direction**. By this is meant direction in the practical sense of that given, for example, by a production manager. It requires knowledge of the raw materials, and of tools in the fullest sense. It has much to do with quality and efficiency. Management is required throughout production but this is rather different. The primary function at this point in the cycle is to direct the transformation of raw materials into a finished form. This is not its only function but it is sufficient for the present.

Things are normally made to be sold. The next step in the production process is the **seller** who sells the goods to a consumer. The seller may be the manufacturer or a retailer who anticipates the final desires of the consumer.

6 Some are now considering that 'thorium' may replace uranium as a cleaner, more abundant and less politically sensitive fuel. This requires new knowledge in the form of research and study (see *The Economist*, 10th December 2009).

7 Tools may be thought of as capital as long as it does not become confused with money (money will be introduced in Chapter 7). Although some tools can be of a general nature, others are quite specific and especially relevant to specialisation.

To sell the goods there must be someone who wants them and will pay for them. This is the **purchaser**. Without a purchaser production would be pointless and could never even start. Many may dream of having a Ferrari or a Rolex but few can afford them.

In a modern community there may be specialists at each step, often many. Very few producers complete more than one or two steps in the cycle. Even vast chemical companies do not generally produce their own raw materials or sell their products to the final consumer. At each stage there is specialisation: the research chemist, the prospector, the miner, the toolmaker, the organisation and methods adviser, the market researcher, the advertiser and the retailer.

However, the important thing to grasp is not the breakdown of production into its components, but rather the way in which all the diverse aspects interlock. By doing so, they take their part in a cycle that covers the whole of production from natural resources through to the final consumer. Indeed, at the true completion of the cycle, the product, whatever it may be, returns to the earth to take a new place in the universe from where it may one day again become available as a natural resource. These days there is a huge industry in waste disposal, which assists this process or extracts raw materials directly from the waste.

At each point labour is needed. So also is land.

Natural resources may come from anywhere in the universe and not only from dry land, but access to them always requires land. Land is needed for a quarry, a fishing harbour, or a uranium mine. It is needed for a water supply, to pasture animals or to benefit from the fertility of the soil. Wireless internet connections do not obviate the need for land. The user still needs a chair and table on which to work effectively and more particularly space to situate them.

Land is needed for the storage of **raw materials** and for their transport to the place where they are wanted. Land is required for people to work with the humblest of hand tools and more for their factories, power stations and office blocks.[8]

For **direction** very little land is required but it is still necessary.[9]

---

8 Even though an office block does not on the face of it require much land 'per person', it can only be useful if there exists a power station to provide electricity, a dam and catchment to provide water, and land around it for roads and recreation. The amount of land used is greater than at first appears even when used efficiently.

9 For instance when a large office block is being built temporary offices are often set up adjacent to the site to direct construction.

The **seller** certainly needs land in abundance. Consider the number of retail shops and shopping malls.

The **purchaser** is a special case to be considered separately.

The conditions at the point of interaction where land and labour meet (Diagram 1) strongly influence the man-made world. Another look at the cycle illustrates this.

Access to natural resources is often controlled by a landowner. Before a mine can be started, land for a pithead must be bought or leased, as well as securing the rights to the minerals under this or the adjoining land.

The same applies to drilling for oil. In Texas and in the countries of the Middle East the mineral rights are being enjoyed by the land-owners and rulers. The result is the oil billionaires of the USA, and some Arab sheiks and princes, who previously lived in lands of great poverty but now travel the world with retinues that would shame King Solomon. On the other hand in Alberta, Canada, the mineral rights are vested in the Crown, and in Alaska mineral rights are vested in the State. In both cases royalties go to the community and this has resulted in the development of roads, schools and hospitals of a high standard.

The industrial revolution brought a great increase in the importance of **tools**, largely replacing handwork by machinery. Industry has become more and more mechanised as sophisticated machines carry out operations that previously required large numbers of workers. This has resulted in large movements of labour as workers become redundant in one industry and another expands to offer them work. Seen on a national scale, the land and work are unchanged but the change at the point of interaction has wide repercussions. These include both a rise in the standard of living and the problems of redundancy, unemployment and depressed areas.

For the **seller**, advertising has critical effects on sales, boosting branded goods and mass production at the expense of small producers and small retailers, with consequences which affect the whole community, particularly in villages and small towns.

Finally, in considering the **purchaser** we come to one of the greatest tragedies of the modern world. A great proportion of the earth's population is living on the breadline or at starvation level,[10] whilst for many years industries could not sell their produce because of so-called over-production. In parts of the world, to sustain market prices at

10 850 million people were undernourished 2006-08. See Food and Agricultural Organisation of the UN, *State of Food Insecurity in the World*, 2011.

a level which will give the small farmer a living, there are quotas on agricultural production, stock piling and burning of excess crops. All this is done because there is no purchaser, not because no one wants the products, but because those who want them cannot pay for them.

During the potato famines in Ireland in the 19th century, peasants died from starvation while their wheat, barley, butter and meat were being exported. The real cause of the trouble was not the failure of the potato crop but the peasants' poverty, which prevented them from buying the foodstuffs produced in their own country.[11]

If the conditions at the point of interaction are based on knowledge of natural law, the community will truly serve its members and bring them toward fulfilment of their potential. If these conditions are based on ignorance, the community will fail in its true purpose and its members will suffer accordingly.

1.6 Community

What is meant by community? If one looks at the way in which the human race is organised a hierarchy is evident. This hierarchy stretches back beyond recorded history and dominates human activity. It may be represented diagrammatically as shown in Diagram 3.

It is evident at once that the human race has contained numerous civilisations and that each civilisation has contained a number of cultures. For example, the Christian civilisation has included the medieval culture with its cathedrals and castles and the scientific culture with its aeroplanes and computers.

Within a single culture nations rise and fall, their capital cities flourishing and decaying with them. Nations seem to be the basic unit of human organisation. The capital cities are the nerve centres.[12] In these cities population is dense and every major activity in the nation is represented. They are the natural meeting places of the nation.

Next in size and importance are the great ports and commercial centres. In the United States they include New York, Chicago, Los Angeles and San Francisco; in the United Kingdom Glasgow, Liverpool, Manchester and Birmingham; in continental Europe,

11 The potato blight affected other European countries, but only led to famine in Ireland.
12 The centre of government is frequently divorced from the major city of a nation especially in newer nations. Thus the centre of government in the USA is Washington but the nerve centre is New York; similarly in Australia with Canberra and Sydney. The classic cases here would be London, Paris, Madrid and Tokyo.

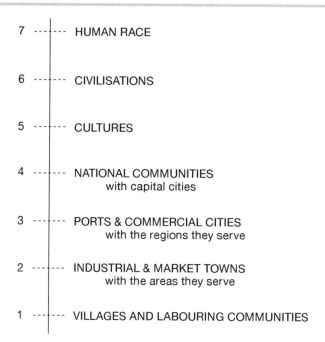

7 ---|--- HUMAN RACE

6 ---|--- CIVILISATIONS

5 ---|--- CULTURES

4 ---|--- NATIONAL COMMUNITIES
              with capital cities

3 ---|--- PORTS & COMMERCIAL CITIES
              with the regions they serve

2 ---|--- INDUSTRIAL & MARKET TOWNS
              with the areas they serve

1 ---|--- VILLAGES AND LABOURING COMMUNITIES

Diagram 3 – The Hierarchy of Society

Rotterdam,[13] Hamburg, Marseilles. They are to the regions what the capital is to the nation.

Smaller centres, the market towns, grow around specific industries and markets, forming a natural focus for the neighbouring areas and facilitating exchange of consumer goods and supplies or services for the industries they support. They provide specialisation and are centres of skill.

Last are small communities centred on villages or on some basic industry like fishing, mining or quarrying.[14] The village looks to the town, the town to the city and all to the capital. The pull exercised by these centres grows with their place in the hierarchy. This pull is one of the major factors in Economics, and needs to be understood.

The hierarchy facilitates specialisation. With trade flowing through the whole nation it is possible for villages to concentrate on agriculture in one area, mining in another, fishing in a third, forestry in a fourth. All these turn to the market towns to sell their produce and

13 Note here that ports and commercial cities can serve regions beyond national boundaries; for instance Rotterdam serves vast areas of the Rhine valley.
14 The 'City' of Broken Hill (see page 28) in Australia, although it has a population of 21,000 exists solely due to the mines in and around it. In this context it is a village.

buy their daily needs. Market towns may also specialise. In the United Kingdom, traditionally Greenock on the River Clyde concentrated on ship-building, Rochdale near Manchester on cotton goods, and Huddersfield in Yorkshire on woollen goods.[15] They in turn looked to the regional centres of Glasgow, Manchester and Bradford from where their goods could be marketed throughout the world. These cities provide all that is especially required for the principal industries of the region, including wholesale markets and full banking and insurance facilities.[16] Together Levels 1, 2 and 3 compose the economic organism which is primarily concerned with the production and distribution of wealth.

Finally, there are the capital cities, the great centres of world trade: London, Tokyo, New York, Singapore. Here are the global commodity markets, the trading and banking houses, the money markets, the stock exchanges, as well as law courts and the seats of government.

This great hierarchy enables the human race to function fully so that at each level the person, village, town, city and nation may develop their native genius to the full to the mutual benefit of all.[17]

1.7 The Significance of Land

Considering land in relation to Diagrams 2 and 3 together, it is clear that just as men have their particular qualities and talents, so different places have their particular qualities and advantages. Land which is ideal for one use may be quite unsuitable for another. The qualities of land which are important to the first two steps of the cycle of production are the presence of natural resources with easy access: for agriculture, fertile land with good drainage but no steep gradients; for mining, mineral-bearing land which can be worked in large seams on or near the surface; for hydro-electric power, fast-flowing rivers in deep valleys which can easily be dammed.

The next step on the cycle is the industrial town. Here are found the raw materials and the tools of industry: factories, railway marshalling yards and shipping container terminals. The special advantages

15 As transport and trade have become more global manufacturing has moved to cheaper locations, especially to the Far East. These towns, like similar specialist towns in the United States (eg Detroit for car manufacture), have lost much of the industry with which they became synonymous, but new areas of specialisation are developing, the best-known example being 'Silicon Valley' in the United States. In many areas public authorities have attempted to attract new industry but many are still vulnerable and looking very depressed.
16 Banking and insurance is likely to be adapted to the needs of the region.
17 The hierarchy is dealt with more extensively in Chapter 19.

needed for land to be suitable for the development of an industrial town are often largely historical. Villages grow up at road junctions, river crossings, on natural harbours, in sheltered valleys, at water supplies. Where conditions are favourable villages may grow into towns, towns into cities.[18] Once established, areas close to transport facilities and labour supply may be most favoured for industry, while central sites will be preferred for markets, shopping and business purposes.

English cotton mills tended to be located in Lancashire because the climate there is humid and the water soft. The raw materials came from America, Egypt (cotton) and Ireland (flax). They were transported through the nearby port of Liverpool and, once the ship canal was completed in 1894, through the port of Manchester. Other industries were attracted by the cotton industry including those manufacturing the special machinery needed in the mills and the chemical industry.

At the beginning of the Industrial Revolution in the mid-18th-century, steel-working functions such as milling, forging, casting, and the spinning industries were located in well-wooded western and northern valleys of England where streams gave water power and forests provided charcoal for fuel; thus the original iron mill of Lloyds – later to be the famous family of iron masters and bankers – was at Pont Robert in the heart of Montgomeryshire.[19]

Industry in the 18th and 19th centuries was drawn to the English Midlands and the 'Black Country' by the presence of coal, after the coking process for steel and later the steam engine had been discovered and developed. Where there were no satisfactory roads for industry to use, rivers provided an attractive means of transport,[20] though once canals had been constructed industry was no longer tied to the navigable rivers.

The invention and development of railways provided industry with an alternative to the canals. When electricity became a practicable source of power, industry began to move south to the great

18 Along transport routes in Eastern Australia, where almost any journey once involved many days travel, hotels grew up at about one day's journey apart. Some of these locations developed into towns and regional centres, but as transport has improved the requirement for rest places has diminished and only the larger towns remain.
19 Montgomeryshire is in North West Wales. The Lloyds family had operated coal mines for some time, but began producing steel using the new 'hot blast' technique (1823). They benefited from both 'ironstone' and lime being available side by side as well as nearby coal. The company continued until the steel industry was nationalised in 1967 with facets of the company still surviving. Lloyds Bank was also established by the family in the late 18th century.
20 Before 1850 a map of England shows no significant centres of population far from the coast, except along the chief navigable rivers.

25

population centres, facilitated by the development of roads and road transport. Nowadays canals have largely dropped out of commercial use.

There will be differences in what is required for different industries. The essential requirements for any particular industry mean that the right kind of land may be scarce – sometimes very scarce. For example, in an article entitled 'Why this site was chosen', the managing director of Richard Thomas & Baldwin Ltd had this to say about the new steel works at Llanwern in South Wales:

> Geographical conditions set a limit to what could be done at Ebbw Vale to increase production ... and plans were drawn up for a new works at Llanwern, near Newport, 20 miles from Ebbw Vale. The site was chosen after long and careful investigation of a number of possible places. Wherever the plant was to be built, certain essential conditions had to be met. First, the new plant must be capable of integration with the existing main activities of the company, and it must be able to supply steel slabs on an economic basis to Ebbw Vale ... Secondly, it must be suitably sited in relation to consuming markets, of which the two main centres are the Midlands and the London areas. Llanwern is 90 miles from Birmingham and 164 miles from London, with good rail and road facilities. Thirdly, there must be easy access to raw materials of suitable quality: coking coal, iron ore and limestone. Llanwern fulfills this condition in that it can obtain good quality coal from Welsh coalfields, iron ore from Oxfordshire and limestone from quarries in Monmouthshire and Glamorgan. A fourth condition to be satisfied is that the plant must have reasonable access to a good seaport ... The port of Newport is only five or six miles from the site. Another essential condition for the site is an ample supply of water. Vast quantities of water are used in a modern steelworks ... Spencer Works will require about 14 million gallons of replacement water every day ... With the cooperation of the local authorities and the river board, soft water will be drawn from the Usk ... while hard water will be pumped from the famous springs in the Severn Tunnel, eight miles to the east. Lastly, the area and facilities should provide for expansion, should economic conditions warrant such a step. No other site investigated satisfactorily fulfilled all the above requirements.'[21]

Together Diagrams 2 and 3 explain much of the world's economic history. The several points on the cycle of production have pulled populations hither and thither in pursuit of opportunity. At this time we are living in a period when the pull of the big centres is more insistent than ever.

21 Source unknown, probably around 1938.

Underlying all the previous considerations is the fact that output of an undertaking will vary with the land on which it is located. Miners produce more coal when working a thick, straight, easily accessible seam and less when working a poor seam awkwardly placed and miles from the pithead. Potatoes are easier to grow in Lincolnshire than in other parts of England and the gross receipts for the crop are greater for less effort than for other growers. Differences in soil, sunshine, rainfall and shelter make a difference to the vines that can be grown. The wine produced may be white or red, sweet or dry, and may sell at very different prices. What the growers obtain will be different for the same effort.

Before transport was as cheap as it is today, iron smelters in Australia were situated on the east coast adjacent to the coal seams at Newcastle and Wollongong, because three times as much coal as iron ore was used in steel production. A smaller smelter was built near the iron ore fields at Whyalla (a journey of 2,000 miles from Newcastle) so that the ships did not return empty.

On the other hand, when producing perishable goods, such as bread, it might be advantageous to be nearer to the customers than to the raw materials. Again, the retailer in a busy shopping centre will expect a greater turnover for the same effort than the owner of a little shop on the corner of a housing estate.

These examples show that not every piece of land is necessarily suitable for any purpose. Bearing in mind the cycle of production (Diagram 2), it will be seen that in order to obtain the most economic advantage from production it is important for any industry to be located in the right place. This means that the undertaking must obtain control of the land required and to do this the owners of the business will have to pay. The more suitable the site, the more they will be prepared to pay. Clearly one advantage of the land may quite outweigh another. In the centre of a town or city it is not the fertility of soil that is important. As towns expand land may change use several times to meet the most profitable requirement.

Table 1 on the next page shows land prices (in 2010) to indicate the scale of the different sums that people will pay for sites of varying advantage in a highly developed community. Here the example is from the State of New South Wales in Australia where all land is officially valued. Table 1 lists values for land between Sydney, and Broken Hill, 1,116 kilometres west of Sydney as shown on the map below.

The differences in price are staggering.

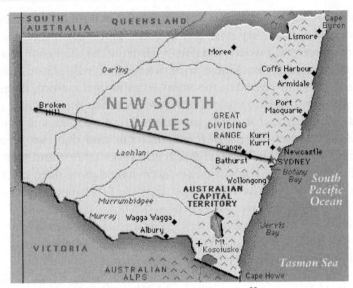

Map of New South Wales[22]

Price of Land per Hectare

Location (km from Sydney)	Population	Retail Sites	Small Industrial Sites	Wheat Farms	Grazing Farms
Sydney	4,119,190	$216,494,845		urban	urban
Burwood (12)	In above	$102,459,016		urban	urban
Parramatta (26)	In above	$96,000,000		urban	urban
Blacktown (38)	In above	n/available	$3,144,494	urban	urban
Penrith (56)	172,140	$38,424,658	$2,061,424	urban	urban
Katoomba (102)	7,623	$30,300,000		mountains	mountains
Lithgow (141)	19,756	$10,000,000		mountains	mountains
Bathurst (203)	35,339	$21,481,481	$404,290		$3,411
Orange (257)	35,844	$21,020,408			$5,672
Parkes (357)	14,280	$5,530,303		$1,125	
Condobolin (458)	2,849	n/available		$508	
Broken Hill (1116)	19,360	$4,750,000		desert	desert

Table 1 – NSW Land Prices

22 Extracted from NSW Valuer General's Blue Book 2010 http: //www.lands.nsw.gov.au/ valuation/nsw_land_values. Note: prices for retail land are quoted as the length of the street front. To create an area comparison a standard depth of 20 metres has been assumed. This may undervalue the most expensive sites. Prices in Australian dollars. The values are for rating and taxation purposes and typically less than the price a site might sell for.

When paying for land people are paying for the advantages they hope to derive from living or working in a particular place. The great differences in the prices paid are a measure of the economic and social advantages to be gained from location. The price of land rises sharply as one moves up the hierarchy from village to town, from town to city and from city to capital.[23] It varies greatly from one part of the country to another, from one part of a town to another, and from one part of a city to another. These variations in land price are related to the points in the cycle of production and reveal important facts about our economic life. Plainly, businessmen would not make these payments if they did not have to, and if they did not expect to recoup the expense.

1.8 The Importance of Location

The land prices shown in Table 1 ranged from $508 to $216,494,845 per hectare. What causes one hectare of land to be four hundred thousand times more expensive than another? The explanation is to be found in the interplay of the various influences shown in the three preceding diagrams.

The triad (Diagram 1, page 15), showing the three points necessary to the creation of the man-made world and the three necessary connections between them, is on a vast scale. To think on this scale is not easy, but it is valuable to try to see in their grand simplicity the great forces which shape the man-made world. In so doing, we may glimpse the fundamental principles which permeate every detail of human activity, for vast as the triad is, its principles are to be found operating in all productive activity and its effects are felt by everyone.

The significance of these principles in everyday activity can be seen in two ways: on the one hand, land is of no use for production if there is no labour to work on it. People would hardly pay high prices for sites in the middle of the Sahara or in Greenland. On the other hand, a person's willingness and ability to work are of no value if they are unable to obtain access to suitable land to work on – hence the horrors of unemployment.

One reason for the present population movement is the attraction of a warmer climate. Traders in London will pay significantly higher

---

23 Which will be generally true, and particularly where this has evolved over long periods of time, but in Table 1, using the definitions in this book, Sydney would be a capital city/port, Bathurst, Orange and Parkes towns, and all the rest villages.

prices for sites on the north side of Oxford Street because that is the sunny side preferred by shoppers. Americans migrate to Florida when they retire, Englishmen to Malaga and Australians to Surfers Paradise: all to take advantage of the warmer climates. The population growth in these areas has caused land prices to rise accordingly. These are also examples of **direct influences** combined with the nature of human beings.

The next diagram in order of scale shows the hierarchy of the human race (Diagram 3, page 23). It is useful to connect the importance of location with this hierarchy and to consider why things are located where they are: for instance, national communities with capital cities at Level 4.

Why is London located where it is? It has certain natural advantages: a well-watered valley, an inland port connected to the sea by an easily navigable river and until recent years the first crossing place of the river. But these natural advantages alone would not have ensured the development of a capital city on this site. There is also its relative proximity compared with other UK cities to the centres of culture and civilisation – first Rome, later Paris.

The practical business advantages given by civilisation, culture and community are very great. The influence of a high level of civilisation permeates the whole community, expressing itself as a sense of justice, moral standards, honest dealing and fair play. Business in London has thrived on trustworthiness: 'My word is my bond' is the motto of the London Stock Exchange.[24] In turn cultures encourage natural abilities, develop the mind through education and learning, and raise standards of taste and conduct. By encouraging men and women to develop their natural talents the whole community benefits.[25]

Community is the medium through which the benefits of civilisation and culture reach its members. A particular community may also confer its unique qualities that may be beneficial or a positive impediment. Its laws may be tyrannical, its officers corrupt, its customs degenerate. All this makes a substantial difference to the practical advantages of working in one community or another and has important economic repercussions.

24 'Dictum Meum Pactum'. The other extreme is in South Africa where there are anecdotal reports that some farmers choose to grow cotton despite the poor return, because it is the only crop that will not be stolen.
25 Reading and writing for working people was a cultural influence. In England it was a result of the rise of the Protestant church in the 19th century, not a vocational requirement. One consequence was to raise workers' expectations and raise the lowest acceptable level of earnings.

The benefits conferred on land by civilisation and culture vary greatly from place to place within the community.[26] In the city the benefits will be greater than in the town, in the town greater than in the village. Similarly, within each, the benefits will vary from one place to another, largely according to the interplay with the cycle of production (Diagram 2, page 18).

The least benefit is to be found in land used for access to natural resources: agricultural, forestry and mineral-bearing land. Then comes land suitable for work on raw materials and with tools: industrial sites, which tend to be situated in towns and on the perimeters of great cities. Finally comes land suitable for bringing together seller and purchaser: markets, shopping centres, the great exchanges and trading houses. For these purposes easy access for large numbers of people is important, hence the use of central sites, whether in village, town or city. Generally, the larger the population the greater the advantages these sites confer.[27] The most sought-after land is that occupied by banks and finance houses for their head office functions, where the value of being near their kind is extremely high.

All this illustrates a fundamental fact about Economics which is not generally appreciated. The same work, skill and equipment produce quite different results in different locations. The differences are startling and are reflected in the range of land prices shown in Table 1. Very little of this range results from natural advantages such as fertility, but arises generally from the presence of the community.[28] From one street to another in a city a glimpse may be gained of how differently these forces work. The holder of each piece of land has no doubt as to its advantages and limitations but is less likely to see the causes from which they spring.

Production and trade vary with location as shown diagrammatically on the next page. Diagram 4 represents the results of the same knowledge, skill and effort expended on sites in different locations. The base line is land, the columns represent production net of goods or services on each site, that is, the total produced less the costs of

26 Refer to Table 1, page 28. Prices of retail premises are broadly in line with the size of the community. Katoomba is the exception perhaps largely due to the very high tourist trade.
27 Housing land is to be found at all levels of the hierarchy and is essential to support production – generally its value tends to increase with the size of the population.
28 That is not to say that natural resources do not confer enormous benefits on some sites such as the location of an oil well. This however is the exception rather than the rule, and this too is often subject to the existence of the community around it.

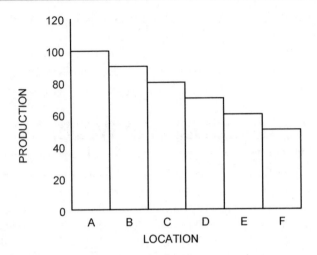

Diagram 4 – Variable Productivity due to Location[29]

goods and services produced on other sites.[30] The numbers are quite arbitrary but are given to help show the relationships. Thus a shop located in the middle of a shopping centre would do much better than one in a side street, or a factory with good road and rail links would be better placed than one in a rural town.

Diagram 4 illustrates how the same work produces more on some land than on other land. If a person works on the least productive land in use production will be the least. On better land (to the left) the same person will produce more for the same effort. This is inevitable simply because the site is more productive. Without work there can be no product, but is the product due solely to their work?

In the light of the first three diagrams this question poses no difficulty. Land plays a part alongside work; so do direct influences. The producers' locations bring them under more or less influence from civilisation, culture and community. The location gives more or less access to natural resources, to the supply of raw materials and tools, and to the market. A farmer close to a town requires less time and effort to deliver the product to market than a farmer on equivalent land in a remote location.

29 The diagrams here and later show the principle of variation and are not indicative of amounts. For actual amounts see Table 1 on page 28.
30 For example, if the business is engaged in making shoes, this amount would be the sales revenue less the costs of leather, electricity etc.

CHAPTER 2

The Division of Wealth

THIS CHAPTER will begin to look at how the elements of production interact, especially how wealth, once produced, is divided. Rather than looking at companies, which may operate from multiple locations, the focus is on conditions at the specific location where wealth is produced. The business operator (the company) in economic terms is the tenant of the site and for clarity will be referred to as such.[1]

The initial division here is between those who work and those who control the site. Other claims on production which affect the distribution of wealth will also be considered.

Although numbers are used for some of the examples in this chapter, by wealth and production is meant goods and services not money. Once again, by production is meant net production: the total produced, less the costs of goods and services produced on other sites.

2.1 The Primary Division of Production

If the land is not controlled by those who work on it, the product will pass naturally into the hands of the tenant who holds the land and is the operator of the business. By law and custom the product normally goes to those in control of the land on which it is produced rather than to those who make it. The law and custom are based on convenience. The person in control of the land naturally finds the wealth within their power and so their claim has come to be recognised. This fact underlies all economic institutions.

Wages, salaries and other earnings have their roots in nature. *Wages are not properly a cost of production.* There can be no production without

---

1 The business may own the site but from an economic perspective he is the tenant. If the business owns the site, the business will also be the recipient of the rent.

work, and so the labourer has a primary claim to part of the product and receives this from the tenant. If a person is to retain all they produce, they must not only work but have control of the land on which to work.

Consider the case of a shoemaker. If he has his own shop and works alone he will own the whole proceeds of his work. But if he stops working himself and employs another, though he loses the employee's wages, any surplus over wages will still be his *because he is the tenant.* If the shoemaker loses his workman and again does all the work himself he gains the man's wages. Out of the total product some comes to him because he works and some because he controls the land.

This is the primary division of wealth (Diagram 5): between what someone gets by virtue of their work and what comes to them through holding land; between labourer and tenant, even though this may be one and the same person. As we have seen, production varies enormously with the nature of the land on which it is produced. It also varies, although very much less, with the quality of work. What determines how wealth is shared between the primary claimants varies in different communities depending on custom and tradition and on the prevailing theories, opinions and beliefs.[2]

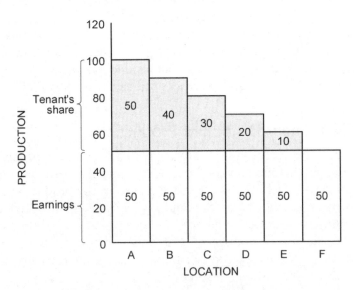

Diagram 5 – The Primary Division of Wealth

2 The variations in the distribution of wealth can be seen in the statistical tool known as the GINI Index. The World Bank publishes these for most countries.

Only when the labourer is also the tenant of the land[3] does he own what he produces. In modern society the overwhelming majority of the working population work on land controlled by others, using other men's tools upon other men's materials, producing wealth which will never be their own.[4]

2.2 Determination of Earnings

How the product is divided between those who work and those who control the land is of fundamental importance. First, how are earnings – net wages and salaries – determined?

Consider any occupation, the earnings in one branch of an occupation are related to those in another. A train driver's wages are related to those of other railwaymen and these are related to the earnings of a bus driver and a lorry driver.

The facts show that although earnings do vary they are related to a general level throughout the whole country. Wage rates in major cities are a little higher than provincial wage rates. Wage rates in urban areas are higher than those in rural areas. Earnings also vary from occupation to occupation. Wage rates vary within the same occupation and within the same business, but they are related to a general level for each occupation, and the rates for different occupations are related one to another. But they do not vary from site to site. Retail sales staff in prime city locations do not get greater earnings than retail sales staff working at adjacent, less productive locations. Farm labourers are not paid more for working on good land than on poor. This relationship is not static and may vary from time to time.

The highest point to which the general level of earnings can rise in the productive community is represented on Diagram 6 as the product of the least productive site (F). In our model community the highest point to which the general level of earnings can rise is 50. If men will work for 50 on the least productive site there is no reason why the tenants of the better sites should offer more. If they did, the rush to move would soon persuade the tenants to reduce the wages offered.

Therefore the general level of earnings cannot exceed the net product of the least productive site in use. In a society in which land, not

3 In more common parlance a 'sole trader'.
4 Self-employment represented 10.9% of all employment in the US in 2009. See *Monthly Labour Review Online*, September 2010, Vol 133, No 9. In other English-speaking countries it appears to be higher but the figures are not directly comparable.

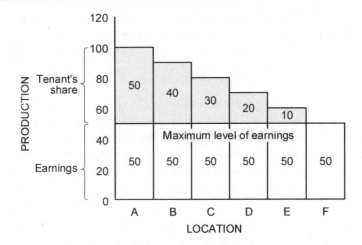

Diagram 6 – The Maximum Level of Earnings

in use, was freely available for anyone who wanted it, the general level of earnings would equate to the net product of the best land open to use free of charge.

2.3 Determination of the Tenant's Share

What then of the tenant's share? How is that determined?

Having paid wages, the tenant holds whatever is left. This is the tenant's share because the tenant holds the land. There are some risks in that position but generally these are far outweighed by the advantages. Both the risks and the advantages arise from the control of land and this control, so long as it lasts, gives economic freedom to the tenant. It is tenure of land not their knowledge, skill and work that frees people from economic servitude. The ablest scientists, engineers or executives, who are not tenants of the site where they work, are necessarily servants, whereas the ignorant, untrained workers who tenant their own premises are free.

The tenant's share in the productive community represented on Diagram 6 will be 50 on site 'A' and nothing on site 'F'. The tenant's share on any site is what is left after earnings have been paid.

We see then that although the general level of earnings does not vary from site to site the tenant's share varies vastly. It varies with location, with benefits derived from civilisation, culture and community, with access to natural resources, raw materials, tools and customers.

This division between tenant's share and earnings is fundamental. There is no part of the economy that is not affected by it.[5]

2.4 Secondary Claims on Wealth

So far we have considered the primary claims on wealth, earnings and tenant's share, but there are others who are able to claim some part of the product: the landlord, the money-lender and the tax collector, for example.

As shown in Diagram 7, the product naturally passes through the hands of the producer to be controlled by whoever tenants the land by the very nature of the productive process. The claims of landlords, money-lenders, tax collectors and others do not arise from production but are claims on the tenant arising from law and custom. Ultimately these are all claims upon the product of industry, paid by the tenant.

What are the secondary claims? A leasehold tenant will have to pay rent to the landlord; interest will have to be paid to the money-lender for finance borrowed to purchase the site or the buildings, equipment and stock. The tenant may also have to pay rates levied on the site, import duties on raw materials, licenses, road charges and petrol taxes for vehicles used, and social insurance contributions and taxation levied on employees' wages.

Suppose that every tenant, including the tenant on the least productive land – location 'F' on Diagram 7 – has to make payments to a landlord, a money-lender and inevitably the tax collector. Suppose the payments add up to 10. This will have the effect of reducing the maximum level of earnings to 40 on all sites, as shown in the diagram, because the level of earnings in the community is determined by the amount available for earnings on the marginal land, which has now been reduced. If earnings are reduced by secondary claims at the margin of production employers need not pay more on the other sites, and the maximum level of earnings throughout the community must also fall.

The important point to watch is not the central site with its great buildings and bustling activity but the least productive site in use, called the marginal site, where small exactions make a big difference. The secondary claims falling on production at the margin reduce earnings there and, consequently, throughout the community. If, as a result of secondary claims, tenants

5 For example, if earnings are high, production will be oriented to serving the population with good quality goods. If earnings are low, mass production will produce cheap goods.

at the margin of production are limited in what they can earn, tenants of more productive land need not pay their employees more, but they cannot reduce wages and salaries below what can be earned on the least productive sites. So the maximum level of earnings is fixed by the margin of production.

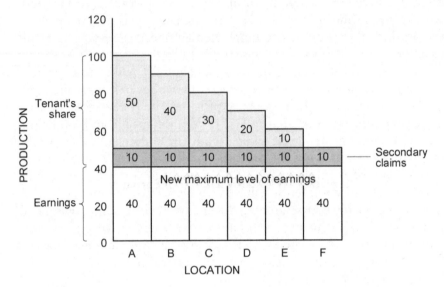

Diagram 7 – The Impact of Secondary Claims on Earnings

2.5 Lowest Level of Earnings

What is the lowest point to which earnings can fall?

People will not work for nothing. They must at least be able to eat. Some men work for a loincloth, a bowl of rice and little else. Others go on strike if their wages are insufficient to buy beer and cigarettes. There is a level below which earnings cannot fall. It is different in different occupations, in different countries, and at different times in the same country. Custom has a lot to do with fixing it and law may influence it. On Diagram 8 below, this is shown as the lowest acceptable level of earnings.

Taxation is a major factor in depressing earnings. Diagram 9 shows how a 10% tax on the net product reduces earnings but allows all sites to be worked. However, where marginal land barely produces an acceptable level of earnings, only a little taxation will be enough to put the site out of production.

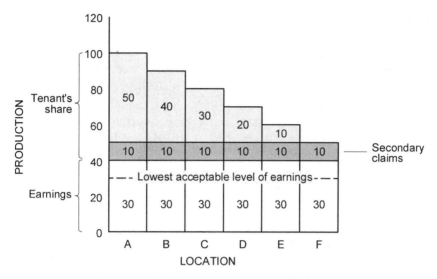

Diagram 8 – The Lowest Level of Earnings

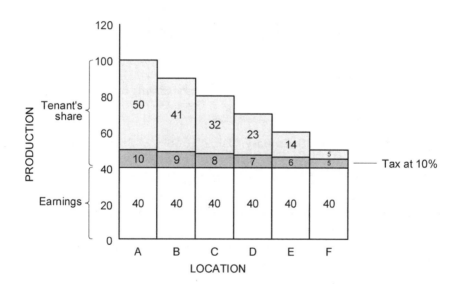

Diagram 9 – Tax at 10% of Production

In Diagram 10 where secondary claims, including tax, amount to 50%, sites D, E and F produce an acceptable level of earnings but not sufficient to pay the additional secondary claims, thus forcing land out of use. If taxation were reduced, the land could be brought back into production. This is true on other sites if industry is burdened not only by taxation but by other heavy secondary claims, such as landlord's claim, high interest charges, heavy rates, etc.

In many countries large areas, which once yielded a good livelihood to a substantial population, have gone out of use under the heavy burden of taxation. In England the Cornish metal mines, many hill farms and almost the entire coal industry have closed down. Although these 'marginal' lands are said to be 'uneconomic' they could still produce enough goods and services to afford a livelihood were it not for the burden of taxation.

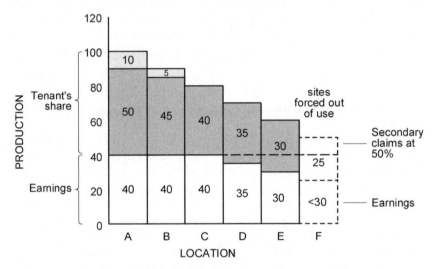

Diagram 10 – Secondary Claims at 50% of Production

Wealth is produced by the application of work on land. But not all land enjoys the same advantages, so work produces more on one site than on another. *Nevertheless natural law ensures that what a man earns by way of reward for his individual labour on the best site is related to what he may earn on the marginal site.* The rest, which we have called the tenant's share, is created by the existence and activity of the community. That being so, it is reasonable that taxes should be levied by the community on what it has created. It is unjust to levy taxes on the fruits of an individual's labour.

2.6 An Historical Perspective

To watch in imagination the growth of a community, from the first primitive cooperation of a few villagers to the intricate combination of men and women which makes a modern city, may help to show how the economic laws governing the level of earnings work in practice. To take a European example would mean tracing the growth of some city over many centuries. In America this growth happened within a lifetime and was reported by writers who saw it all take place, from the first covered wagon arriving on the deserted savannah in the West to the establishment of Chicago or San Francisco.

Economic Development in the United States

The following are the observations of the American economist, Henry George.[6] Diagrams have been interspersed amongst the text to illustrate the development. Like the diagrams above, each column assumes an equal-sized piece of land worked with equal skill and effort.

> Here, let us imagine, is an unbounded savannah, stretching off in unbroken sameness of grass and flower, tree and rill, till the traveller tires of the monotony. Along comes the wagon of the first immigrant. Where to settle he cannot tell – every acre seems as good as every other acre. As to wood, as to water, as to fertility, as to situation, there is absolutely no choice, and he is perplexed by the embarrassment of richness. Tired out with the search for one place that is better than another, he stops – somewhere, anywhere – and starts to make himself a home. The soil is virgin and rich, game is abundant, the streams flash with the finest trout. Nature is at her very best. He has what, were he in a populous district, would make him rich; but he is very poor. To say nothing of the mental craving, which would lead him to welcome the sorriest stranger, he labours under all the material disadvantages of solitude. He can get no temporary assistance for any work that requires a greater union of strength than that afforded by his own family, or by such help as he can permanently keep. Though he has cattle, he cannot often have fresh meat, for to get a beefsteak he must kill a bullock. He must be his own blacksmith, wagon maker, carpenter, and cobbler – in short a 'jack of all trades and master of none'. He cannot have his children schooled, for, to do so, he must himself pay and maintain a teacher. Such things as he cannot produce himself, he must buy in quantities and keep on hand, or else go without, for he cannot be constantly leaving his work and making a long journey to the verge of civilisation; and when forced to do so, the getting of a vial of medicine or the replacement of a broken auger may cost him the labour of himself and horses for days. Under such circumstances, though nature is prolific, the man is poor. It is an easy matter for him to get enough to eat; but beyond this, his labour will only suffice to satisfy the simplest wants in the rudest way.

6 Henry George, *Progress and Poverty*, Book IV, Chapter 2.

Soon there comes another immigrant. Although every quarter section of the boundless plain is as good as every other quarter section, he is not beset by any embarrassment as to where to settle. Though the land is the same, there is one place that is clearly better for him than any other place, and that is where there is already a settler, whose condition is at once greatly improved, and to whom many things are now possible that were before impossible, for two men may help each other to do things that one man could never do.

Another immigrant comes, and guided by the same attraction, settles where there are already two. Another, and another until around our first comer there are a score of neighbours. Labour has now an effectiveness which, in the solitary state, it could not approach. If heavy work is to be done, the settlers have a log-rolling, and together accomplish in a day what singly would require years. When one kills a bullock the others take part of it, returning the favour when they kill, and thus they have fresh meat all the time. Together they hire a schoolmaster, and the children of each are taught for a fractional part of what similar teaching would have cost the first settler. It becomes a comparatively easy matter to send to the nearest town, for someone is always going.

Each new arrival adds a bit to what everyone earns. Though newcomers have to resort to less productive land, their presence increases the efficiency of each member of the community, and they too are more efficient despite producing less than they would on the better land.

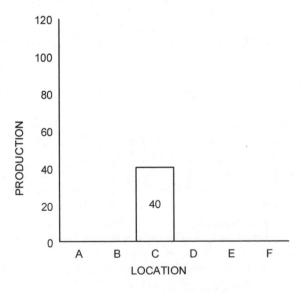

Diagram 11 – The First Settler

42

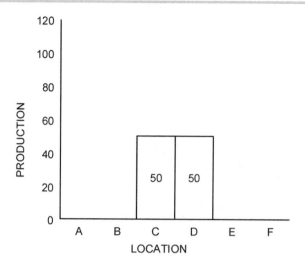

Diagram 12 – The Second Settler

As land giving less and less advantage is brought into use, earnings as a proportion of production are lower and lower. The best-situated family produces more than the last-comer by reason of the land they work on – not by reason of their work. Production goes up as population increases but a growing proportion of it is unearned by those into whose hands it falls. Nevertheless earnings will be greater.

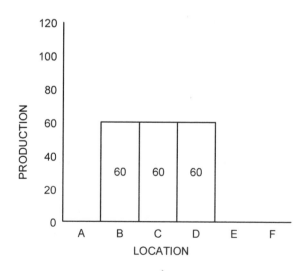

Diagram 13 – The Third Settler

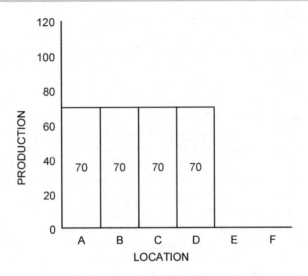

Diagram 14 – The Fourth Settler

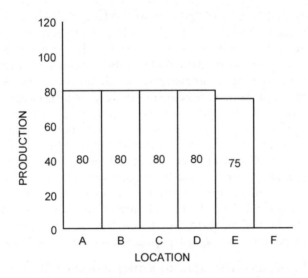

Diagram 15 – The Fifth Settler

Test it this way: move A on to E's land; he would produce less. He would lose the extra that had come to him simply because he was able to claim the best land. That extra had nothing to do with his efforts: put E on A's land and he would get it instead.

The story continues:

A blacksmith and a wheelwright soon set up shops, and our settler can have his tools repaired for a small part of the labour they formerly cost him. A store is opened and he can get what he wants as he wants it; a post-office, soon added, gives him regular communication with the rest of the world. Then comes a cobbler, a carpenter, a harness-maker, a doctor; and a little church soon arises. Satisfactions become possible that in the ordinary state were impossible ... Population still continues to increase, and as it increases so do the economies which its increase permits, and which in effect add to the productiveness of the land. Our first settler's land, being the centre of population, the store, the blacksmith's forge, the wheelwright's shop, are set up on it, or on its margin, where soon arises a village, which rapidly grows into a town, the centre of exchanges for the people of the whole district. With no greater agricultural productiveness than it had at first, this land now begins to develop a productiveness of a higher kind. To labour expended on raising corn, or wheat, or potatoes, it will yield no more of these things than at first, but to labour expended on the subdivided branches of production, which require proximity to other producers, and, especially to labour expended in that final part of production, which consists in distribution, it will yield much larger returns. The wheat-grower may go further on, and find land on which his labour will produce as much wheat, and nearly as much wealth; but the artisan, the manufacturer, the storekeeper, the professional man, find that their labour expended here, at the centre of exchanges, will yield them much more than if expended even at a little distance away from it; and this excess of productiveness for such purposes the landowner can claim, just as he could an excess in its wheat-producing power. And so our settler is able to sell in building lots a few of his acres for prices which it would not bring for wheat-growing if its fertility had been multiplied many times. With the proceeds, he builds himself a fine house, and furnishes it handsomely. That is to say, to reduce the transaction to its lowest terms, the people who wish to use the land, build and furnish the land for him, on condition that he will let them avail themselves of the superior productiveness which the increase of population has given the land.

Where will the specialist want to settle, and why? Where there is access to the greatest number of customers – in the centre of the community. The first settler unwittingly chose the site for the specialist. Perhaps the site of the biggest skyscraper in town was in fact decided by the first settler's choice of site for a log cabin! The nearer it is to the centre the more customers can reach it and the greater the income.

This extra income will be the result of possession of land.

What effect will the arrival of the storekeeper have? Where will he settle? The storekeeper is a super-specialist, who brings far-off communities into cooperation with the growing little settlement. Through the storekeeper, boots, ploughshares, clothing arrive from England, cutlery and binoculars from Germany, and so on. Co-operation and specialisation so increase production that now there is a surplus of goods – corn, hides, timber – to send over the Atlantic in return. The storekeeper, like other specialists, must settle in the centre to be accessible to the whole community. By then people will have got the habit of trading in what has now become 'Main Street'. When they come to have horses shod they will call in at the nearby store for a drink, to make some insignificant purchase, or just to chat. Each may only spend a few cents but when hundreds do, it adds up. In time the storekeeper – so long as he owns his land – will be the richest person in the community, receiving the most cooperation from others; and not only from this little community but from Lancashire, the Ruhr, and the Eastern States of America with whom he connects it. Without the store both this community and the industries of England and Germany would earn less. But with the help of all three the storekeeper takes more and more.

> Population still keeps on increasing, giving greater and greater utility to the land and more and more wealth to its owner. The town has grown into a city – a St. Louis, a Chicago or a San Francisco – and still it grows. Production is here carried on upon a great scale, with the best machinery and the most favourable facilities; the division of labour becomes extremely minute, wonderfully multiplying efficiency; exchanges are of such volume and rapidity that they are made with the minimum of friction and loss. Here is the heart, the brain, of the vast social organism that has grown up from the germ of the first settlement; here has developed one of the great ganglions of the human world. Hither run all roads, hither set all currents, through all the vast regions round about. Here, if you have anything to sell, is the market; here, if you have anything to buy, is the largest and the choicest stock. Here intellectual activity is gathered into a focus, and here springs that stimulus which is born of the collision of mind with mind. Here are the great libraries, the storehouses and granaries of knowledge, the learned professors, the famous specialists. Here are museums and art galleries, collections of philosophical apparatus, and all things rare, and valuable, the best of their kind. Here come great actors, and orators, and singers, from all over the world. Here in short, is a centre of human life, in all its varied manifestations.

What part in the economic life of a growing community do the missionary, doctor, lawyer play? Probably the missionary comes first and combines the roles of lawyer, doctor, teacher, midwife, marriage-broker and undertaker. The community establishes order and peace in which to work and trade and people begin to find satisfaction for their desires beyond a mere subsistence. Visiting actors, a circus, a lecturer, add to this. Later the schoolteacher, the newspaper editor, etc. all arrive to join the community. Cooperation depends on established human relationships. The lawyer and the parson help to determine and regulate these. Gradually the hierarchy shown on Diagram 3 (page 23) builds up. But the higher levels are still missing. The young nation feels the lack and turns back to its roots in the Old World. Europeans are often amused by American tourists trying to acquire as much 'culture' as they can in a short visit to Europe.

Such then is the growing community. There is always land to be had free where an enterprising family can set up for themselves as farmers, sheep graziers, small ranchers, etc. As long as there is a living to be had on the free land no one will work for a master for less than they could get working for themself. Wages and salaries are high.

So enormous are the advantages which this land now offers for the application of labour, that instead of one man with a span of horses scratching over acres, you may count in places thousands of workers to the acre, working tier on tier, on floors raised one above the other, five, six, seven and eight stories from the ground, while underneath the surface of the earth, engines are throbbing with pulsations that exert the force of thousands of horses.

All these advantages adhere to the land; it is on this land and no other, that they can be utilized, for here is the centre of population – the focus of exchanges, the market place and workshop of the highest forms of industry. The productive powers which density of population has attached to this land are equivalent to the multiplication of its original fertility by the hundred fold and the thousand fold. ...Our settler, or whoever has succeeded to his right of the land, is now a millionaire. Like another Rip Van Winkle, he may have lain down and slept; still he is rich – not from anything he has done, but from the increase of population. There are lots from which for every foot of frontage the owner may draw more than an average mechanic can earn; there are lots that will sell for more than would suffice to pave them with gold coin. In the original streets are towering buildings, of granite, marble, iron, and plate glass, finished in the most expensive style, replete with every convenience. Yet they are not worth as much as the land upon which they rest – the same land, in nothing changed, which when our first settler came upon it had no value at all.

...The valuable quality of land, which has become a centre of population is its superficial capacity – it makes no difference whether it is fertile, alluvial soil like that of Philadelphia; rich bottom land like that of New Orleans; a filled in marsh like that of St. Petersburg, or a sandy waste like the greater part of San Francisco.

And where value seems to arise from superior natural qualities, such as deep water and good anchorage, rich deposits of coal and iron, or heavy timber, observation also shows that these superior qualities are brought out, rendered tangible, by population. The coal and iron fields of Pennsylvania , that today are worth enormous sums, were fifty years ago valueless. What is the efficient cause of the difference? Simply the difference in population. The coal and iron beds of Wyoming and Montana, which today are valueless, will, in fifty years from now, be worth millions on millions, simply because, in the meantime, population will have greatly increased.

It is a well-provisioned ship, this on which we sail through space. If the bread and beef above decks seem to grow scarce, we but open a hatch and there is a new supply, of which before we never dreamed. And very great command over the services of others comes to those who as the hatches are opened are permitted to say: 'This is mine!'[7]

These observations were written in 1879. Since then scientific progress has more than fulfilled these prophecies of plenty. New sources of energy and boundless natural resources, together with increasing population, have made the United States of America one of the richest nations the world has ever known. And yet in 2009, amidst this affluent society more than 42.8 million people were living in poverty.[8]

How can this be? In the early pioneering days life was certainly hard and primitive but there was no poverty. Today, amidst the enormous cities with their towering buildings, there is abject poverty[9] and the unfortunate minority is increasing rather than diminishing. What are the economic factors that have been overlooked? The increased population enables specialisation to effect greater and greater efficiencies, and there is no doubt at all that the nation as a whole produces more than enough for everyone. Sometimes it is suggested that the population has grown too large. Can that be true when millions of dollars

7 Henry George, *Progress and Poverty*, Book IV, Chapter 2.
8 See US Census Bureau, *Income, Poverty, and Health Insurance Coverage in the United States: 2009*.
9 The poverty rate in the US was 14.3% in 2009 (42,868,163 people living below the poverty line). – see US Census Bureau, *Poverty: 2008 and 2009 – American Community Survey Briefs*, issued September 2010.

are paid out every year to farmers in order to keep land out of production?[10]

A little earlier the English writer, Gibbon Wakefield, wrote:

When land is very cheap and all men are free, where everyone who so pleases can easily obtain a piece of land for himself, not only is labour very dear as respects the labourer's share of the produce, but the difficulty is to obtain combined labour at any price ...

In the northern states of the American Union it may be doubted whether so many as one-tenth of the people would fall under the description of hired labourers ... In England the labouring class compose the bulk of the people ...

Nothing is more common in the US as a whole (excepting New York, Pennsylvania and New England) than for proprietors to work in the field at the same occupations as their servants.[11]

But all is now changed. The actuality of today and the reminiscence of the past are brought out by this passage from an American commentator:

The ladder that began with the apprentice ended with the Presidency of the Federation. Americans still believe this to be true; but in fact, as in the Old Country, the ladder which begins with the labourer now ends with the foreman...[12]

The legend still persists from the days of free land but the facts have changed and this is being recognised reluctantly by Americans. From such a promising start, is it not strange that a large proportion of the American population should be living in poverty?

When the first settlers came, they took only as much land as they could cultivate – it was pointless to take more. But when the central sites began to bring great advantages and there was a demand for more and more land at the margin, some began to enclose the land that they did not want for their own use but could sell or let to others. The effect of this on newcomers to the community was that they could no longer find free land to work on. The alternative they had to settling beyond the enclosures or starting a new community was to buy or rent land from the existing speculators, or else go and work for existing

10 A great deal of this is now expressed as environmental protection. See for instance the US Food, Conservation, and Energy Act of 2008.
11 Gibbon Wakefield, *England and America, A comparison of the social and political state of both nations,* page 247.
12 Attributed to Raymond Gram Swing 1887-1968, radio commentator and journalist.

occupiers. In either case what they had for themselves would be greatly reduced. They would have to work in part for a landlord or for a new master.

In America great belts of land were enclosed on the outskirts of any community and left unused. As a result people had to travel onwards to the West, sometimes hundreds of miles, before they could find free land on which to settle. Consequently the Far West was being settled long before the Mid-West and the East were fully developed. There were vast areas of empty land between settlements then – and so it is today.

The enclosure of land could be a very profitable venture for those who practised it. Gibbon Wakefield wrote in 1838[13] describing the sale of enclosed land:

> Thus it frequently happens, that when one of the western states of America or some land-jobbing company fixes on a spot as fit for a town, marks out the future streets by notches on the trees, and fixes a day for selling the district in lots by auction, hundreds of people congregate and make ready for the sale by estimating the future different values of the different lots.
>
> Captain Basil Hall describes admirably one case of this sort, in which 1,200 people had assembled in the forest weeks before the day of the sale. The different lots of land sold at such auctions are, generally, of pretty equal natural fertility, being equally covered by dense forests of the same kind of trees, yet while still covered by the forest they sell for very different prices.

This practice still goes on today. Land can be bought now in Brazil and held with a view to selling a few years hence at a good profit. The anticipated demand for land exists because development has already taken place to form the nucleus of a new community. The promoters are well aware of how attractive such an investment can be.

One recent advertisement stated:

> **Land** is the purest investment of them all and **Brazil** is the hottest **opportunity** available in today's emerging markets, where land prices in key areas have increased by up to 50% in the last 12 months. **Land** is a simple and uncomplicated investment in today's complicated world. For many years it has been considered an attractive asset and solid investment, and has long been a favourite of professional fund managers as well as shrewd individuals. With **land** prices in the UK and Europe already maturing, sophisticated investors, bankers and other

13 Gibbon Wakefield, *Collected Works of Gibbon Wakeflied*, page 415.

investment professionals have delivered a clear verdict: invest elsewhere or be doomed to mediocre returns. So the big question on everyone's lips is – 'where next?'. **Land prices in Brazil** are rocketing and now is the time to invest alongside some of the most well-known names in international leisure and real estate including' (a list of prominent companies follows).[14]

It is in anticipation of *future* land values created by a community that land is bought as a speculation.

What effect did land enclosure have on the level of earnings of the American settlers described by Henry George? If the settlers went further they could make less and less on the best free land open to use. This being so, in order to settle in an existing community they were willing to pay a land speculator more and more to be allowed to occupy his land. Or if they worked for a master they would be forced to accept less and less. But note, it is what can be earned working for oneself where land is freely available, that fixes the level of earnings.

This is in fact what happened. Slowly the stories of high earnings in America got back to Europe. People of a softer sort than the early pioneers went out to seek their fortunes. But they found they had to travel great distances before they could find free land on which to settle. It meant starting a new community from the beginning, which was not at all what they had intended and the advantages were not sufficient to tempt them. The only alternatives were to pay the speculators for use of their land or, if they could not afford this, to work as hired labourers for the existing occupiers, where the prospective employer need offer only enough to discourage the new arrivals from taking up free land. When the free land left was not good enough to attract a settler by providing him with a living, the criterion by which wages were fixed disappeared.

When there is growing competition for work those who ask the lowest wages will get the jobs. But wages cannot fall below the least that labourers are willing to accept. Enclosure of land reduces earnings to the lowest acceptable level while the tenant's share is increased to its maximum.

Economic Development in Europe
The same development occurred in the British Isles and in continental Europe but over a much longer period. Records show that in Saxon England the landless man was very rare, apart from the serfs who were

14 http://www.purchasebrazil.com/why_invest_in_land.php sighted 19/11/2010.

relatively few. With the development of feudalism, which was intensified by the Norman Conquest, each man still had a holding of land, though it was probably held subject to doing service for a lord, such as working on his land.

Gradually the lords of the manor began to encroach upon the common lands enclosing them for their own use, though at first this had little effect. In the 15th and 16th centuries the high price of wool led to a great increase of enclosures both of wasteland and arable land for conversion to pasture. This brought wealth to the lords and deprived many men of their holdings, driving them to search for work.

In the 18th and 19th centuries came a further period of enclosures – this time with parliamentary consent. Nine million acres were enclosed under the Enclosure Acts and probably nearly as much again without troubling to obtain official blessing.[15] Cottages were destroyed and the countryside largely depopulated, until only the landlords and their hired labourers remained. Those labourers who were left found themselves working long hours for very low wages, whilst the rest were driven to the towns which were growing with the industrial revolution. Here they met great competition for work and in order to make a livelihood men, women and children alike worked long hours in dreadful conditions for low wages.

Material conditions have improved greatly since those days.[16] But today there is almost no free land in any part of the English-speaking world. Consequently a vast majority of the working population are employees[17] and earnings are low as a proportion of production.

Land enclosure lies behind the changes from the early days of settlement in America to the present day, as it does behind the changes in Britain from the 13th century. Scientific progress has brought great advantages, which have tended to obscure the picture. But it is shocking that, despite all these advantages, there is still poverty and hunger even in the richest countries of the world. This need not be if people truly understood the natural laws which govern communities.

15 See footnote 4, page 55.
16 In terms of wages and the quality of the working environment. Working hours decreased progressively until the 1980s but have been increasing since then (they never dropped to the level before the C18th enclosures). Other aspects of work may have deteriorated.
17 In the original notes the word here was 'servants'. No doubt this was intended to be provocative and highlight the difference between free men and women and those who depend on others for a livelihood.

CHAPTER 3

Civil and Economic Freedom

I T IS OFTEN said that the English-speaking world is made up of free countries. What do we mean? What is the measure of a country's freedom?

The English-speaking world certainly enjoys a high standard of civil freedom: free speech, free press, freedom from unlawful arrest, all of these are greatly prized and are the envy of many other nations. But what of economic freedom? Why does the government supply a health service, state education, state pensions and unemployment support? Is it not because earnings are too low to enable men and women to meet the cost of these services for themselves? As nations we can afford them but as individuals we cannot. Why should this be? Why is the level of earnings so low as a proportion of the national product?

Here is a description, in Thomas Moore's *Utopia* (1516), of England during the great land enclosure movement in the 15th and 16th centuries when vast amounts of agricultural land were converted to pasture for sheep:

> Forsooth my lord, ... your sheep that were wont to be so meek and tame and so small eaters, now ... be become so great devourers and so wild, that they eat up and swallow down the very men themselves. They consume, destroy and devour whole fields, houses and cities. For look in what parts of the realm doth grow the finest and therefore dearest wool, there noblemen and gentlemen, yea and certain abbots, holy men no doubt ... leave no ground for tillage. They enclose all into pastures; they throw down houses; they pluck down towns, and leave nothing standing but only the church to be made a sheep house ... those good holy men turn all dwelling places and all glebeland[1] into desolation and wilderness. Therefore that one covetous and insatiable cormorant ... may enclose many thousand acres of ground to within one pale or

1 Glebeland in this context means a field or a meadow.

53

hedge, the husbandmen be thrust out of their own, or else either by fraud or by violent oppression they be put besides it, or by wrongs and injuries they be so wearied, that they be compelled to sell all. By one means, therefore, or by another ... they must needs depart away, poor, silly, wretched souls, men, women, husbands, wives, fatherless children, widows, woeful mothers with their young babes, and their whole household ... Away they trudge ... out of their known and accustomed houses, finding no place to rest in. All their household stuff, ... being suddenly thrust out they be constrained to sell it for a thing of nought. And when they have wandered abroad till that be spent, what can they then else do but steal, and then justly pardy be hanged, or else go about a-begging? And yet then also they be cast in prison as vagabonds, because they go about and work not, whom no man will set a-work, though they never so willingly proffer themselves thereto.[2]

What wages would such men receive? It has been shown that at the root of a low level of earnings lies land enclosure. Gibbon Wakefield said:

Where land is very cheap and all men are free, where anyone who so pleases can easily obtain a piece of land for himself, not only is labour very dear, as respects the labourer's share of the produce, but the difficulty is to obtain combined labour at any price.

This is written from the employer's viewpoint and indicates that under such conditions earnings are very high.[3]

What are the prerequisites for high earnings? The first is that land is very cheap and anyone who so wishes may easily acquire a piece for themselves; the second, that men and women are free. In terms of Diagram 6, on page 36, this means that where land may be had without charge and all men and women are free, the level of earnings tends to rise to the full product of the best land to be had free of charge. Assuming that land producing 50 may be obtained without charge, the level of earnings would tend to rise towards 50. The tenant's share would be what was left on better sites after earnings were paid. In these circumstances labour takes a large share of the product, amounting to the whole on the marginal land.

Where people and land are free earnings are high and master-men are numerous. The opposite extreme is where all land is enclosed and

2 Sir Thomas Moore, *Utopia*.
3 Gibbon Wakefield (1796-1862) was amongst other things a British politician who was deeply involved in the colonisation of New Zealand and South Australia. One of his concerns was that to get 'gentlemen' to migrate to the colonies either servants must be available on low wages or there must be bonded servants, i.e. convicts.

none can be had without coming to terms with the landowners. In these circumstances there are many who cannot acquire land and there is always unemployment, more or less, but ever-present. Earnings tend towards the lowest acceptable level (Diagram 8, page 39).

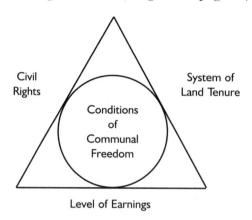

Diagram 16 – Communal Freedom

There are then three fundamental factors affecting a nation's freedom: civil rights, the level of earnings, and the system of land tenure. This may be illustrated diagrammatically, as in Diagram 16 above. In 13th-century England there was a large measure of economic freedom. People were tenants in their own right. What was produced belonged in the first instance to the tenant. There were tithes and feudal dues to be paid but most of what was earned could be kept, and earnings were comparatively high. Apart from the serfs, who were slowly being freed, citizens also enjoyed a fair measure of civil liberty, though it did not compare with what is enjoyed today. Through land enclosure economic freedom has now been lost and wages are comparatively low.[4] Who can say whether England enjoys more freedom now than then?

So it is throughout the world and throughout history. In any community at any period, the conditions of freedom derive from the interplay of these three factors. This applied in ancient Egypt, it applied to Roman Britain, as it did to the early settlers of America; it still applies to America today, and equally to Zimbabwe or North Korea. In each case the conditions of freedom are quite different but the underlying laws that give rise to them are the same.

4 For details of the effects of land enclosure on wages in England in the 18th and 19th centuries see J.L. Hammond and Barbara Hammond, *The Village Labourer* and *The Town Labourer*.

3.1 The Importance of Earnings for Civil Rights

Civil rights may secure freedom of the person, freedom of thought and speech, and freedom of conscience. Freedom of the person enables anyone to go where they like, provided they do not trespass, and meet whom they like, provided those they meet do not object. But going where one likes may involve paying the fare; meeting whom one likes may mean keeping pace with their expenditure on living. Freedom of thought assumes thought, and freedom of speech, something to say. Poverty and ignorance often march together. Nothing blinds and gags like ignorance.

Tenure of land often involves responsibilities for the upkeep of buildings, fixtures and furniture and for preserving the condition of the land. Poverty may render people unable to meet these liabilities and so deprive them of the full benefit of their tenure, or even of the tenure itself.

A little thought will show how civil rights and land tenure are related to one another. Law may give freedom of movement, speech and conscience; but if the exercise of this freedom is punished by notice to quit, the law is of small use. Conversely, the law may give security of tenure but if the tenant is liable to be beaten up or thrown into prison this security is of small avail.

All three conditions, civil rights, land tenure and level of earnings act on each other. By their interaction they determine the communal conditions of freedom. To look at any one alone may be wholly misleading.

The conditions of this triad underlie the structure of modern industry. High regard for civil rights, complete enclosure of land, and low level of earnings began in Britain, then spread to the northern states of America. These underlying conditions have been carried across the world to give the industrial structure its shape, its strengths and its weaknesses.

Modern industry has risen on the advance of science, the development of new techniques and special skills, and the vigour of daring enterprise; to do this it needs the free air of civil rights. It also relies on a mass of landless servants[5] and a reserve of the unemployed that results from land enclosure. It needs a level of earnings low enough to leave a substantial margin for rents, taxation, interest, insurance

5 This has been the basis of the rise of Brazil, Russia, India and China as economic powers at the beginning of the 21st century.

premiums and investor's profit even at the margin of production. The modern industrial structure is the pragmatic solution to the basic conditions of civil rights, land tenure and level of earnings. Different basic conditions would deliver a different result.

The particular answer of a particular era is necessarily transient. Changes in the deeper conditions must change everything which depends on them. These deeper conditions are the work of law, both natural and human. Civil liberty rests on simple foundations however elaborate the machinery that ensures it. It rests on the enforcement of three duties against all equally. By the law of most English-speaking countries everyone from the president or prime minister downwards owes three fundamental duties to everyone else:

- Not to assault another person;
- Not to imprison another person;
- Not to libel or slander another person.[6]

These three duties are the foundations of civil liberty. They protect our persons, our movements and our reputations. No breach of these duties is permitted except in certain closely defined cases, as for instance, assault in self-defence, arrest for an offence against the law, and defamation under some overriding public or private duty, such as a parliamentary debate.[7]

The central fact is the simplicity of it all. Simple universal duties ensure freedom of thought, speech, association and conscience. They do so because they are a recognition of natural facts. If men and women may go, do or say what they like without fear of assault, imprisonment or defamation of character they are assured of civil freedom.

The way civil rights are maintained is instructive. The action of protecting them by enforcing three fundamental duties is of profound effect. Declarations of rights are useless if these duties are not observed. The enforcement of these fundamental duties is of far-reaching economic importance. For example, in the United States in the 19th century it was in the North, where a high level of civil freedom was enjoyed, that industry developed and not in the South, where slavery existed until the end of the civil war in 1865.

---

6 Blackstone puts it that our rights 'may be reduced to three primary articles: the right of personal security, the right of personal liberty, and the right of private property …' and of the first he goes on to say: 'The right of personal security consists in a person's legal and uninterrupted enjoyment of his life, his limbs, his body, his health, and his reputation'. Sir William Blackstone *Commentaries on the Laws of England – The Rights of Persons*, Volume 1, page 125.
7 Parliamenary Privilege, or protection under Article 1 of the constitution in the United States.

What then of the economic sphere? Our concern here is to take things from first principles. The following two principles might provide a basis for economic freedom:

1 That all have equal rights to the use and enjoyment of the elements provided by nature (land, water, air and sunshine).
2 That each has an exclusive right to the use and enjoyment of what is produced by his or her own labour.[8]

The economic history of the human race reflects the fundamental importance of the tenure of land, an element to which by nature all have equal rights. All economic systems have been founded on a combination of a system of land tenure and a system of civil rights. These are the points of effective action. Direct action at the level of earnings involves much effort for small result.

In conditions of full land enclosure the level of earnings, slowly and arduously raised over decades, can collapse overnight at the outset of a period of bad trade. In periods of exceptionally good trade the level of earnings rises despite all efforts to hold it down.[9] Even then, however, the rise is not very great for earnings cannot rise above the limits set by the margin of production. Any attempt to push them beyond that point is defeated by a general rise in prices or the failure of the marginal site, with consequent unemployment.

This is the inconvenient truth: the level of earnings moves within limits set by natural law. Natural law cannot be defied. It springs from the very nature and essence of things. The law is that the primary division of wealth between earnings and tenant's share depends on two things: first, the degree of civil freedom; second, the conditions of land tenure. We are now in a position to state with precision the law that governs the distribution of the tenant's share and earnings, commonly referred to as the law of rent:

1 Where land is free and anyone who so wishes may easily acquire a piece for themselves, the level of earnings rises to the full product of the marginal land. The tenant's share is what is left over on the better land (see Diagram 6, page 36).
2 Any charge put on the marginal land decreases the level of earnings and increases the tenant's share (Diagram 7).
3 Where land is all enclosed earnings tend to a customary minimum, rising in times of good trade, falling in times of bad trade.

8 Henry George, *Protection or Free Trade*, Chapter 26.
9 See Diagram 21, page 69.

4 Earnings cannot fall below the lowest acceptable level (Diagram 8).

This is natural law and has duties associated with it in the same way that natural law in the civil sphere has associated duties. These will be called the economic duties and will be discussed further in Chapter 18.

3.2 Natural Law

The law of rent illustrates one aspect of natural law, showing the relationship between tenant's share and earnings. Sometimes the labels are altered and it is spoken of as the law of rent and wages.[10] Call it what you will, it remains universal in application. It applied in ancient Rome; it applies everywhere today and will still apply in years to come.

Natural law cannot be changed. It is part of the order of creation, one of the principles of harmony, which welds all things into a coherent and purposeful whole. Understanding of it shows what can and cannot be done. Natural law may produce widely different results depending on the conditions under which it is acting. It is highly intelligent and allows for all circumstances. If the people and the land are free, one result follows; if the people are slaves, another; if marginal land is subjected to secondary claims, another; and if land is all enclosed, yet another. The same law gives different results in different conditions. The very laws, which bring a badly designed or badly flown aircraft crashing to the ground, keep a well designed, well flown aircraft airborne.

The English common law of the highway for example is simplicity itself. It states that no one should conduct themself on the Queen's highway in such a way as to put another in danger. That is all. It is simple and intelligent. It allows for all circumstances. It says nothing about keeping to the left or the right, not exceeding the speed limit, dipping headlights and so on. On the contrary, it envisages circumstances when it would be a driver's duty to go on the wrong side of the road so as to avoid endangering someone; or to accelerate rapidly; or not to stop at a major intersection, and so on. It applies with equal force to those on foot, on horseback, bicycles, wagons, cars and lorries, acting quite differently in different circumstances. This law has the quality of natural law. It will remain when all the rules and regulations have been forgotten. It will survive the motor vehicle as it has survived the horse.

10 The law of rent and wages is referred to by a number of economists. Here the terms used are 'earnings' and 'tenant's share' because wages and rent can have so many meanings that they can lead to confusion.

Unfortunately, we are not yet intelligent enough to follow this intelligent law, so government has found it necessary to make thousands of rules and regulations to keep some order on the road.

Human communities may live under conditions of slavery, serfdom, political tyranny, or civil freedom. The system of land tenure practised today is by no means the only system that has existed, still less the only possible system.

It is difficult to envisage how land can be free, although we do know that people can be free for we experience this condition. Yet the ancient Greeks could not envisage freedom for all. Two thousand five hundred years ago Aristotle, in his *'Politics'*, wrote:

> But is there anyone thus intended by nature to be a slave, and for whom such a condition is expedient and right, or rather is not all slavery a violation of nature? .... There is no difficulty in answering this question on grounds of both reason and fact. For that some should rule and others be ruled is a thing not only necessary but expedient; from the hour of their birth, some are marked out for subjection, others for rule.[11]

And further:

> And indeed the use made of slaves and tame animals is not very different: for both with their bodies minister to the needs of life... It is clear then, that some men are by nature free, and others slaves, and that for these latter slavery is both expedient and right.[12]

It is only one hundred and fifty years since slavery was abolished in the United States.[13] Until 1807 the slave trade had been a great source of revenue to England and on it was founded the prosperity of the city of Liverpool. The slaves did not find their way into England, for with total land enclosure there was plenty of cheap labour and they were not needed, but English ships carried many of them from Africa to the American continent. To own shares in the slave trade companies was perfectly respectable, for slavery was accepted as necessary and inevitable.[14]

In learning to understand how land may be free it is first necessary to study the foundations of civil freedom. If people were able to assault one another when it suited them this would not be freedom.

11 Aristotle, *Politics*, Book 1, Chapter 5.
12 *Ibid*.
13 The 13th Amendment to the Constitution, finally ratified 6 December 1865.
14 Slavery was legally abolished throughout the British Empire by the Slavery Abolition Act of 1833.

In such situations no one would be free to go where they wished, say what they liked or meet with such people as they chose. Nor is it freedom if people can be thrown into prison to suit the convenience of others, or may freely slander and libel one another and thus subject one another to hatred, ridicule and contempt. To secure freedom such abuses of one person by another must be prevented. The duties which each owes to another to ensure freedom must be enforced.

Human freedom implies human laws based on understanding. It is not easy for a community to achieve a high level of civil freedom: such understanding does not belong to the common run of popular opinion, theories and beliefs. It is not surprising that those fortunate communities, which have achieved a high standard of civil freedom, have guarded it so jealously against attack from within and without.

Let us consider all of the above in the context of the hierarchy shown in Diagram 3, page 23. The natural law that governs the division of wealth in a community acts on the population as a whole. Part of the machinery of creation, it is neither right nor wrong, neither good nor bad; it acts impartially on every human community. There are other forces at work. These do not act directly on men in general but through particular individuals and groups. Such are the forces of culture and civilisation, and they possess great power. It is to these that we must look in order to gain the necessary understanding of how true freedom may be achieved.

How do we meet the influence of these higher forces? The treatment here may have aroused what for want of a better term may be called moral questions: questions of right and wrong. At these times something may tell us that things we have previously taken for granted are wrong and unjust. But although in a moment of unusual awareness we may feel a thing to be wrong, it is not so easy to see what is right, for we lack the necessary knowledge. Such knowledge is to be found in the forces of civilisation and culture working through individuals and groups. Throughout history these groups may be found scattered in no easily apparent pattern. What is surprising is how their work has lasted through the centuries so that their influence is still felt today. There are the ten commandments of Moses; people may scoff at some of them but they cannot ignore them. They are as much an influence in the 21st century as they were when Moses came down from the mountain to deliver them to the Israelites.

The English common law is the basis of the United Kingdom's reputation for high standards of civil justice, as it is in the whole of the English-speaking world. The common law was formulated by the lawyers of Henry II (reigned 1154-1189), who were undoubtedly men of great understanding though little is known of them now.

It is not only through the legal system that these forces work, but through the influence of great figures such as Shakespeare, Leonardo, Mozart, or Lao Tse, Buddha and Mohammed. And in our particular civilisation there can be no doubt of the fundamental influence of the teachings of Christ.

CHAPTER 4

Further Divisions of Wealth

I N CHAPTER 2 it was stated that the primary division of production is between earnings and tenant's share (see Diagram 5, page 34). This is governed by natural law. It is a primary division because the two claimants control directly the two essential factors of production: work and land. Any other claims on production cannot be made directly but only indirectly against earnings or tenant's share; they will be called secondary claims.

In the capitalist system these secondary claims are principally taxation, rates, interest, landlords' claims, and insurance.[1] They arise as claims against production because the claimant has the power to make such claims, not because of any contribution made to production. Anything that is left to the tenant after meeting all these claims is his profit.

This chapter will first consider the origins of secondary claims and will then examine them in more detail.

4.1 The Rise of Capitalism

It has been stated above that where land may be had free of charge and people are free, the level of earnings tends to rise to the full product of the marginal land. Under these conditions earnings are high and master-men are numerous (see Diagram 6, page 36).

The opposite extreme is where all land is enclosed so that none can be had without coming to terms with the landowners. With the resulting competition to get work, wages are driven down to the lowest acceptable level. If anyone tries to rent a plot of land so as to work

---

1 In some situations other claims may arise, copyright and patents particularly. In recent times there have been attempts to patent things which occur in nature; testing this in the courts is still in the early stages.

on their own account, they will find that the landlord's claim is very high. After paying landlord's claim and taxes, there will generally be no tenant's share left and the earnings will be no greater than could be obtained as an employee.[2]

Two divergent lines of development may occur in a community where all land is enclosed. The choice the particular community makes will depend much upon its traditions and native genius. As wages are down to the lowest acceptable level, (see Diagram 8, page 39) workers will not be able to supply themselves with more than the most rudimentary tools. And so they are denied the natural human advantage of extending and refining the power of body and mind by the development of instruments to aid work.

If matters rest thus, most people will be obliged to work for their more fortunate fellows; or else they will rent little holdings from the owners of the land and work as small farmers, or carry on their trades in cottage workshops, generation after generation. Production will be low, the lion's share will go to the landlords and the tenants, and employees will be pitifully poor. There will be little incentive to enterprise, for increased production is likely to mean increased demands by the landlords.[3] Nor is the landlord normally interested in changing the status quo.[4] The failure of a crop or of the market may mean that the landlord cannot be paid, with the consequent likelihood that he evicts the tenant. Such is the situation in large parts of what we refer to as the third world today.

In such a community the division of wealth is represented in Diagram 17 on the next page.

There is another way in which the conditions of full land enclosure may be met. For convenience let us start from the conditions shown on Diagram 17.

Where industry is working with such simple tools and equipment as the workers are able to provide, production will generally be low. In this situation the effect of fully equipping workers on a good site will be a rise in production. If production on site 'A' rises from 100 to 150, the increase will go to the tenant, for the greater part at

---

2 Or even in some cases less, for some men will prefer to be their own master rather than employed by another and will accept somewhat less to maintain that situation.

3 The fate of much aid to the third world. Even when farmers are enabled to produce more the rent rises again to absorb everything except the lowest acceptable level of earnings.

4 See Adam Smith, *The Wealth of Nations*, Book III, Chapter II: 'To improve land with profit, like all other commercial projects, requires an exact attention to small savings and small gains, of which a man born to a great fortune, even though naturally frugal, is very seldom capable.'

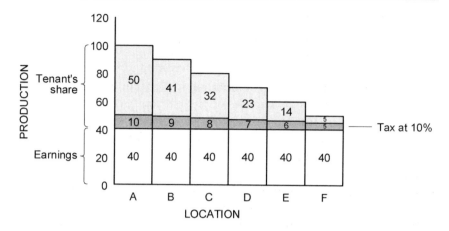

Diagram 17 – The Division of Wealth – Full Land Enclosure

least. This may make it profitable for a tenant to employ and equip workers.

To set up as a master of industry, an entrepreneur will have to obtain land, workers and equipment. To obtain the right land, he may have to offer more than the 50 which the landlord is now obtaining for site 'A' above.[5] To ensure success, he will want the best employees. To induce them to give up their present employment or their independence as tenants of their own land, he must offer them slightly more in wages[6] than they are already earning. To equip a site fully requires a large sum of money. If the would-be entrepreneur is a worker or salary earner this can only be obtained by borrowing. People will not lend money for nothing. They will require interest or else a share of the profits. Higher taxes are likely also. All this is shown in Diagram 18.

Having taken on these greater liabilities, success will depend on whether increased production more than covers the additional financial burdens. If there is no margin of profit the undertaking will fail even though production may have increased very considerably.

---

5 Or in countries like America he may purchase land, as Henry Ford did for the Highland Park plant where the Model 'T' Ford was first manufactured. The principle, however, remains. Henry Ford became both landlord and entrepreneur. Note that the location was selected because it had access to railways for distribution of the product and was outside the Detroit taxation regime (He later decided to move production to a site where both rail and shipping were available).

6 Again, Henry Ford in 1913/14 doubled wages of his production line workers to $5 per day (and reduced working hours). His stated objective was to eliminate attrition and retain his trained workers but his hiring practices were refined to identify the best workers.

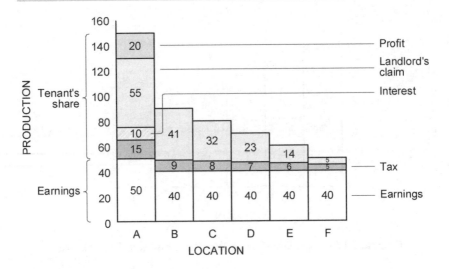

Diagram 18 – The Division of Wealth – The First Entrepreneur

This type of undertaking provides great opportunities for those with the right talents. The successful entrepreneur or captain of industry needs a clear vision, an ability to judge people, deft negotiating skills, and a capacity to squeeze the last ounce out of production. Over the years many have made vast fortunes, but as many have gone to the wall.[7]

If the undertaking is successful both production and earnings go up but production rises faster. The increased production that does not go in earnings goes in the first instance to the tenant, and earnings as a proportion of production fall. Seeing the success of early undertakings, others will be attracted by the possibility of a larger margin of profit. In order to obtain a site, they will offer landlords more than an ill-equipped tenant can afford, and gradually the latter will be forced out of all the good sites. These changes are shown on Diagram 19.

This is what happened in England at the start of the industrial revolution. Aided by the Enclosure Acts[8] and the new inventions,

7 The failure rate of new businesses is relatively high. Figures available for the US show that where they were employing staff 69% of new businesses survived two years and only 51% survived 5 years. U.S Dept. of Commerce, Census Bureau, *Business Dynamics Statistics 2009.*
8 The 'Enclosure Acts' were bills passed by the Parliament of the United Kingdom whereby land, previously held in common was deemed to be owned by a single person, to the exclusion of all previous users. Between 1700 and 1844 approximately 4000 Enclosure Acts were passed, enclosing some 6,000,000 acres of land, see J.L. & B. Hammond, *The Village Labourer*, Chapter 2. Wages rose only where workers had special skills but for the masses they fell dramatically.

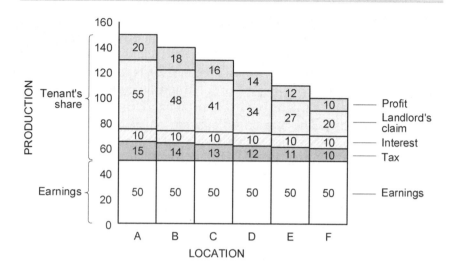

Diagram 19 – The Division of Wealth – Subsequent Entrepreneurs

entrepreneurs were successful in starting new undertakings. With the discovery of the steam engine, there was a great demand for coal to replace water-power and charcoal, and many mines were opened up. Canals, and later railways, grew at a rapid rate.

As time goes on and competition for the best sites becomes keen, the landowner is in a strong position and can sell or lease land to the highest bidder. Landlords' claims tend to the most the tenant can pay, and profits drop to the least on which an entrepreneur is willing to operate. The success of each undertaking depends on the profit margin. If profit margins are low fluctuations in trade will cause industrial distress and add to the risks of industry. The system is vulnerable, especially at the margin of production. At the outset, the effect of organising industry under an entrepreneurial system is a great increase in production, higher wages, and good margins of profit. As the system matures, competition for sites reduces profits and land-owners grow rich. In England this stage was marked by a period of building great country mansions, especially in the late 18th and early 19th centuries. However, during the second half of the 20th century there was a great increase in taxation,[9] largely to provide people with the decencies of life which they had come to demand but which they could not afford out of their earnings. Thus education, national health,

9 For data see page 178.

old age and widows' pensions, public assistance, children's allowances, benefits of various kinds, and all the expense of administering these schemes are met from taxation.

The effect of all this, as shown in Diagram 20, is that increased taxation is levied more-or-less in proportion to production. Consequently landlords' claims tend to drop as a proportion and landlords leave their country mansions.[10] The burden of taxation on the margin is a constant threat to undertakings, which would otherwise be fully capable of showing a profit after all other secondary claims have been met, and the fear of mass unemployment is never far away.

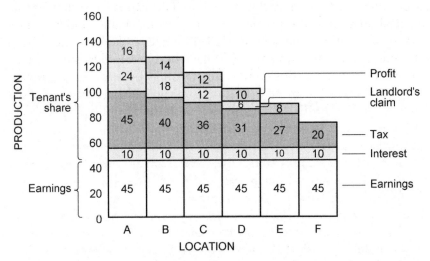

Diagram 20 – Division of Wealth under Capitalism

Undertakings merge into great combines in order to protect themselves against trade fluctuations and to reduce competition, increasing the tendency to private or public monopoly. Marginal industry clamours for protection and subsidy, whilst governments are forced to pass whole series of laws designed to alleviate the situation.

Diagram 20 represents the division of wealth that arises from such a system once it has become thoroughly established – the position in most industrialised countries today. In this system of total land enclosure, the chief advantages are increased production and higher earnings (though lower as a proportion of production). The chief failings are vulnerability to trade fluctuations, high taxation to subsidise low earnings and difficulty in operating on the margin of production.

10 A phenomenon particularly observable in England in the post World War II period.

Using a term coined by Karl Marx, we call this 'the capitalist system'. What is capital? It is very simply the tools, buildings, machinery and equipment required by industry to promote further production. Capital is wealth used to create more wealth. It comes out of production and, like all wealth, arises from human labour on land.

When early man devoted himself to making the most primitive of tools he was producing capital. With the aid of this capital production of wealth was greatly increased. All that has changed today is the scale. Capital is still wealth used to create more wealth. It is very simple. To confuse capital with money, stocks and shares or entries in balance sheets only leads to muddled thinking. The capitalist system is the practical answer to the problem of how to mechanise industry in a system of total land enclosure. Had the system of land tenure been different, some other system would have been devised to suit the particular circumstances. But there is no reason to believe that the advantages made available by scientific progress would have been checked in any way, even though the pattern of industry might have been very different.

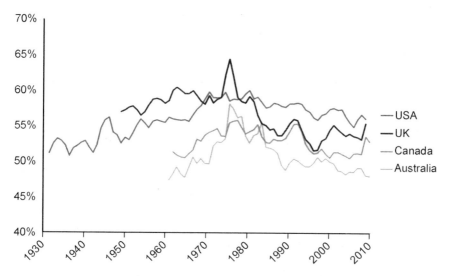

Diagram 21 – Gross Wages as Percentage of GDP[11]

11 Gross Wages and salaries as a percentage of GDP. Note these are not 'earnings' as defined in this book and include taxation paid on wages and salaries. Source: – For Australia, Department of Census and Statistics (series A2302467A and A2302401K); for UK, Office for National Statistics (GDP by type of Income, Series DTWM and YBHA); for Canada, Statistics Canada (Gross domestic Product Income based, Table 380-00001); US, Department of Commerce, Bureau of Economic Analysis (Gross Domestic Income by Type of Income).

Under the capitalist system earnings are relatively low. As a proportion of total production in the English-speaking world, they probably peaked in the mid-1970s at less than 50% and have tended to fall since, although as an amount they have increased. It is not surprising that people are not satisfied with this position: they want a larger share of the national cake. Under these circumstances this can only be achieved by subsidising earnings – hence the welfare state.

All this is obscured behind a cloud of rising prices as wage claims and increased taxes are passed on to consumers, themselves the various claimants on production.

In the period following the Second World War, at least until the collapse of the Soviet Union at the end of the 1980s, there were two main political schools of thought. One supported capitalism, seeing increasing production as the answer to all our problems. Its solution was to exhort everyone to work harder. The other school opposed capitalism, deploring the low level of earnings and blaming this on the entrepreneur. Its solution was to increase taxes and subsidise the wage earner. But as each in turn fought to gain power, each stole the other's weapons so that there was little to choose between their policies when in government.

It used to be claimed, for example in the UK, that the nationalisation of industry was the solution to economic problems.[12] But this only replaced the tenant by the state. It did nothing to increase earnings and the records showed no marked improvement in labour relations in those industries that had been nationalised.[13]

It is no good blaming capitalism. With all its failings, it is an extraordinarily ingenious mechanism and has brought in its train a great improvement in standards of living since the early 19th century. It arose to meet the economic situation which then existed, and this it has done to the best of its ability. Low earnings are not the fruit of capitalism. No lasting solution can come from trying to influence the level of earnings. They are the inevitable result of total land enclosure. If the community desires economic freedom that is the only point where action can prove effective. Anything else is but a patchwork attempt to mitigate the workings of natural law.

12 Hence the nationalisation of various industries in the United Kingdom (the coal mines – 1947, the railways – 1948, the steel industry – 1967, British Airways – 1974, and the motor industry – 1975. This led to inefficiency and considerable cost to the tax payer. When these industries were privatised the cost to the consumer dropped in real terms.
13 See UK Office for National Statistics, *Labour disputes: working days lost, 1901 to 1998: Social Trends 30,* which shows that the period of highest post-war industrial unrest coincides with the period of government ownership of British industry.

4.2 Secondary Claims

Chapter 2.4 introduced the charges of rent and interest that an entrepreneur must pay to develop production when land is enclosed. It was suggested that taxation would also inevitably increase.

The terms 'rent' and 'economic rent' are widely used in the study of Economics, and have acquired a number of different meanings. In order to avoid any confusion with the wider use of these terms, we shall call the payment to a landlord for the use of land the **landlord's claim**.

Two other claims can be made on the entrepreneur in this situation. The first is insurance and the second is rates (or property taxes). Rates we shall look at separately from taxation, generally because these have a quite different effect.

The Landlord's Claim

The landlord's claim always rises to the maximum the tenant is prepared to pay. When the other secondary claims have been met the landlord's claim absorbs what is left, except for the minimum margin of profit sufficient to keep the entrepreneur in business. This is the particular nature of landlords' claims. Rates and taxes may increase, interest charges may rise or fall from time to time, trade may be good or bad, but always the landlord's claim will tend to adjust to take up whatever is left, save only the least the entrepreneur is prepared to accept.[14]

There is of course a time lag before landlords' claims can rise to absorb any increase in profits beyond the minimum acceptable. When a tenancy is granted the landlord's claim is almost invariably fixed for a period and cannot be increased until that period has expired.[15] Tenancies may be monthly, quarterly or yearly, or for a number of years but at the end of the term the landlord has an opportunity to increase his claim to the maximum again. And if over the years production has been constantly increasing, prices rising, and business is expected to continue to increase there is usually room for some increase in the landlord's claim – sometimes a very substantial one.[16]

14 Adam Smith observed: 'As soon as the land of any country has all become private property, the landlords, like all other men, love to reap where they never sowed, and demand a rent even for its natural produce'. *The Wealth of Nations*, Book 1, Chapter VI.
15 Contemporary leases for retail premises may contain agreements to take a proportion of the gross sales as well as a fixed amount, thus the landlord's claim continues to increase as trade improves.
16 When the tenancy comes up for renegotiation the landlord is usually at a significant advantage because the cost of moving and re-establishing the business can be very great.

It may happen that a tenant cannot meet the landlord's claim and the other secondary claims out of the tenant's share. It may be that prospects have been over-estimated or that trade has declined after the claim was fixed. In this case the tenant may be forced out of production, or the landlord may agree to reduce his claim to a figure that the undertaking can just carry. The latter avoids the risk of having premises vacant for a long period.[17] But generally the landlord's claim must be regarded as a fixed charge during the term of the tenancy, with the prospect of an increase at the end of the term if there is any elbow-room at all.

On the other hand, where a tenant is in occupation under a long lease and the tenant's share has risen steeply over the years, the landlord's claim cannot be increased. This puts the tenant in nearly as good a position as if he were also the owner of the site. An effect of this can be that the undertaking is allowed to run below full efficiency, and this is quite common with old family businesses. When eventually the lease does run out the landlord may be able to increase his claim very substantially, perhaps as much as tenfold or more. If the firm is to survive there is no longer any room for inefficiency; the site must be used to maximum advantage. When traders put in new shopfronts or build extensions and generally extend the scope of their business, this is often a sign that the lease has just fallen in and been renewed at a much higher figure.

We begin to see why land is considered to be such a good investment. The entrepreneurial system has increased production all round and has accentuated the advantage of one site over another, producing very substantial tenants' shares. This has given enormous scope to the landlords and, although taxation has eaten deeply into their claim, what is still available for them is a very big proportion of the total wealth produced in the whole community.

Interest

The nature of money and interest are dealt with in more detail in Chapter 9. What can be said here is that in starting a new venture, in addition to land, the entrepreneur needs equipment and machinery, which is capital. It will often be necessary to borrow to obtain this, getting as much credit as possible from the banks, but beyond that, as

---

17 Similarly, landlords seeking new tenants during difficult times may offer to pay for fitting out office premises or offer rent holidays at the beginning of the tenancy, although the tendency is for the amount of rent to remain at the higher rate.

things are, the remainder must be borrowed from someone with those resources. Generally speaking, these funds can only come out of the tenant's share of other undertakings. In other words, the entrepreneur will borrow from those who have had a claim on other undertakings, either by way of interest, landlord's claim, or profits.

What is borrowed is a claim on present wealth – usually in the form of money. In return the entrepreneur will give a similar claim on future wealth and will in addition make a regular payment for this facility. This payment is called interest.

The entrepreneur may also borrow in this same way to buy a piece of land or to pay off debts. In these cases there is no capital involved but interest is paid on the loan. Interest therefore arises from the relationship of debtor and creditor and is in no way connected with capital as such.

Lending money at interest, or 'usury' as it used to be called, was forbidden in Judaic law. The early Christians also frowned upon usury. The letter of the law, however, did not forbid the Jews from lending to gentiles and so from early times they tended to become the money-lenders. At first money-lenders were despised and redress against their debtors could be somewhat precarious. But slowly, as land enclosure took its toll, it was realised that conditions had been created whereby usury was an inevitable part of economic life. Labourers could not equip themselves with capital and so they had to be equipped by entrepreneurs, who in turn had to borrow money from those who held the claims on wealth – at that time mainly landowners and merchants.

As time went on the view completely changed; usury became first 'money-lending' and is now 'investment'. It is a respectable activity and indeed is regarded as a service to the nation in that it provides work for many landless citizens. Perhaps Judaic law was right in its condemnation of usury.

The important thing to note here is that interest arises because of the power of the lender over the borrower, enabling the lender to extract some part of the tenant's share.

Insurance

In its simplest form insurance is a provision against possible disasters at some future date, including unforeseen liabilities arising from the use of the businessman's premises, products or services. The extent of the provision required will depend on the nature of the business, but it is worth noting that the requirement for capital continues to grow as tools become more sophisticated, and the provision that is needed against disaster increases proportionately.

As a commercial facility insurance arises naturally as a service because what remains to the entrepreneur after all the other secondary claims have been met is insufficient to accumulate reserves against this provision.[18] Commercial insurance therefore becomes a prerequisite for production. Historically landowners in many countries have been able to live well by staking their estates as security against possible insurance claims.

In the context of this discussion nothing further needs to be said, except to note that the business is expected to insure the landlord against any damage to his property as well as any damage to the businessman's own property, further increasing the potential liability.

Property Taxes (Rates)

Property taxes[19] are known in some parts of the English-speaking world as 'rates' and are sometimes called local taxation. They are a form of taxation based on land and buildings rather than on production, profits, prices, incomes, etc. The history of rating began with the Poor Law Act in England in 1601.[20]

From this a system of local taxation has developed across the world to deal with all the expenditure of local governments: roads, drainage, refuse collection, education, libraries, police, and local administration. Today this expenditure has grown to such a vast extent that it may include public housing, greatly increased education, health clinics, parks, sports grounds, fire brigades, police forces, urban planning, public transport, and so on.[21] The financial burden has become too great for the rating system and local authority expenditure is subsidised by the state from national taxation to an ever-increasing extent; indeed there is a body of opinion that would transfer the burden entirely to central government.

In most countries an assessment is made of the market value of each separate land unit together with the buildings or other

18 And similarly for wage earners in relation to their own property.
19 For an analysis of Property Taxation, its variations and consequences, see Francis K Peddle, *Cities and Greed*. This book focuses on Canada which has extremely diverse systems of property taxation.
20 The Poor Law Act 1601 stipulated that the parish should provide the 'impotent poor' (those too sick and old to work) with items of food and clothing and to be cared for in 'almshouses'. The 'able bodied poor' were to be set to work in a house of industry more commonly known as a 'workhouse'. The 'idle poor' were sent to a 'house of correction'. Pauper children were to become apprentices.
21 What is administered by local authorities varies enormously from country to country.

improvements upon it. Rates are paid at some percentage of that value.[22] There are some important features that should be particularly noted. First, rates are commonly based on what land, together with the buildings and improvements on it, would let at. Second, rates are often based on the use to which the land and buildings are actually put. Third, it is common that no rates are paid if the property is unoccupied. What are the effects of this?

If rates are payable on current use and the land is left vacant,[23] no matter how much that land might fetch in the market, no rates will be paid. Since the same also applies to taxation, conditions are conducive to speculation and to holding land out of use, thus creating an artificial scarcity. This is against the public interest.[24]

What happens to the rates if land is already in use and the tenant improves it further? If a bathroom is added to a house that had none, a factory modernised by adding central heating, new toilets and a canteen, or a new extension added to an existing building, then the rating assessment is likely to be increased. The result is that the full use of land is actually penalised while to hold it out of use is rewarded. This must inevitably check the improvement of buildings and hamper the expansion of industry.[25]

Under this system, if land worth hundreds of thousands an acre is covered with slum dwellings, the rates will only be assessed on the present use. And if the slums are allowed to deteriorate, the rating assessments will probably be decreased so that even less rates are paid.

In the case of a house with a garden in the main street of a town, the rates will be assessed on a letting as house and garden, ignoring not only what the land is worth as a site, but even what the same house would let for if it were used as shops or offices. This provision, where it exists, discourages the full use of land and enables owners to obtain an income from their land whilst waiting for it to become worth even more. When a site has been developed and a brand new building erected, still no rates will be paid until it is occupied. Thus it is that from time to time in many great cities there are new blocks of offices

22 In New Zealand and some parts of Australia and Canada rating is done on the 'unimproved' value of the site and rates are payable irrespective of whether the land is used or not.
23 Or any buildings on the land are unoccupied.
24 Consider for instance the residential areas in the 'rust belt' of America where there has been a massive population exodus. Notwithstanding the depression in house prices, what were once vibrant communities have become depressing and unattractive places to live.
25 In some jurisdictions local taxes have been removed or reduced to encourage industry or agriculture (a phenomenon common in depressed areas), and especially to try to attract 'international investment'.

standing empty.[26] It is not that no one wants them but that owners are happy to wait until some undertaking will pay their figure.

Though the effect of ensuring that rates were paid on unused as well as used sites would not necessarily be great, it would tend to reduce landlords' claims a little by putting more developed land into use, since landlords would be loath to suffer outgoings for land which produced no income. To rate vacant land as well as vacant buildings would be far more effective in bringing land into use and preventing speculation.

Who bears the burden of the rates? In commercial leases they are levied upon the occupier.[27] But the rates are closely related to landlords' claims. As has been described, the landlord's claim tends to absorb the balance of the tenant's share after all other claims and profit have been met. When leases are renewed and landlords' claims agreed, these will reflect the amount of the rates. The point is clearly demonstrated by the operation of the English De-rating Act of 1925, which relieved agricultural land from paying any rates and relieved industrial premises of a large proportion of their rates. The intention was to boost agriculture and industry and this was the initial effect. But when leases fell in rents rose to reflect the savings in rates, and so what was intended as a subsidy and encouragement to the tenants became a gift from the exchequer to the landowners.

Within its limitations, the principle underlying the rating system has certain advantages over other forms of taxation. Unfortunately its proper working has been greatly handicapped by these artificial modifications. This being so, it is little wonder that it is today regarded as an anachronism and overripe for reform.[28] But it is more than probable that reform without understanding the underlying causes of the inadequacy of the system would worsen rather than improve the situation.

26 Or in some cities, when the commercial real estate market has turned down, developers will suspend building projects, leaving vast holes in the ground or skeletons of new buildings standing for years, with a detrimental impact on business conducted on surrounding properties. Some city authorities have required such sites to be converted to public amenities (parks etc) to avoid those consequences.
27 It is customary for commercial tenants to pay all outgoings, although where a business uses only part of a site (as is common for an office block or an industrial estate), the landlord must pay for the whole site. Residential leases vary from one country to another depending on the legislative arrangements. In England it is the occupier, in New South Wales (Australia) the landowner who pays.
28 The concept that the user should pay has become widespread, so that a flat rate is often charged for waste collection, water supply, sewerage and other services.

Taxation

In order to raise the enormous sums required for government spending each year taxes are levied wherever conceivably possible. They are levied on individuals' incomes, sales, profits, prices of commodities, capital gains, internal combustion engines, legal agreements, conveyances, licences, betting, dead men's estates, and so on. Despite this apparent diversity the revenue all comes out of production – which is the only source of wealth. Whether the tax is paid directly from production by the tenant or the employee, or indirectly by the landlord or money-lender out of secondary claims, it is clearly still issuing out of production.

Take the case of a tax on capital gains: someone buys shares for $10,000 and sells them later for $20,000. They are taxed on the profit of $10,000, which is either a credit at the bank or a number of bank notes. But money is still a claim on wealth and whoever bought the shares had to forego a claim on wealth to do so. Eventually that claim can be traced back to a direct claim on production by an employee, money-lender, landlord, entrepreneur, or other secondary claimant.

Having established that taxes are paid out of production, let us see how they are divided between tenant and employee. In a system of full land enclosure, as shown in Diagram 8 on page 39, earnings are already reduced to the lowest acceptable level. Any increase of tax on earnings will bring them down below this minimum. This will lead to pressure for increased wages and after a little while net earnings will be re-established at the old level. In this way the incidence of taxation on earnings is passed on to the tenant's share. Despite this, tenant's share is the one basis on which taxation is not assessed at all. Income tax is levied on earnings, interest, landlords' claims and profits. Purchase tax is levied on prices, which are a reflection of total production. The others are less easy to place but in general taxes are assessed in proportion to production, becoming more complex and confused each year.[29] In fact all taxation, including that based on earnings, comes out of tenant's share. If taxation comes out of the tenant's share of production, would this not seem to be the natural basis on which to assess it?

Let us assume a community where unused land is freely available, and consider the possibility.

---

29 Although the proportions paid in different industries may vary, depending for instance on how labour- or capital-intensive the industry is and the relative mixture of taxes, especially those calculated on wages.

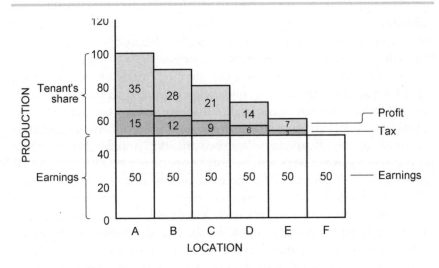

Diagram 22 – Tax at 30% of Tenant's Share

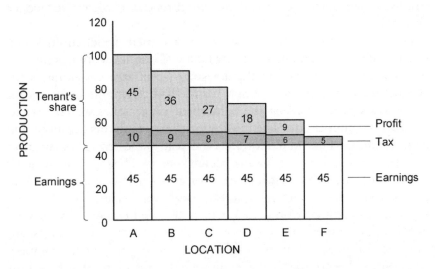

Diagram 23 – Tax at 10% of Total Production

Diagram 22 shows tax revenue calculated as 30% of the tenant's share and Diagram 23 shows tax revenue calculated as 10% of total production. In each case the total tax raised is 45. This is of course a trick: the important thing is the difference in the burden of taxation from site to site. Because in Diagram 23 tax is paid on the least productive site, earnings are reduced on all sites. Although the total tax raised is the same, total earnings on Diagram 22 are 300 and total earnings on Diagram 23 are 270; total profit after tax is 105 on Diagram 22 and 135 on Diagram 23.

The effect of all this, as we have seen before, is to put an undue burden on the marginal sites. Such sites will tend to be occupied by tenant farmers, independent craftsmen, and small traders. They will usually be ill-equipped, and in order to make a living the tenants will have to be prepared to work hard for long hours. Often in times of pressure their families will help in the business, for hired labour is too expensive to take on if it can be avoided.[30]

We see then that indiscriminate taxation has the same effect as land speculation in that it leads to land being held out of production or under-used. In so doing it tends to exert a downward pressure on wages and acts as a deterrent to production. This is one of the conundrums of modern politics: if taxation is increased, production is discouraged and earnings will not purchase so much; if taxation is reduced, it is not possible to maintain the social benefits that are needed to support a reasonable standard of living when the level of earnings is low.

Taxation is a very powerful tool of government which, used aright, can be of great benefit to a community. When its workings are not understood, it becomes a clumsy strait-jacket causing unnecessary hardship and frustration at every turn and defeating its own objects. Every attempt to patch up the deficiencies only makes matters worse. In order to put this right one must go back to basic considerations and align taxation to that out of which it is paid – the tenant's share.

30 For example, the small local shop so common among immigrant populations in many advanced countries.

CHAPTER 5

Value

*An economist is someone who knows the price of everything
and the value of nothing.*[1]

OSCAR WILDE

S O FAR the main focus of attention has been the great fundamental forces which shape the economic life of communities. These forces act on the whole population and do not concern themselves with individuals.

In this Chapter our focus will be on another force, which acts in every individual and governs relations with other individuals. This force expresses itself as human values.

It is values which determine how each reacts or responds to the great fundamental forces to which all are subject. Setting aside the element of chance, it is his values which will decide whether a man without means will struggle to make a precarious livelihood on a marginal site, or offer his services to an employer to work on a more advantageous site. It will depend on what he values more highly, independence or security, the possibility of making a fortune one day, or the certainty of a steady income now. The great fundamental laws will maintain the balance between what the average worker may earn independently at the margin and what he or she may demand by way of earnings on the better sites. These fundamental laws set the framework but individual values largely determine how it is filled.

Human values can also change the conditions in which the fundamental laws work, producing quite different results. In many western countries civil rights are highly prized: in Russia, even today, the concept of the State is highly prized. The fundamental laws operate

1 A popular joke, adapted from Oscar Wilde's play *Lady Windermere's Fan.*

to produce quite different results. At the root of these differences lie the human values that determine whether a man is a tinker, a tailor, a soldier or a sailor – provided all are needed by the community. These values decide whether production concentrates on housing or motor-cars, food, fashion or computer games. They also decide whether a nation enjoys civil freedom or tyranny, economic freedom or total land enclosure.

5.1 What are Values?

People buy things because they have desires and they have desires for more than they can afford to buy.

Suppose you particularly want a new television and also a new computer, each costing $1,000, and suppose you have only $1,000 to spare. If you buy the computer it signifies that at that time your desire for the computer was stronger than your desire for the television. In this situation you are comparing the strength of your desires one with another, whether you value a computer more strongly than a television. Value then is related to desire.

Care must be taken to avoid confusion between value and price. The prices of both are the same but to the purchaser the values are clearly different. Values are not directly related to price. It is not correct to say that the value of the computer is $1,000. By the potential purchaser the computer may be valued at more than $1,000 but less than $1,200. Price is fixed by the interplay of individual values in the market and these values will determine whether the sale takes place.

Two people apply for a job at $50,000 a year; both are earning considerably less at present and both find that the job would suit their capabilities and the work would be interesting and congenial. There is only one snag: the job involves going overseas for a year to a place where they cannot take their families. Both are offered the job, one refuses, one takes it. Why? It is all a question of values.

Things can only be measured against their like. Three metres is three times as long as one metre and two kilograms is twice as heavy as one kilogram. Similarly desire can only be measured against desire. That I desire one thing more or less than another is a question of intensity. Value is a measure of that intensity, a measure of preference or esteem. If I value a thing very highly it means that there are few things I desire more intensely.

In buying a carpet to fit a room, it is possible to take a large quantity and cut off what is needed. But this is not very practical.

81

If, however, we adopt the metre as a standard of length and measure the room in metres, the number of metres needed can be calculated and that precise amount ordered. Because the metre is a recognised standard of length, the storekeeper will be able to measure off the right amount of carpet without ever having seen the room.

However, if we want to tell a neighbour how much we value a book on Economics, there is no absolute standard of measurement[2] because each individual's values are personal. The neighbour might put a very low value on a book on Economics.

Any one thing may have as many values as there are people to desire it. It is not a quality of the object. Things do not have intrinsic value. For example, if I am shipwrecked alone with a treasure chest of gold it will have no value for me except the gold is in the shapes of useful tools or vessels. I might gladly swap the lot for a glass of water. Yet gold is normally thought to have great intrinsic value and water to have little.

Value resides in the individual preference not in the object. A thing nobody wants is valueless; but for anything to be valuable there need be only one person to value it. Its value will depend upon that person's estimation of its worth which will be based upon a personal standard.

The confusion over intrinsic value arises from the fact that an object may be valued for its different properties. Paper money is generally valued only for what it can buy, but gold coin is valued not only for what it can buy but also as a precious metal. A necklace may be valued by its owner for its associations, as a thing of beauty, as an investment, or as a status symbol. A painting may have little value as a piece of canvas and a frame but be greatly prized as a work of art.

The values of an individual also reflect the civilisation and culture in which that individual is reared, the traditions and customs acquired from the community and from the family. Each person's own bent is also important; it would be unreasonable to expect a musical genius to have the same values as a great general. It is important that this should be so or exchange would not be possible.

Assume for example that I have a camera and that you have a pair of binoculars. I would only part with my camera if I preferred your binoculars, and equally you would only part with them if you preferred

---

2 Even if we compare the value of a book to some other item, say, 'I would rather read a book on Economics than Shakespeare's Hamlet', the comparison is weak because the other person may have a completely different set of values around the text of Hamlet.

my camera. If we agree to exchange it means that I value the binoculars more than the camera, and you value the camera more than
the binoculars.

Exchanges are possible because people value things differently.
Normally each party to an exchange expects to get better value than
they give. Every exchange involves at least four values, two on either
side. Unless each set were valued on different standards neither could
gain and no exchange would take place. What then is meant by
exchange value or market value? The only conclusion can be that there
are no such things. They are unhappy synonyms for 'price' and can be
most confusing. An exchange involves four separate values – not one
value shared by both objects of exchange. Such thinking obscures the
relationship between values and price.

5.2 Values in Operation

Values are important and far-reaching. Apart from things like cameras
and binoculars, values are also placed on behaviour and relationships,
other people's opinions, education, the arts and so on; and, higher still,
on justice, goodness, truth itself. On the other hand, people may value
highly praise from someone, encouragement, skill in some craft, a day
at home with the family or a day away from them, a good night's sleep,
or a day's hard work. Day-dreams, hopes and ambitions, learning,
honour, nationality, happiness, are all valued, as well as a sense of
justice and the desire for truth. It is strange to realise that these are
things not normally spoken about; no doubt we will recognise that in
fact we seldom speak of the things we value highly. We must study our
own values first, for it will be more difficult to study other people's
when they are so very well hidden.

Nor are values always the same: what we value one minute, we may
be indifferent to the next, and quite opposed to the next. It all depends
upon our desires at the time. One person may agree to exchange
a cigarette lighter for a pen. They would not have considered it for a
minute the previous week but since then have given up smoking! Yet
another week and they may be regretting the impetuosity!

A lady described how, when she married, her mother gave her a tea
service which she had always thought was silver plate. Her mother had
always hated the thing as it needed constantly to be cleaned. The lady
liked her tea service; she thought it very pretty. Then one day she took
it to a silversmith and found it was solid silver. He offered to buy it
from her. Here are three quite separate values: to the mother, the

daughter and the silversmith. But the tea service was not sold so there was no price.

As personal values dominate the way individuals live, so the values in a community dominate its influence upon community members and upon other communities. The civilizing and cultivating forces in society work through value; thence spring justice, loyalty, honesty, plain dealing, and good workmanship. The debasing and disintegrating influences also work through value; thence spring tyranny, treachery, crime, deceit and bad workmanship. A community reaps as it sows and its values are the seed.

6

Price

Diagram 24 – The Factors of Price

PRICES EXIST when goods are bartered in the same way that they exist when money is used as a means of exchange. If you had agreed to exchange your binoculars for my camera, the price of the camera would be the binoculars, and the price of the binoculars would be the camera. If there had been agreement to exchange a television for one thousand $1 notes, the price of the television would be one thousand $1 notes, and the price of the one thousand $1 notes would be the television.

In each transaction there are two prices and four values. The prices equate but not so the values, for each party values more highly that which they receive than that with which they part.

Confusion between price and value arises easily. The practice of exchanging goods for money and money for goods has become so general that the word price is usually restricted to the money price for goods. For example, we say the price of a packet of biscuits is $2, the price of a computer is $1000; but this is a partial view for money is only a claim on wealth which enables the receiver to obtain what they really want in exchange for goods on a later occasion.

There is another point to watch in relation to price. Two farmers exchange five tons of chicken meal delivered to a farm for eight tons of wheat to be collected from that farm. Here the price of the five tons of chicken meal is eight tons of wheat, and the price of the eight tons of wheat is five tons of chicken meal plus delivery.

What then is price?

Price only arises on an exchange; it is all that is given, done or promised by one party in return for all that is given, done and promised by the other. Unlike value, price is tangible since it is the very thing that passes between the parties to an exchange.

6.1 Setting the Price

Free exchange only takes place if each party values what they receive more than they value what they are offering. If Alan has a pot of jam but would be equally happy to have ten of Betty's eggs instead, and if Betty has twelve eggs but would be equally happy to have Alan's pot of jam, then an exchange is possible. If Alan gets eleven eggs for his pot of jam then both parties will be well pleased. The price of the jam is eleven eggs and the price of eleven eggs is a pot of jam.

There are three factors that lead to the establishment of price: the seller, the buyer, and the conditions at the point of exchange. Betty may be able to persuade Alan to part with the pot of jam for only ten eggs, or he may persuade her to hand over twelve eggs. It all depends upon the conditions at the point of exchange. But before examining these conditions in detail, consider what happens if dollars are substituted for eggs.

This does not significantly change the picture. Alan will accept ten dollars and Betty will happily part with twelve dollars. The price will be somewhere in that range. By convention the buyer is the party whose part of the bargain is fixed in terms of money, whilst the seller's part is the goods given in exchange. If a shop offers money in exchange for second-hand jewellery, the shopkeeper is considered to be the buyer and the customer is the seller, although it could easily be argued that the shopkeeper is selling money in exchange for goods.

What are the conditions at the point of interaction using the example above? What determines whether Betty pays ten or twelve dollars for the jam? There can be many factors at work at the point of interaction. Betty may need the jam now for a cake she is baking whereas Alan is in no hurry, in which case Betty easily parts with twelve dollars. On the other hand Betty may be a good haggler and persuade Alan to accept only ten dollars. Similarly Betty may willingly part with twelve dollars without argument because she likes Alan or feels sorry for him.

By far the most important of the conditions at the point of inter-action is the alternative market. Betty may equate a pot of jam and twelve dollars in her valuation, but if she can get it just as easily from some other source for ten dollars she will be reluctant to pay more to Alan. Similarly if Alan can get twelve dollars for his jam from another buyer he will be reluctant to sell to Betty for less. Thus the market for any commodity sets a level of prices. This is not to suggest that all prices are set rigidly: they clearly are not and may vary for many reasons including of course lack of knowledge of the market by buyers and sellers alike.

Care must be taken when considering prices to compare like with like. A pot of jam sold by the shop on the corner is not the same thing as a similar pot of jam sitting on the shelf in a supermarket. A customer may well pay more quite willingly for the convenience of purchasing close by instead of having to drive to the supermarket, queue up and then drive home. Jam ordered over the internet and delivered to the door is another thing again.

Time can be a factor in a different way. Some people like to purchase the latest technological devices as soon as they are available. Others bide their time. The price at different times is often not the same.[1] Equally, in many transactions cash may be quite a different proposition to the seller than a credit card or three months' interest-free credit. We need to be very clear as to what is the price on both sides of the bargain before considering the conditions at the point of interaction.

There are many different forms of bargain but this basic triad of seller, buyer and conditions where they meet lies behind them all. The only real difference is the way in which the price is settled within the

---

1 Prices of many food items, for example, vary with the seasonal availability. Some such as ham and turkey vary with the cycle of feast times, even though suppliers are able to produce according to anticipated demand.

range possible in any individual exchange. In an eastern market every individual bargain is settled by haggling, whereas in a western shop haggling does not usually take place – the goods are on display, the price required is indicated and the customer either buys at that figure or tries another shop. But when it comes to buying a second-hand car or a house then we have no qualms about haggling and every bargain is settled individually. This is a matter of custom at the point of interaction.

Auctions vary enormously. In an auction the seller offers to sell a certain commodity to the bidder who offers the best price, almost always in terms of money, very often with a reserve price which represents the least the seller will accept. The auction may be of a Leonardo painting which is the only one of its kind, or a couple of brass pots and a lawn mower from an old house which is being sold up. On the London market vast quantities of grain or metal are auctioned, unseen by buyer or seller, described entirely by specification. In each case the price is fixed by the highest bidder. The conditions at the point of interaction play a large part. Someone may be carried away with the idea of having the brass pots and pay far too much for the lawn mower. In the case of the Leonardo all sorts of values come in. For grain on the London market there is likely to be more level-headed bargaining. At some wine auctions there is even greater variation. Here the highest bidder may choose how much wine will be purchased at that price. The next highest bidder may choose how much to buy of what is remaining, at his highest price, and so on until either all the wine is sold or all the bidders are satisfied. The price here varies with each buyer.

There is another form of price setting in which purchase is done by tender. Those who may be interested are invited to tender in writing the amount they are prepared to pay. A piece of land may be sold by tender. Shares are sometimes sold by tender, as are government treasury bills. It is common for building contracts to be based on tender.

These are all different means of fixing a price. They are different conditions at the point of interaction on an individual basis. But there is rarely just one seller and buyer. What effect does this have? A seller wants to sell a pair of shoes. Let us say he will sell them for $100 a pair. The buyer is prepared to pay up to $200 for a pair of shoes. It would seem that a deal must take place here, but what happens if the buyer finds somebody willing to sell shoes for $80 and somebody else for $60? What will the buyer pay now?

When there are a few million pairs of shoes on one side and a similar number of people on the other side, the market strikes a balance. There may be an occasional customer willing to pay $200, but more usually there is a market in shoes that establishes a general level of prices. A seller comes along who knows he can sell a certain type of shoe for $100. If he knows he can make them for $80, he is in a good business. Someone else will realise that and follow him, selling the shoes for $90. Then the first manufacturer will drop the price. All the time the market is being established.

Wages today are expressed in terms of money. When selling their labour though, each employee considers the standard of living he or she is prepared to accept in terms of goods and services. The prices paid when doing the daily shopping and the other expenses become the conditions entering into the triad.

This is very simple but very far-reaching. Every individual transaction arises from this triad whether the price appears to be fixed by the seller, to result from bargaining or to be settled by auction or tender. In all cases there will only be a sale when the method to be used is acceptable to both parties, and when the lowest price the seller will take is not more than the highest figure the buyer will pay.

6.2 Monopoly and Price

In a healthy free market prices will be kept down by competition so that profits tend to the least the tenant will accept. But if there is no competition, if one business manages to eliminate all or at least the greater part of their competitors, it can then increase prices without fear of losing sales to competitors. As prices increase some potential purchasers will be lost – those whose evaluation of the product is less than the increased price – but unless the demand is very sensitive to price changes[2] the entrepreneur will increase total sales in money terms or will at least increase profits.[3] Thus for a time increased prices lead to increased profits, until the point comes where a further increase in price would so much reduce demand as to begin to reduce profits again. The art of the monopolist is to manage supply so as to produce optimum profits. In the case of pepper, for example, a large increase in price has little effect on the amount that will be sold; on the

2 That is, demand is 'elastic' if small changes in the price have a large impact on the amount sold, and 'inelastic' if large changes in price have very little impact on the amount sold.
3 In some situations it may still be more profitable to increase prices even when sales reduce significantly.

other hand, the demand for motor vehicles is very sensitive to price increases.

There is no such thing as a perfect monopoly, for this requires complete control of supply either through elimination of competitors or by entering into a price-fixing agreement with them – a cartel; it also requires that there be no acceptable alternative for the goods or services available. This latter requirement particularly cannot be met in practice.[4] A monopoly in coffee for example cannot be fully effective in that a sufficient rise in price will drive people to drink more tea or other beverages instead. Similarly, a monopoly in copper turns buyers to zinc, steel, or other substitutes. But even an imperfect monopoly can have serious and undesirable effects upon the market by forcing up prices to the detriment of the public at large.

Monopolistic tendencies arise in many forms. There may be a full monopoly, or an agreement between competitors, as in a cartel.[5] Another form of monopoly is retail price maintenance[6] whereby a manufacturer lays down the retail price at which goods shall be sold. This gives monopoly advantages to the smaller customers by protecting them from fierce competition from large chains of stores. The latter can afford to charge lower prices or to slash prices on certain items as a draw to customers, willingly facing a loss in the expectation of increased turnover on other goods. Again, monopoly may give rise to discrimination in prices asked of different customers with a view to obtaining optimum profits.[7]

In order to establish a monopoly a trader will sometimes reduce prices quite drastically, and face heavy losses for a period with a view to forcing weaker competitors to go into liquidation or to sell out. Once a monopoly has been established prices will be increased again so as to maximize profits.

Monopoly power is not always deliberately exploited. It may act merely to protect a tenant from the forces of competition that would

4 Visa and Mastercard currently have an effective monopoly over payment for retail goods by international travellers. However, cash is always available if these two were to increase their prices to an unacceptable level – albeit much less convenient.
5 Most cartel behaviour these days is illegal. Currently the most enduring cartels are OPEC (Organisation of Petroleum Exporting Countries) which attempts to set prices for crude oil; the international payment systems operated by the banks – Visa, Mastercard and SWIFT, and international telecommunications groups.
6 Retail price maintenance is illegal these days in most countries but the influence of dominant suppliers still has the effect of keeping prices consistent, albeit they 'recommend' prices rather than dictating them.
7 For example, some airlines offer different prices for the same journey on the same date depending on when the booking is made, so that all seats are filled.

compel him to produce with greater efficiency. Prices in this situation may be unnecessarily high without the monopolist enjoying any great profits.

The attitude of governments toward monopoly has much changed over the years. There was a time when monopolies were commonly granted by the sovereign as royal favours in return for services rendered or for payment: the famous East India Company and the Hudson Bay Company were both given monopoly powers by royal decree.[8] Airlines throughout the world were granted various forms of monopoly in the years after World War II. Today monopolies are regarded as highly undesirable except where they are necessitated by the nature of the undertaking, as in the case of utilities,[9] railways, water supply, post,[10] etc., and these are often in the hands of government or are regulated private businesses.

Although in recent years a number of takeovers and mergers have been prevented by governments, monopoly is not always easy to detect and defeat in practice. Consider for instance the power of Microsoft and the attempts by authorities in a number of countries to break up its market dominance.[11] As firms become ever larger through mergers and takeovers and as new processes require vast plant and equipment, the likelihood of monopoly in many products continues to grow. There may be fierce competition between the new variants in relation to their principal products but many sidelines are likely to end up under one control.[12] Monopoly is clearly not in the public interest but is one inevitable consequence of the capitalist system. It may be condemned by government but once established the return to a really free market is very difficult to ensure. Where land is enclosed without payment of the full rent, the conditions at the point of interaction are

8 In 1600 and 1670 respectively.
9 Electricity supplies, gas and telephone have been subject to 'competition' in recent years. In some cases this simply means that the consumer can choose who invoices them for supplying the service, in others the supplier must provide additional services (managing the reporting and repair of faults, or in the case of telephone companies, supplying some of the infrastructure). There are rarely multiple services running down the same street for obvious reasons.
10 Although even the postal service is now subject to competition on the one hand from international parcel delivery companies and the other from the internet.
11 Or Mastercard and Visa which have in many countries escaped scrutiny. In some however contracts forcing retailers to charge the same price irrespective of the means of payment have been declared illegal.
12 For example in the field of computers there are essentially only two main products: Apple or Microsoft. The lattter are supplied by a number of manfacturers. Inside either of these many of the component parts are identical.

propitious for monopoly to arise. Without changing the basic conditions it is not possible to do more than curtail the worst excesses of monopoly: it cannot be eradicated completely.

6.3 Advertising and Price

Before considering advertising, here is a little story.

In 1790 or thereabouts a Mr Brown owned a small dispensary in York and invented a product which he called Doctor Brown's Liniment – he never was a doctor but the prefix gave a ring of authenticity to his product. He made outrageous claims for his liniment, as was the custom of the times, and came to sell 500 bottles a week to the citizens of York. News of the efficacy of his medicinal compound was passed on by word of mouth until the limit of his sales was set only by the number of people who could reach his shop. And there matters might have rested but for the advent of the railways.

With rail transport it became possible to approach a wider market. When the railway reached Sheffield, Mr Brown went there offering his product to suitable retailers. But at first no one in Sheffield was very interested in selling his unknown remedy. However, Mr Brown promised that he would advertise his liniment in the *Sheffield Telegraph*, telling the public of the approbation of the citizens of York for his famous remedy; in this way he would entice customers to their shops. Very soon Mr Brown had doubled his production. From then the pattern repeated, governed only by the spread of the railways and the availability of suitable advertising media.

But if the railway helped Mr Brown to reach a larger public in Sheffield, it also helped another dispenser in Barnsley to offer his compound in Sheffield, and in York as well. So now the public were offered two virtually identical products, both competing for their custom. Mr Brown immediately increased his advertising, while his competitor cut his prices and put his product into a more elaborate packaging. The battle might well have spread to further devices such as the introduction of a new improved variety of Dr Brown's Liniment, a bonus coupon, and so on; but before they reached these lengths the two rivals decided to merge and so cut all these advertising costs. Then other competitors appeared and the new partners had to start battling all over again.

In relation to Diagram 24 on page 85, the purpose of advertising is to influence the buyer's values so that he will wish to buy the advertiser's products in preference to those of competitors or in preference to other commodities. This enables the advertiser to obtain a higher price, or at least to gain a sale.

Advertising is basically simple but tends to divide into two types. There is the informative type of advertising to make known what is on offer. This is entirely desirable for otherwise potential customers would not know what was available. On the other hand, there is the blatantly competitive advertising aimed solely at persuading customers to buy one brand of goods in preference to any other. The success of this lies largely in making sure that the product name becomes a household word. All other things being equal, which brand would you buy: one you had never heard of or one with a name that was familiar?

The costs of advertising are today enormous and can only be recouped out of the resulting increases in profits. The situation has been reached where without advertising many goods are virtually unsaleable. It is estimated that in the grocery trade well-known brands of food cost on average 25% more than unbranded foods of the same quality. It is quite an indictment of shoppers that names remembered subconsciously replace quality as the criteria by which goods are chosen.

Apart from a monopoly, one effective alternative to advertising is for a company to control the retail outlets and sell its own produce. Little advertising is needed by supermarket chains to sell products they brand as their own. Some retail chains have made such a virtue of this that it has become the key to their success. Oil companies work on the same principle through petrol stations owned by or tied to the company.

Where the range of suppliers is small but sales are over a vast field, as with detergents, then advertising has become essential and products must be constantly given new appeal. So it appears that well-known brands of washing powder wash whiter every year and pain relief products become ever more efficacious.

Advertising these days is a huge industry and a subversive one. Apart from its informative function, it gives no direct benefit to the public but rather takes away people's capacity to exercise discrimination. It contributes very little to human wealth but has a profound effect upon human values, and thus upon the pattern of production.

6.4 Taxation and Price

What is the effect of taxation? Imagine that in a shop window you see a watch for which you would be perfectly happy to pay $200. The salesman would be glad to sell it to you for $180. It would seem that there must be a deal. But purchase tax is imposed and the law stipulates that if the watch is sold for $180, the seller must give the government $36. So for the seller to obtain $180, the price will have to rise to $225.[13] Since you are only prepared to pay $200 there can be no sale. Everyone has experienced this whether they realize it or not.

6.5 The Law of Supply and Demand

In every sale the buyer is influenced by the knowledge of what he will have to pay someone else for the goods or for a substitute. Similarly, the seller is influenced by knowledge of what he can sell for elsewhere. The effect of a large number of transactions carried out, with each party having an eye to the alternative market, is to set a general level of prices for each commodity. Statistical law acting through this triad sets the market price. The least the seller will accept is influenced by what the goods cost to produce;[14] the most the buyer will pay is influenced by how much he has available to spend on this or other merchandise. This is the basis of supply and demand.

The 'law of supply and demand' is one of the main planks of current economic theory. In effect this says that the quantity demanded for any good or service will increase as prices fall. Conversely suppliers will increase the quantity of goods and services offered for sale as prices rise. These two statements can be expressed as lines on a chart and the market price is said to be set at the point where these lines cross, as shown in Diagram 25 on the next page.[15]

By themselves these graphs are of little practical value since they always assume that other factors remain constant – which they never do.[16] In fact, this triad of buyer, seller and conditions where they meet is the law by which all prices are fixed, in conjunction with statistical law – the law of large numbers. These three factors settle the market and the conditions of supply and demand for all commodities.[17]

13 That is say, a tax of 20% of the total sale price.
14 Seller may accept less if for instance cash is urgently needed, but this cannot be sustained.
15 Economists are often able to express the lines as a mathematical formula, an expression of statistical law.
16 Economists use the term '*ceteris paribus*' or 'other things being equal'. External issues which may affect price include such things as the price of possible substitute products (such as Vegimite for Marmite), the availability of complementary products (such as software for computers, re-charge stations for electric cards, etc), changes in the consumer's income, or in taste, or in confidence levels in the community, etc. Such movements change the shape and positions of the lines on the chart.
17 The curves and angles of graphs vary with the susceptiblity of price to changes in supply and demand.

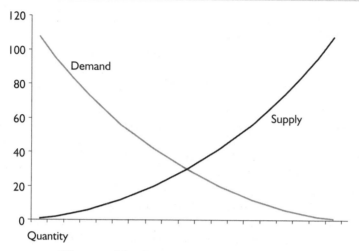

Diagram 25 – Demand and Supply Graph

The significance of price being expressed in terms of money is that money is a claim on other wealth, and it is this claim that is in effect being exchanged for the goods purchased. Any rise or fall in the market price of a particular commodity must be considered against the amount of wealth it will command. An increase in an undertaking's sales measured in terms of money does not necessarily represent an increase in production: it may arise from general inflation or, if the prices of other goods remain steady, from a real increase in price due to a change in the conditions at the point of interaction in favour of the seller, such as the elimination of a competing supplier.

6.6 Production and Price

Some further clarification is required on the relation between production and price. Production provides the goods and services which are wealth. Claims on production are measured in terms of money. The production of wealth can only be reconciled with these claims by equating money with wealth. However, production can only be measured accurately in terms of goods and services produced. To say the United States' Gross National Product is $14,586 billion[18] is misleading – in 2000 it was $9,898 billion[19] but it clearly has not increased by 40% over ten years. Changes in both the purchasing power of

18 World Bank *World DataBank* figures cited 9 May 2012.
19 *Ibid.*

money and variations in the relative prices of goods and services make comparison almost impossible.[20]

Consider landlord's claim, usually spoken of as rent. The rent on different sites clearly varies considerably. When leases are renewed the rent may increase very substantially. But rent does not enter into price.[21] The price that can be charged for goods on one site, as opposed to the price that can be charged for the same goods on another site, may affect the rent, hence the high rents for shops in some locations. Prices of goods and services may enter into rent but rent does not enter into price.

Prices in the English-speaking world have been relatively stable in recent years. Governments have increased their borrowings to pay for the mitigation of poverty and overseas military adventures instead of increasing taxation, and are only now increasing taxation to repay their debts. Consequently, there is a clamour for increased wages despite poor trading conditions.

It is widely held that prices are continually chasing wages, that is to say, producers increase prices because their wage costs have risen. But it was noted earlier that wages are determined by the least the employee is prepared to accept. In fact, wages are continually chasing prices, as is clear when it is realised that earnings are falling rather than rising as a proportion of production.[22] Increases in the standard of living are largely due to social services – a poor substitute for higher real earnings – and to the continual reduction in prices of manufactured goods imported from emerging economies.

20 For comparison purposes, figures for GNP are commonly adjusted for inflation, usually using consumer prices. In the English-speaking world, population and participation in the workforce are increasing – although not at the same rates – and this inevitably elimates most of the apparent gain. Other factors should be noted. First, many goods produced today were not available in previous years and so cannot be compared; second, as specialisation has increased much production has been commercialised and counted in GNP that was previously produced but not counted; third, GNP calculated by income includes monetary income such as capital gains on real estate and financial assets, which are not the result of production; finally GNP is a measure of what is produced, CPI is a measure related to consumption, and in a trading economy these may not equate.
21 Of the secondary claims, interest, taxation and insurance directly increase costs, and wherever possible the entrepreneur will increase prices to cover the increased cost. Rent however absorbs the difference between the least the business will accept and net revenue.
22 Note: 'earnings' as defined in this book. As an indicator, gross wages have been falling since the mid-1970s. See Diagram 21, page 69.

7

The Means of Exchange

A COMMUNITY allows people to specialize and find the calling that suits them best. To satisfy their desires specialists must exchange and, if everyone is a specialist, each must trade with the entire community. What the community provides in exchange is money and credit which are the subject of this chapter. The reality is very different from the outward appearance – and far simpler. But in order to recognise the reality, we must be prepared to set aside what we have come to take for granted about money, banking and trade, and take a fresh look.

7.1 What is Money?

Chapter 5 considered value and concluded that values were individual and could not be measured by any standard: an article has as many values as there are people who desire it. Consider again a simple proposition of barter – the exchange of my computer for your television. There will be four values in this example: an exchange takes place if I value your television more than my computer and you value my computer more than your television. Barter of this kind can only be very limited. It may be that I would gladly exchange my computer for your television, and that you would not be sorry to exchange your television if only I had a mobile phone to offer but, since I want to keep my mobile phone, no trading can take place. What is needed is some medium of exchange, something that is readily in demand by everyone – or at least by the majority.

Suppose I offered you one hundred packets of cigarettes for your television. You would consider your values and if you were happy with the suggestion we would do business. You could then smoke the cigarettes. But let us assume that you keep them and later find someone

97

willing to exchange them for a mobile phone. In the meanwhile I might find someone who would take my computer and give me another one hundred packets of cigarettes in exchange. At the end of the day you have gained a mobile phone in place of a television. I have gained a television in place of a computer – and I still have one hundred packets of cigarettes. The cigarettes have facilitated the flow of trade and have acted as a medium of exchange. In fact, the cigarettes have played the role of money.

Throughout history there have been countless forms of money. Cattle have very commonly been used in this way for the major purchase, such as a slave or a horse. The word 'impecunious' stems from the Latin 'pecunia' meaning money, which in turn derives from 'pecus' meaning cattle. Also used as means of exchange have been salt, rice, honey, oil, silk, skins, cloth, beads and other ornaments, and metals such as gold, silver, lead, bronze and copper. The cowrie shell has been used in this way for centuries in some Pacific islands. As for our example of cigarettes, these were a common form of money in Germany during the collapse of the deutschmark after World War I, and also by occupying troops in Europe during World War II.

The next step is self-evident. Metal is minted into coins, which have the guarantee of the State[1] and then there is no need to doubt the worth of your exchange medium. You have a handful of coins to make your purchases with greater ease and more surety than if you had to trail around a couple of oxen and an assortment of other exchangeable goods of varying shapes and sizes.

Coins were originally of precious and semi-precious metals which had an alternative use as well as being used as money, just as the cigarettes, in addition to being used as a medium of exchange, could always be smoked. Gradually it was realised that the alternative usefulness of money was not really important provided people trusted it as a means of exchange. Currency today consists of paper notes and coins of inexpensive alloy which fulfil the role of money perfectly because

---

1 The credibility that the State provides here is extremely important, as noted by Marco Polo: 'In the City of Kanabalu is the mint of the Grand Khan who may truly be said to possess the secrets of the alchemists, as he has the art of producing paper money ... when ready for use he has it cut into pieces of money of different sizes ... the coinage of this paper money is authenticated with as much form as if it were actually made of pure gold or silver ... and the act of counterfeiting it is a capital offence. When thus coined in large quantities, this paper currency is circulated in every part of the Grand Khan's dominions; nor dares any person, at peril of his life, refuse to accept payment. All his subjects receive it without hesitation, because wherever their business may call them they can dispose of it again in the purchase of merchandise they may have occasion for such as pearls, jewels, gold or silver. With it, in short, every article may be procured.' *The Travels of Marco Polo*, circa 1295.

people have confidence in them. So, if we go back to our earlier example, I could offer you one hundred five pound notes instead of one hundred packets of cigarettes for your television and the deals could all go through as before.

So long as people have confidence in bank notes as a medium of exchange, that is all that matters, and it really is as simple as that. But should anyone question the significance of that scrap of paper, let us see what they will find. Written on the English note are these words: 'I promise to pay the Bearer on demand the sum of Five Pounds', and underneath is the signature of the Chief Cashier, 'For the Governor and Company of the Bank of England'.[2] It is, then, a promise to pay, an acknowledgement of a debt. But to pay what? To pay five pounds. You certainly will not get an amount of gold in return for your five pound note; you will only get five one pound coins or a new note in exchange. There is, then, no such thing as a pound – it is a standard of measurement, a measurement of indebtedness. All that matters is that you should be able to exchange the bank's indebtedness to you for goods and services when you require them.

Consider the example again. I have one hundred five pound notes, each of which is an acknowledgement that the Bank of England owes me five pounds. I exchange the notes for your television. The Bank of England now owes you five hundred pounds instead of owing it to me. You in turn use the notes to obtain the mobile phone and the debt passes on again. What could be more convenient than a debt as a medium of exchange – provided everybody trusts the debtor?

Instead of the five pound notes I might give you a cheque on, say, Barclays Bank. This is an instruction to the bank to pay you five hundred pounds. Pay it into your account, assuming you also bank at Barclays, and the bank credits your account by five hundred pounds, thus increasing their indebtedness to you, and they debit my account, thus decreasing their indebtedness to me. If, when I sell my computer, I pay the proceeds into my account, then Barclays Bank owes me the same amount as originally.

Instead of using cigarettes as money we have used debts, either debts from the Bank of England or from Barclays Bank, as the case may be. Why is it necessary to bring them into the picture? If I had written out a promissory note for five hundred pounds – that is an

2 In the United States, we speak of a 'dollar bill', reflecting that it is a bill of exchange (a debt). Other currencies often have wording to the same effect, eg: Australian, Canadian and New Zealand paper currency says 'This ... Note is legal tender ...) where 'note' is banking shorthand for 'promissory note' (a debt).

I.O.U. – would not that have met the case? Well, it might have done, if you could have been sure that the mobile phone owner would accept it in payment, but he might not trust the note if he did not know me well; or even if he did, he might be unsure of finding anyone else to take it from him.[3] But everyone knows Barclays and trusts their promise, so the cheque is accepted, provided they are satisfied that I have sufficient funds in my account to meet it, that is to say that Barclays owes me sufficient funds to cover the transaction. And if they do not trust Barclays, they can always cash the cheque and get hold of bank notes – a debt from the Bank of England.[4]

Clearly there is no such thing as a pound. Just as there is no such thing as a yard or a pint or a ton. Pounds, dollars and euros are scales of measurement and what they measure is indebtedness. But there can be no fixed standard of indebtedness for it has no physical form. Length can be measured against the standard yard, which may take the form of a rod of fixed length, or the distance between two marks on a piece of stone. Similarly with volume and weight. But there can be no true standard of indebtedness for all to see.

Nonetheless, money provides a very useful scale of measurement for purposes of trade. Gifts and theft apart, nothing can be acquired without either producing it for ourselves or exchanging other goods, services or promises for it. To go back to the earlier example, you are willing to exchange your television for one hundred five pound notes, that is for a promise to pay five hundred pounds – a measure of indebtedness. In deciding whether to agree or not you will be assessing all those goods and services which that degree of indebtedness from the Bank of England will enable you to command. If you value one or more of these more highly than the television, you will accept the hundred five pound notes. If you value none of them as highly, you will not accept the notes and the deal is off.

Price, as was said earlier, only arises on exchange. It is all that is given, done or promised by one party in return for all that is given,

---

3 In the early days of the British colony in Australia insufficient coins were brought to the colony to satisfy domestic trade. Merchants would produce I.O.U.s to fill this gap, and these were traded as money. But because they were not as trustworthy as the coin of the realm they were discounted, giving rise to the concept of 'sterling' for coin, and 'currency' for the ad hoc notes of the same denomination.

4 Coins are simply tokens representing smaller currency units or proportions of them. They may be changed into bank notes anywhere. Coins are often not issued by the banking authorities but by government itself. This is simply a product of history arising from when coins were the predominant form of money. Coins represent a very small proportion of the money in circulation.

done or promised by the other. In the earlier example the price of the computer, the television and the mobile phone is, in each case five hundred pounds. Our values were all different. I valued the five hundred pounds more highly than my computer but less highly than the television, whilst you valued the television more highly than the computer but less than the mobile phone. Nevertheless, by equating five hundred pounds with the price each was prepared to pay, trade was enabled to flow.

So it is throughout the whole of society. Everyone's earnings are a primary claim on production. But it is extremely inconvenient and impractical to be paid in our actual produce. Fishermen do not want to be paid in fish; car assembly line workers do not want to be paid in cars, or even in spare parts. In a service industry such as building or insurance the position becomes quite impossible anyway. Everyone is quite content to be paid money – that is, a debt from the Bank of England or one of the ordinary banks – knowing full well that with this money there will be no difficulty in claiming the equivalent in whatever form of goods and services. The wages and the wealth acquired will equate to the price received for the work and given in exchange for goods and services. And at any time this price, being paid in debts, may be expressed in terms of pounds, dollars or euros.

This in essence is the secret of money. It is a medium of exchange. It can be in any form, provided people will accept it. In the modern world, with its enormous complexity and specialisation, the only really convenient form of money is that of debts:[5] debts acknowledged by an institution in which people have trust. The nature of our familiar pounds and dollars is quite ephemeral. But as long as people believe in them they are safe – far safer than salt or cowrie shells. In fact, as safe as the Bank of England.

7.2 Credit

Credit is the belief or trust that a man will fulfil his economic obligations. This trust is essential to all trade. Even in a simple case of barter there has to be trust between the two parties or neither will part with their goods for fear the other will snatch them and run away. But most forms of trade require a little more trust than that. For instance, if a builder orders a thousand bricks to be delivered on site, is he to pay

---

5 A product of the Renaissance culture which invented double entry accounting and established the concepts of duty and trust which allowed the banking system to flourish.

as the first brick is unloaded or the last? Either way there has got to be trust on the part of the one party or the other, and in practice it is more than probable that payment will not be made until the end of the month. In the meantime the builder enjoys credit.

When someone 'gives credit', they are in fact accepting in return for goods given a promise by the purchaser to pay. Equally, if a purchaser pays in advance for goods to be delivered, this is also giving credit and relies on a promise to deliver the goods. During the period between the fulfilment of the two parts of the exchange the parties are bound by obligation – one is the debtor for the purchase price and the other is the creditor. The debt is the duty arising on the promise to pay; the credit is the right to have that duty performed.[6]

This debt can be extinguished in various ways. First, by **release**, in which the debtor is relieved of obligation; secondly, by **satisfaction**, in which the promise is fulfilled (as when goods are delivered or a service discharged); third, by **set-off**, where one debt is off-set in part or whole against another; and, fourth, by **novation**, where one debt is substituted for another, as when payment is made by cheque or bank notes and the debt of a bank or of the Bank of England is substituted for that of the debtor.[7]

As society develops and production becomes more complex with ever-increasing specialisation, so credit becomes ever more important. When we look at industry we see people working on ventures which will not reach fruition for long periods. It may be months or years before payment is made but meanwhile the workers must eat, be housed and clothed. Simultaneously with their efforts others will be producing food, clothing and shelter for the whole community. They will gladly provide for their fellows working on long-term projects but they will want to be paid in cash. In wanting cash they are wanting 'a promise to pay' either from an ordinary bank or from the Bank of England In fact, a promise from the long-term producer would meet the event equally well if only there were sufficient trust in that promise. In practice what happens is that the banks set up as specialists in credit. They take over their customers' promises and give

6 Strictly, the belief that it will be performed, from the Latin 'credo', I believe.
7 Release – may be voluntary or by an order of the court if a contract is declared void. Satisfaction – applies in the case of an obligation relating to some specific goods or service, where no substitute is acceptable – such as an agreement to sell a specific car or a ticket is to hear a particular singer. Set-off – is used where there are obligations in both directions. Thus, when you trade in your old car against a new one there are debts each way which can be off-set against each other leaving only the balance as an unfulfilled debt.

their own in return. Because the credit of the banks is good, their promises are readily acceptable and production can go forward.

Imagine a shipbuilder who has on hand an order that will take two years to complete. He must buy his raw materials, meet his other costs of production and then pay wages and meet secondary claims such as interest charges on his plant, landlord's claim and rates. All these expenses must be met, starting from the day the keel is laid and mounting higher and higher all the time. Yet he will not be paid in full until the ship is completed, although he may get one or two payments on account during the course of the work. If the bank manager is satisfied that this is a sound project with an assured purchaser at the end, he will be willing to give the shipbuilder credit as the job proceeds. This means that when the shipbuilder writes out cheques to pay for raw materials, the bank increases its debt to the payee (the supplier of the raw materials), even though a corresponding decrease in the debt to the shipbuilder will leave an adverse balance. The shipbuilder is now working on an overdraft. As the job proceeds and more payments are made by the shipbuilder, whether by cheque or by cash drawn from the bank, so the overdraft increases. Eventually the contract is completed, the purchaser pays up in full and this more than covers the shipbuilder's payments. The purchase price is paid into the bank and the overdraft is wiped out, leaving the shipbuilder with a favourable balance once again. Money has been created, has served its purpose and been extinguished. The bank has lost nothing; in fact it has gained by charging for its services; production has been enabled to take place and the flow of trade has been facilitated. It is all so simple.

By granting an overdraft in this way the banks have created new debts against themselves and thus have created new money.[8] This may seem a little alarming at first and suggests that if banks want to raise funds for any purpose, such as to rebuild their offices or increase staff wages, they can do so just by making the necessary entries in their books. But it is not like that. Notwithstanding the regulations, banks that did that sort of thing would soon run into trouble. People would lose faith in their reliability and credit-worthiness.

When a bank gives credit against production the money is created in step with the production of wealth, for a half-finished ship is worth more than its component parts. The money is backed by wealth and

---

8 It is not the approving of the overdraft which creates the money, but the drawing of cheques against the overdraft limit. In this situation, deposits to the shipbuilder's accounts extinguish the money. This will be discussed in the next chapter.

is perfectly sound. When the ship is eventually sold the shipbuilder pays off his overdraft and the new money is extinguished. Thus money appears with production and is extinguished with consumption. What could be sounder?[9] There is no fear that giving this credit will jeopardise the currency; it cannot result in too much money in relation to wealth for it grows and disappears with wealth.

In the early days banks were able to print notes[10] and make money almost at will.[11] Many failed, and governments limited this right to approved banking institutions[12] or created banking institutions to fulfil this role.[13]

A four-dimensional view of production is required. It is not an instantaneous process. The farmer takes six months or so from the time he sows to the time he reaps. To build a house may take a year, to build a bridge may take five years or more. Despite the speed of modern production, the average time from when the cycle of production starts with the extraction of raw materials from the earth until it reaches the consumer is seldom less than a year and often very much more. Then again, consumption is hardly ever instantaneous – except perhaps in the case of fireworks. Food may be bought to last a day but clothes may last a number of years, a ship decades, and buildings and bridges centuries.

If at any point in time a snapshot is taken of production it will reveal various stages of completion evenly spread (in normal times of normal trade at any rate). As one ship sets out on her maiden voyage, so another is launched and the keel is laid of another. At the other end of the scale yet another ship is edging its way into the scrapyard. Whenever the snapshot is taken we shall also find that people are eating, burning fuel and being transported from place to place.

This is the large view. People are specialising. Production is running smoothly. But to the individual it does not look like that at all. Put ourselves in the shoes of the mechanic in the shipbuilder's yard or the clerk in the office. We have done our work and we expect to draw our

9 It could be argued that consumer finance – credit card debt, personal loans – is not backed by production and may be considered undesirable for this reason. But often even this is backed by wealth not yet consumed, as in the case of a loan to buy a car or to repair a house.
10 In some countries they still do. Hong Kong and Scotland are examples.
11 This did not occur in the United States where in 1781 an act was passed that established the Bank of North America as the sole issuer of bank notes for the newly independent nation.
12 Such as the Bank of England, which was a private commercial organisation until it was nationalised in 1946.
13 Such as the Federal Reserve system (1913) in the United States and the Reserve Bank in Australia (1959).

wages. Where they come from is not our concern. We are not interested in the fact that the ship will not be finished and paid for until next year; that is the employer's worry. Nor are we concerned as to how the shipping company will pay for the ship when it is finished. We are not interested in buying ships; all we want is our money to pay the rent and other bills and to provide the weekly housekeeping. Living in Europe, perhaps it does not occur to us that the bananas we eat come from the Caribbean, the oranges from Israel and that our clothes are likely to be made of Australian wool. We do the work we are given and in return ask only for our wages, which we want to be able to spend – now! This applies to all of us in one way or another.

These then are the two viewpoints – that of the community and that of the individual – and they are quite different. The link between them is credit. Banking thus has a special part to play in industry. Banks are specialists in credit. When they operate well they are in the best position to judge the credit-worthiness of their customers. If they are satisfied, they accept the customers' credit and give their own in exchange. This is acceptable everywhere – at least within their own country. Once again, money facilitates the flow of trade. This is the soundest form of money, for it is created and extinguished in unison with the production and consumption of the wealth by which it is backed.

SECTION 2

The Capitalist System

S O FAR we have looked at the elements of the creation and distribution of wealth from first principles and, although examples were used from the contemporary world, our concern has been primarily with the essence of things, irrespective of whether the economy is organised as a capitalist, communist, feudal or other system.

In this section we shall consider the specifics of the capitalist economic system as it has manifested in the English-speaking world over the last couple of centuries.

To begin with we shall consider money, the banking system and inflation.

Although there are some differences,[1] broadly speaking the monetary and banking systems are similar in most countries in the English-speaking world. A large number of other countries have followed this model.

1 The United States being the furthest from the common approach largely because they were reluctant to adopt a single banking and monetary authority (The Federal Reserve System involves a number of 'Reserve Banks'). Until recently restraint was exercised against banks growing too large by legislation against interstate operation of banks.

CHAPTER 8

Money

A simple invention it was in the old-world Grazier, sick of lugging his slow Ox about the country till he got it bartered for corn or oil — to take a piece of Leather, and thereon scratch or stamp the mere Figure of an Ox (or Pecus); put it in his pocket, and call it 'Pecunia', Money. Yet hereby did Barter grow Sale, the Leather Money is now Golden and Paper, and all miracles have been out-miracled: for there are Rothschilds and English National Debts; and whoso has sixpence is sovereign (to the length of sixpence) over all men; commands cooks to feed him, philosophers to teach him, kings to mount guard over him, to the length of sixpence.

THOMAS CARLYLE
Sartor Resartus

CREDIT ARISES from the need to bridge the time gap between production and consumption. It is the belief that a man will fulfil his economic obligations. Money as we know it today is a means of measuring these economic obligations which are incurred in trade and production, and of transferring them from one person to another. Thus money arises from production and trade.

For any form of money to be sound, people must be able to accept it safely in exchange for a claim on production, keep it and then hand it over to others for the same purpose. Provided people trust one another and have confidence in the working of the economic system, the soundest monetary system will be one in which the volume of money expands and contracts with the volume of trade and production. This cannot happen where money takes the form of gold or silver, for the amount of these commodities available is not connected to the volume of production and trade.

In Chapter 7 we said that pounds, dollars and euros are all measures of indebtedness. They operate efficiently as mediums of exchange as long as people trust the institution that issues the debt and trust that the paper on which the debt is expressed is provided by that institution.

In the modern monetary system money takes three forms: private money (bills of exchange, etc); bank money (deposits with commercial banks); and public money (the cash issued by government or the central bank).

8.1 Private Money

Bills of Exchange

Bills of exchange[1] have their origin in, and are particularly appropriate to foreign trade where goods may be in transit for several weeks. The seller who becomes the creditor wants early payment; the purchaser will be most reluctant to pay before he has even received the goods, let alone sold them on.

In its simplest form a bill of exchange is a promise to pay the creditor a nominated amount of money on a certain date – usually 90 days hence. This is only of use if the debtor is sufficiently well known. If that is the case the bill may be used as money by the creditor and may be given to a third party in payment for goods and services. Alternatively, it can be discounted by selling it to a bank or other financial institution, some of which specialise in this sort of business, for slightly less than its face value, thus obtaining bank money or public money that can be used to pay for the goods and services required. If the potential debtor is not known to the creditor this will not work.

In the past, to get around this problem, some of the larger, better known merchants started using their credit for the benefit of their less well known brethren by lending their name to the bill.[2] They would 'endorse' bills, standing in as guarantor. The creditor could then either wait for the bill to be paid, pass it on in settlement of his own debts, or sell the bill at a discount.

The merchants who provided this service found that they could charge for it and gradually began to drop their trading activities in

1 For a fuller description of bills of exchange, see Gillett Brothers Discount Co. Ltd, *The Bill on London*, and Oscar R. Hobson, *How the City Works*. These are old books, but the principles are sound.
2 A late renaissance invention. Initially, these were primarily Italian merchants, and in London they congregated in Lombard Street.

favour of endorsing, issuing and trading bills. They became known as merchant banks or acceptance houses.[3] In the early years of the 20th century the London merchant banks, among them Rothschilds, Barings, Schroders, Lazards, Morgans, were exceptionally prosperous and were financing the greater part of world trade in this way.

Trading banks also accept and endorse bills of exchange. Today this business has dwindled but it rises from time to time, often depending on the regulatory regimes governing banks.[4] Money is created by this means to bridge the gap between the time when the goods are shipped by the exporter and are received and probably sold by the purchaser. After the exchange is completed the bill is paid by the debtor, directly or through the acceptor, and the money is extinguished. Until then it is money and may be used in its own right to pay for goods and services.

Like any good bank manager, the merchant bankers know their customers and their creditworthiness. They have local agents all over the world to keep them informed and usually specialise in a particular part of the globe.[5] The reliability of the debtor determines the discount rate applicable to the bills. Bills of exchange are private money, but the system has been formalised so that the risks are assessed to allow these debts to pass readily for money with the appropriate discount.

Treasury Notes/Bills

Treasury notes and treasury bills are bills of exchange issued by the government, having exactly the same form as a commercial bill of exchange. They are not issued to cover trade or production, but to cover the disparities that occur throughout the year between taxation revenues and government expenditure. They permit government to keep ticking over on a day-to-day basis.

Because the government's reputation is very public, these bills need not be endorsed and are sold at a discount on the money market. They can be resold immediately if the buyer needs cash again. They are

3 The terms 'acceptance house', and 'discount house' are almost exclusively used in London where this business is very specialised. In other countries these functions are carried out by a range of other financial institutions.
4 Endorsing a bill does not create a liability on the balance sheet for the bank endorsing it (the technical term is a 'contingent liability' – that is, the bank will have a liability contingent on the debtor failing to meet his obligations). Banks at times have used this as a means of creating credit beyond the rules provided by the monetary authorities. Recent banking regulations require the inclusion of 'contingent liabilities' in bank reporting.
5 Although today ratings agencies fulfill a large part of this role.

usually purchased by banks, other financial institutions and by the central bank.

Treasury bills are thus private money created by government. Although they are not backed by current production and so are not sound money, they are highly regarded and are more readily acceptable than commercial bills. It is all a matter of trust!

Cheques

A cheque is an instruction from a customer of a bank to that bank to pay the person named on the cheque the amount written on it. With a cheque payment must be on demand. A cheque normally has a short life and in practice provides credit only for a day or two. Cheques can be passed from one person to another although this is not common practice these days, especially in commercial situations.

With the advent of credit cards and other forms of electronic banking the use of cheques has been diminishing.

To the extent that cheques circulate they are private money. They are useful only when there is confidence that a bank will accept them, that is, as long as it is believed that the customer has money in his account and that the amount on the cheque is convenient for subsequent transactions.[6]

8.2 Public Money

Cash consists of the coins in our pockets and paper money. The coins are the remnants of a much older monetary system when the coin was a measure of weight of a precious metal. These days they are merely tokens. They do not account for much, being used primarily for change rather than payment.

Paper money in most countries is issued by the central bank[7] and is granted at law the property of 'legal tender'. Legal tender is technically an acknowledgement of a debt owed by the issuer to the holder for the nominated sum. The concept of 'legal tender' means the issuer is only obliged to replace the debt with another identical debt, and all other parties are obliged to accept this paper money in settlement

6 There is still some trade in cheques in America where specialist businesses will cash cheques for a fee. These are referred to as 'check cashing services' and tend to prey on poorly-paid people without bank accounts.

7 In some countries paper money is issued by the government directly, and in some others it is issued by private banks. In the United Kingdom, for instance, paper money is issued by the central bank in England, commercial banks in Scotland and Northern Ireland, and the government in the Channel Islands and the Isle of Man. The principle is the same.

of debts. The central bank still regards this as a debt and as such it is shown as a liability in the bank's accounts.

The amount of paper money in circulation is constantly changing. It tends to rise on the days that government pensions are paid and decreases almost immediately afterwards; similarly it increases to meet the needs of shoppers at Christmas time and declines in January each year.

In recent times the use of cash has diminished and continues to do so because people are paid directly into their bank accounts, and retail as well as commercial spending can be done by transferring money directly from one bank account to another using computers.

Printing paper money is a profitable business. The central bank or any other issuer must have equivalent assets for all the paper money on issue. Central banks typically choose to have as their asset backing a little gold and some foreign currency including foreign government bonds, but the vast majority of the assets are government bonds, that is the debt of the government, for which they receive interest.[8]

8.3 Bank Money

To be money the balance in a bank account must be positive; then the balance in a bank account is a debt owed by the banker to the customer expressed in terms of money. It can be converted to cash (the debts of the central bank) at the whim of the customer, used to pay for goods and services or to settle other debts. The vast majority of money is held in this form. It really doesn't matter whether it is in a savings account or a cheque account, it is still a debt and still available on demand.[9]

It is not the balance which determines how much can be spent, but the remaining amount that the banker has agreed to make available to the customer by way of loans, especially in the form of overdrafts and credit card accounts which can be called on at will.

---

8 The euro as originally constituted was not allowed to hold government debt and the asset backing was short-term commercial debt. The profit was probably greater.

9 Economists measure the amount of money in circulation using the headings M1, M2 and M3 – and more recently broad money. The definitions of these are not the same in each country. Typical definitions of M1 include cash in circulation and the balances in cheque accounts, These accounts were readily accessible, i.e. liquid, whereas savings accounts were a little more difficult to access. A further reason is that institutions with 'savings accounts' maintained 'cheque accounts' with trading banks. Including savings accounts could therefore be counting the same money twice.

8.4 Conclusion

With the exception of coins, all the money we use today takes the form of debt. Money may take different forms and there may be various grades of currency. Private money – for instance bills of exchange – usually has a limited circulation, for its usefulness depends on the known credit of the debtor and any single debtor may be known only to a limited circle of people. Private money strengthened by 'endorsement' may circulate more widely but it can still only be used for transactions of equal size – a £100,000 bill for another £100,000 transaction and so on. Bank money circulates freely among all who have acquired the banking habit, and cheques or credit card transactions can be drawn to equate with any transaction to the nearest penny. But the widest circulation is enjoyed by bank notes issued by the central bank, albeit these days only a small part of total trade. The central bank's notes will be accepted almost everywhere and are in useful small denominations.

Yet there is no essential difference, so far as we have taken the matter, between these different kinds of money. They all begin with production and exchange of goods, which brings into being a debt by a private person who has bought the claim to goods produced. They all end with equivalent production and exchange whereby the debtor sells a claim to production in equal measure and so extinguishes his indebtedness.

A wise banker can therefore always safely take over any private debt so long as he is satisfied on two points. The debt must have been created by wealth or services produced and put into exchange. It must be certain to be extinguished by an equivalent amount of wealth or services produced and put into exchange. There need be no limit to the money created in this way; every time a banker creates money by agreeing to owe his customer £1,000 or £100 or whatever the sum happens to be, he merely creates a claim to supplant another claim. The bank money replaces private debts and the private debts are the outcome of real production and real exchange. In this way the creation of bank money novates[10] debts. Any money created by banks on these principles must be sound money, and the ideal banking system should allow for unlimited money to be created in this way. If money that is

10 'Novate', from the Latin meaning to make new. In contemporary legal usage it means to replace an old agreement or contract with a new one, or particularly to replace an old debt with a new one.

created is not supported by production and exchange it will be unsound.

Credit cards need to be mentioned because they have become ubiquitous since their introduction in the 1970s. A credit card is a token issued by a bank which may be used to identify the bank's customer. The customer can then issue instructions to the bank, usually to transfer money from the customer's account to the account of a merchant. Credit cards are not money but as we are all aware they make trade very easy.

CHAPTER 9

Banking

A LTHOUGH A VARIETY of institutions enjoy the name 'bank', our interest here is in the clearing banks or, as they are sometimes called, trading banks. The clearing banks are uniquely qualified to create credit. Banks constituted as savings banks, building societies,[1] credit unions and other deposit taking institutions[2] have a different genesis, and traditionally perform different roles within the monetary system, as will be discussed briefly below.

The key to successful banking is trust, and that requires personal relationships. Until quite recently bankers were regarded as honourable, and in order to open an account with a trading bank potential customers were required to be introduced to bankers by reputable existing customers and/or to provide references asserting that they were of good repute. This may appear quaint and old-fashioned but the changes over the last forty years have had enormous impacts. Some of these will be considered below.

Many of us may not have a cheque account; we may use credit cards or computer systems to pay our bills. In essence nothing has changed except perhaps that things seem to happen faster. They are all instructions to the bank to pay for the goods and services we have purchased. In the discussion that follows, the term cheque will be used to cover all such forms of instruction.

9.1 The Evolution of Banking

Banking as we know it began in the 16th century in London among the goldsmiths living and doing business in Goldsmith Street. As one

1 Savings and Loans in the United States.
2 This term is used here as a catch-all to include any other businesses that accepts deposits, not as the legal term used in some countries.

would expect, their premises were equipped with strong safes and so became the obvious places to hold in trust the gold of merchants and wealthy individuals. Merchants deposited their gold and were issued with a receipt as proof of deposit.

Because the goldsmiths had a good reputation, it became more practical for merchants to settle their debts by passing on the receipt rather than making trips to Goldsmith Street to collect their gold. Initially the merchant had to countersign the receipt to indicate that he was transferring ownership. The recipient might do the same, but there is a limit to the number of times this can be done on a single piece of paper. So the goldsmiths assisted by issuing paper 'notes' for a predetermined amount, redeemable at their premises for gold or silver coins. If a merchant deposited £100 worth of gold coins, then the goldsmith would provide a hundred one pound notes that could be freely passed from one person to another.[3]

Here is where the magic begins. The goldsmiths started to notice that most of these pieces of paper did not come back to them for redemption, especially after people had tested the system to ensure that the bankers would promptly honour their obligations. The gold remained with the goldsmith but he no longer knew to whom it belonged. The goldsmith realised that he could issue more notes than he had gold in the safe, and that people would pay a fee for this.

Being prudent, the goldsmiths placed a limit on the ratio of notes issued to the gold they held, and experience taught them what this limit should be, for instance, £100 of paper notes for every £10 held in gold.

At the same time as this was occurring, Italian merchants who settled in nearby Lombard Street brought double-entry book-keeping to London.[4] Using this method, the goldsmith's balance sheet would appear as in Diagram 26 on the next page.[5]

In time the cautious goldsmiths found that banking was more profitable than working with gold. They also found it prudent to hold a greater proportion of their assets in a form that was readily available in case the holders of their notes came to redeem them. To achieve

---

3 First used in Europe by Sweden in 1661 and appeared in London at the end of the 18th century.

4 An invention of Renaissance Italy, first documented by Fra Luca Pacioli (1446-1517), in chapters on book-keeping in *Summa de Arithmetica, Geometria, Proportionalitá*.

5 In practice, of course, a goldsmith's balance sheet would show the owner's interest in the business as a liability. In a limited liability company as we know them today the liability is to the owners of the business.

LIABILITIES		ASSETS	
		Gold in safe	10
		Advances to customers	90
Notes in circulation	100		
TOTAL	**100**		**100**

Diagram 26 – Initial Bank Balance Sheet

this, they used some of the notes they had issued to buy easily tradable government securities. This changed the balance sheet to look like this:

LIABILITIES		ASSETS	
		Gold in safe	10
		Advances to customers	70
		Government securities	20
Notes in circulation	100		
TOTAL	**100**		**100**

Diagram 27 – Bank Balance Sheet with Government Securities

As confidence increased, instead of customers holding the bank's 'notes' as evidence of the debt owed to them, the bank simply kept an account of the amounts and allowed customers to give them instructions for settlement of their debts in the form of cheques.

The balance sheet changes to reflect this:

LIABILITIES		ASSETS	
		Gold in safe	10
		Advances to customers	70
		Government securities	20
Notes in circulation	10		
Deposits	90		
TOTAL	**100**		**100**

Diagram 28 – Bank Balance Sheet with Deposits

The final change came from outside the bank. Because of bank failures, the right to issue bank notes was limited to certain approved banks or the central bank. The trading banks sold their gold to the central bank in return for the central bank's notes. As the outstanding trading bank's 'notes' were returned to the issuer, they were burnt and the notes of the central bank used for new advances. Details varied from country to country.

Here in its simplicity is how our contemporary banks evolved. The numbers are somewhat larger and the balance sheet may on the face of it appear more complex. What is important though is that the money was created from advances to customers, and this is possible provided everyone has confidence in the bank and the banks act prudently.

9.2 The Business of Banking

Deposits

When a banker agrees to owe a customer £1,000, the banker gives the customer bank indebtedness that can be used as money. The banker records the debt in his books and calls it a 'deposit'. This same term is used irrespective of whether the £1,000 increases the amount the bank owes you or decreases the amount you owe the bank.

This is misleading for it is not really a deposit in the true sense of the word. A banker does not take 'deposits' from his customers. Deposits are such things as insurance policies, share certificates, title deeds, jewellery, and so on. The banker holds these safely for the customer and will hand back exactly the same items when called upon. These are truly deposits, creating the legal relationship of bailment ('depositum' in Roman law), between banker and customer. The articles deposited remain throughout the property of the customer who has a right to the very article handed over – no substitute will do.

The bank's 'deposits', so-called, arise when the banker becomes a debtor to his customer for a certain sum. In fact banker and customer are then bound together by obligation only – the customer is a creditor and the bank a debtor. Yet it is called a deposit. Apart from loans, which we must consider separately, a banker will only credit a customer – that is give the customer a 'deposit' – in four sets of circumstances.

1 A customer may 'pay in' bank notes. The bank will then record a 'deposit' equal to the amount paid in. The bank takes over the benefit of the debt from the central bank and in exchange gives its own debt in its place. Provided the bank notes were sound money arising from production, so also is the deposit which replaces them.
2 A cheque may be paid in in order to increase a customer's deposit. The bank's indebtedness to the customer will be increased by the amount written on the cheque. Simultaneously the indebtedness

of this or another bank to the drawer of the cheque will be correspondingly reduced and that deposit decreased. Nothing has changed except that bank money has been transferred.

3 The bank may take up a bill of exchange. It may discount it for a customer or buy it from the money market. In either case the deposit of the seller will be increased by the amount paid for the bill. Provided the bill was based on trade and production, the deposits arising from it will be sound.

4 The bank may advance money and deposit it in the customer's account. This creates a debt on one hand and credit on the other. This is largely done for the convenience of the bank and creates the money immediately instead of as cheques are drawn.

Deposits at a bank are not payments into it from an external fund of wealth. They are an acknowledgement of indebtedness by the bank against various forms of money transferred to it. In all cases, one or other form of promise to pay is exchanged for the bank's promise to pay.[6]

Advances

When a business customer needs credit, he approaches the bank manager and explains what he proposes to do. After due consideration the bank manager authorises the customer to withdraw money up to a nominated amount.[7] The bank is effectively saying, 'We will give you credit up to this amount'. Nothing has changed on the bank's balance sheet, but it has agreed to accept liability for the customer's debts should it be instructed to do so (by a cheque). The bank has increased the customer's spending power.

When the cheque is presented at the bank, the bank simultaneously creates an asset against one account and a liability against another. The sum of assets and liabilities held by the bank increases equally and simultaneously.

6 Notwithstanding the above principles, an analysis of the deposits of all the banks reveals that deposits are not entirely represented by loans and that this amount does not vary much. This hardcore has accumulated over the years as a matter of banking history and could be traced partly to gold and silver, now replaced by paper money, and partly to money put into circulation by both the banks and the government with no sound backing. The hardcore appears to align with money balances left in the banks over the years and not yet used to claim current wealth. It may be thought of as a layer of dead water at the bottom of a lake. It is the water flowing through that matters – this is the real basis of our banking system – and over the years the volume of money being created and extinguished with production is far greater than the dead hardcore.
7 Sometimes referred to as a 'limit'.

If the cheque is presented at another bank, the banks settle amongst themselves; a few more accounting entries are involved but the net effect is the same. Repayment of debts to banks reduces the sum of assets and liabilities in exactly the same way.

Fees and Interest

Banks need to charge for their services but unlike other businesses they do not invoice the customer and request payment to be made. Fees and interest are charged directly to the customer's account. In a clearing bank this also creates money. In charging interest to the customer's account the bank increases its assets by increasing the customer's debt. The corresponding liabilities in the bank's accounts are a little more complex, but for simplicity we could say that these end up in the accounts of the staff and the shareholders as a debt owed to them. That is to say staff and shareholders are paid with money created by the bank. This additional money is dissolved by the borrower when the debt, including interest and charges, is repaid.

The Payment System

The other function which banks undertake is called 'the payment system', although in practice there are typically several of these in each country.

When, for instance, a number of householders pay for their electricity using cheques, the electricity provider does not need to go to each bank to collect the money but simply deposits all the cheques at its own bank. This bank will present to all the other banks those cheques drawn on them in exchange for its cheques they have received. There will of course be a difference, and the bank with the least value of cheques to exchange will write a cheque for the deficit on its account with the central bank. This process occurs daily and the amounts involved are vast. Similar processes occur behind the scenes for credit card transactions and other forms of payment.[8]

Participation in this process requires that each party settle its debts immediately. Banks may have to borrow from each other to achieve this. But it is normally only short term because, in the normal course of events, money flows one way on one day and the other way on another day, balancing out over a short period of time. If banks cannot settle debts between themselves, the entire system begins to crack. Banks would be the first to know if one of their number was unstable.

8 This 'settlement' process is not necessarily restricted to banks as defined above, but may include savings banks, building societies and others dependent largely on the regulatory regime.

9.3 The Central Bank

As the banking system has developed, one bank in each country has evolved, or has been created, to act as the central bank, enabling bankers to settle debts arising between them as cheques drawn on one bank are paid into another.[9] The central bank also acts as the principal bank for the government. It has other customers, such as foreign banks, other financial institutions and governments, and some central banks retain a few private customers.

The effect of the central bank acting as banker to the government departments is that, as taxes are paid, indebtedness is transferred from the trading banks to the central bank, and back to the trading banks again as government departments meet their expenditure. As money is paid into government accounts, the central bank's indebtedness to the government rises and its indebtedness to the trading banks falls – so that the central bank's total indebtedness does not vary. Nor does the total indebtedness of the whole banking system vary.

If all the increases in bank indebtedness arise from the current production of wealth and services, then all the money in the banking system will be sound money – it will be a genuine claim to real wealth. This requires that a bank shall only undertake a debt to a private customer, that is, it shall only grant a deposit in exchange for other bank money, central bank money, or private money (for example, bills of exchange), or as an advance against production.

It also requires the central bank to act in a similar way in regard to the government's accounts, which must only be credited in return for sound money.[10] This may arise from production, such as the sale of papers and reports produced by the government, or from what the government may levy from private persons by way of taxation, which itself is a claim on production. Customarily the central bank does not allow overdrafts for government departments, but it does facilitate short-term government debt by purchasing bills of exchange issued by the government.[11] This is common practice in order to bridge gaps between government expenditure and receipt of taxation revenue.

9 Cheques, of course, are not the only settlement between banks, and these days the major credit card companies, SWIFT (Society for Worldwide Interbank Financial Telecommunications), and others also play a role in the settlement process.
10 This is a legal requirement in most countries. The central bank in its charter is given responsibility for ensuring that the currency remains sound.
11 Bills of exchange issued by government are commonly referred to as treasury bills. A variant of these is called a treasury note. These are usually issued for 3 and 6 months respectively. The difference between them is not material here.

Such an advance merely acts in the short term to equate income and expenditure over the year. Advances of this kind are also sound money, being based on a claim to actual wealth and services.

9.4 The Limitations of Credit

As the above discussion has demonstrated, there clearly is no reason why all production should not be entirely financed by credit from the banks. In this way new money may constantly be created to meet people's needs to purchase existing wealth whilst they work on wealth not yet ready for consumption. As new wealth reaches completion, is purchased and consumed, so money is constantly being dissolved. Thus money acts as a catalyst to aid production without itself being affected in any way. It provides the necessary credit, the trust that people will fulfil their promises. It enables them to eat today in exchange for the work they do today although they may not be able to complete their production until tomorrow, and to enjoy the benefits of buildings, bridges, roads and railways built yesterday.

When we consider a single undertaking instead of the community as a whole, the first difference is that the undertaking is very unlikely to traverse the entire stretch of production from natural resources to consumer.[12] Individual undertakings are highly interdependent and generally they will receive partly-completed wealth, add their own particular contribution and then pass it on to the next undertaking. What they receive from other undertakings will have to be paid for, and this we have called the costs of production. What they add is their net product and what is passed on to the next undertaking is their gross product, which becomes part of the costs of production at the next step.

Although production is divided into a very large number of separate operations by undertakings of greatly varying sizes, this does not in itself materially affect the question of giving credit. Each arrangement for an overdraft can be considered by a bank manager with the customer and, unless in the eyes of the bank manager it is based on an unviable proposition, credit can be given. It is true that by the nature of things there may be the occasional failure due to mistakes, but the risks will be widely spread and can easily be carried by the banking system if the other conditions are right.[13]

12 See Diagram 2, page 18.
13 Assuming, of course, that the bank manger understands the business proposition. Conservative bankers are not likely to be associated with the more innovative proposals.

The natural condition – without land enclosure – is that the net product of the undertaking should be divided between the two component factors: land and labour. The community takes the full economic rent for the use of the land; the rest is earnings, the reward of labour (see Diagram 5, page 34).

Where land is all enclosed, earnings are tied to a general level which is established at the least acceptable level, bearing in mind that workers have no access to land of their own and must therefore work for another in order to live. The general level cannot exceed the full product of the marginal site less the secondary claims thereon (see Diagram 8, page 39). Where land is freely available at the margin of production, the difference between what people regard as the necessary level of earnings (the least they are prepared to accept), and the potential level of earnings (the production on the marginal site), is the security for the credit given, in the event that the project fails. With earnings at their natural level the security is adequate and chances of failure small.

Where land is enclosed the tenant is left with the profit, if any, and earnings if he works in the undertaking (see Diagram 20, page 68). This profit is the security for bank credit. If the undertaking fails, the security is reduced: the former tenant cannot usually hope to earn enough as an employee to pay off the debts.[14] In addition to this, the whole structure of industry under such conditions is very vulnerable due to its dependence on a narrow profit margin, and any fluctuations in trade are greatly magnified. Although the individual undertaking may be perfectly sound, assuming normal conditions, a sudden disturbance in general trade may gravely affect its market and lead to failure.[15]

In such conditions banks are clearly unable to give credit without far greater risk than would arise in conditions of free land. Consequently, they normally impose restrictions on their advances and will not finance production to the full. They are also very reluctant to advance credit to those wishing to start a new business but who have no means of their own.[16]

14 Of course, today the debt would usually owed by a business with limited liability rather than by a person.
15 See Chapter 13 below.
16 The essence of the bank overdraft is that it provides short-term finance. Banks in the English-speaking world will not usually make advances on long-term projects (Banks in Germany and Japan do, but in the former banks invariably take some stake in the control of the project, and in the latter banks are often controlled by the institutions they finance). Thus, they will not finance expensive equipment and buildings whose use may be spread over many years unless the undertaking is already financing its own short-term running costs.

The degree of caution will fluctuate: in boom conditions banks are much more generous in their policy on overdrafts. But in times of recession they are very cautious with new lending, and may even wish to withdraw financial support they have already given.

If an advance is not repaid the bank must make it good from its own resources in order to assure its own financial stability, and annual provisions are made for this. The bank cannot take excessive risks.

9.5 Accumulation of Capital

Although bank credit by its nature is ideally suited to finance production, it cannot do so to the full extent in conditions of land enclosure. Yet production cannot proceed in a modern highly-mechanised society without the means of financing the expensive equipment required.

The necessary finance is provided by money-lenders, or investors as they are more politely called nowadays.

All those who have a claim on production will generally be able to exchange that claim for wealth arising from other forms of production, if they so wish. But they may prefer to defer part of the claim until a future time. It is not very practical to buy up a hoard of food and clothing now to be put aside for the future: the food will go off, and if the clothes are not eaten by moths they may well go out of fashion. Besides, one may want to provide for services rather than goods and they can hardly be paid for in advance.

In the community as a whole production must clearly equal consumption except insofar as there is waste or stocks piled up. Therefore current production not taken up by those with a claim on it will balance the current production required by those who have no immediate claims.

Where land is free (and earnings high) the banking system can easily resolve the problem. The needs of those requiring present wealth can be met by credit. The needs of those wishing to defer their claims can be met by converting claims into money in the form of banknotes or, more conveniently, a bank balance which can be held and spent at a later date.

The bank performs the double function of providing credit and enabling claims to be deferred. Each is a service to the parties concerned for which a charge may properly be made. It is not a question of borrowing and lending and would attract no interest charges.[17] The

17 Traditionally service charges were levied on cheque accounts, but no interest was paid on credit balances.

ability to defer a claim on wealth is a service. Imagine the case of a gardener who has a row of lettuces all coming up together. Rather than have a glut of lettuces and then none until the next batch grows, he would be grateful for a service which enabled him to have a fresh lettuce whenever he wanted one.

Where land is all enclosed the picture is obscured. The banks are unable to give full credit, so the people who are wanting wealth now will be all too anxious to borrow money from those who are holding it with a view to deferring their claims. So the relationship of borrower and lender is established. The borrower is in a weak position compared to the lender; he must have wealth to carry on his business whilst the lender can always keep his money in his pocket or in the bank. The lender can demand a payment for his loan – and this payment is what we call interest. If the loan involves any degree of risk, the rate will be commensurately higher, but it will be tied to a basic rate for a safe loan of about five per cent per annum taken over a period of time. This being the case, the banks are encouraged to regard their advances as if they were lending. The banks make a charge for credit that is tied to the interest rate, although in fact they are not lending anything and it costs them no more than the expense of their service. They also pay a much smaller percentage on money left with them on deposit accounts, although they are not borrowing but are enabling their customer to defer a claim.

Where land is all enclosed there will also be a relatively small number of people who have claims to a large portion of production. As a general rule, the least acceptable level of earnings does not provide for deferred claims or as we generally call them, savings. These few will be able to invest large sums and, since they have come by their claims other than by their own efforts, they will be well able to accept a degree of risk in return for a tempting rate of interest. There is also a considerable number of people living on earnings only, who wish to 'put something aside for a rainy day' and who are in a position to invest small sums for interest.[18]

Money-lending is not natural to the economic organism:[19] it arises where land is enclosed. It is not surprising that usury was so frowned on in earlier days, for in a free society it is not necessary to finance production. It would only be practised so that people might acquire money without the backing of their own production. This would be

18 And also these days accrued superannuation savings which are consolidated into *very* large 'funds'.
19 Levels 1, 2 and 3 of the Hierarchy of page 23.

either because their business was in such difficulties that the banks would not help, or in order to live beyond their means. Usury in such circumstances is scarcely a service to the community.

The belief in private ownership of land has affected the customs, traditions and human laws of our nations. Usury, which was despised, has become investment and is now regarded as highly desirable and praiseworthy, and is fully protected by human laws. The repercussions of this run right through the economic organism. They chiefly affect the banking system at Level 3 of the Heirarchy of Society (Diagram 3 page 23), and lead to the creation of the stock exchanges and the money-markets, neither of which would serve any purpose in a free society.[20] Levels 1 and 2 become dependent on investment for their very existence, and are saddled with interest charges as well as the other secondary claims arising from land enclosure.

Some of our most respected traditions and institutions are quite unnatural and arise only to meet the requirements of a society in which the economic duties, which will be discussed in Chapter 18, are ignored. The result is that the economic organism becomes highly complicated and diversified, and is subjected to many laws not natural to it. In the absence of free land, production needs financial backing. In other words, it is necessary for the producer to hold or to borrow a claim on wealth. This idea has been at the back of economic thought in one form or another for many years. It has validity only in a system of enclosed land.

The classical economists observed that people were unable to start a business without either using their own claims on wealth or borrowing someone else's. From this they evolved the wage fund theory, which is still accepted and taught in one form or another in the universities today.[21] This theory is based upon the view that wages, or earnings as we have called them, are paid out of a pre-existing stock of wealth called capital. Consequently, labour is dependent upon this stock for employment and for earnings. On the strength of this theory the political conservatives teach that prosperity depends upon the maintenance of a state of confidence so that rich men will invest their wealth in industry. On the other hand, the socialists used to teach that it is this ownership of wealth that enables the few to control the

20 Since they deal not with production but with claims on production.
21 The wage fund theory is even evident in *The Wealth of Nations*, see Book I, viii. At its most extreme in the early 19th century the theory held that capital was fixed, and wages inversely proportionate to population. Today it is reflected in the constant push to get 'foreign' investment to create new jobs.

many, and therefore the remedy for social injustice is to nationalise production and use the wealth for the benefit of all. The modern centre in politics has found neither view acceptable, and now teaches that the key lies in heavy taxation and extensive social services, backed by planning, to encourage investment into whatever channels the government of the day considers desirable.

All parties agree that employment is increased by encouraging investment and decreased by discouraging investment. This theory appears to have a lot to recommend it, but let us examine it carefully. Are earnings paid out of a pre-existing stock of wealth? The notion that they are, can only apply where earnings are paid by one person to another, for clearly, where someone is self-employed, their earnings do not come from any stock. A farmer's earnings are part of the food he produces. But in fact the same applies where people are employed. Indeed until relatively recent times the crews of whalers were paid off in blubber, and the crews of fishing boats were paid a percentage of the catch.[22] Here clearly they were paid out of the product of their labour. Once it became more usual to sell the catch and pay the crew in cash, nothing had changed; they were still paid out of the product of their labour. And so it is in all cases. Labour applied to land produces wealth: earnings are paid out of that wealth. Production is the mother of earnings: unless men produce more than they receive in wages, the undertaking must surely fail. Wealth owes its existence to labour and not labour to wealth.

Consider the community as a whole and the picture is clear. It is in studying individual relationships that it easily becomes obscured, unless we keep the big view in mind. Those producing food and clothing provide for everyone. The employer does not need funds in order to provide for the employees, but to provide a bridge so that the work contract may be fulfilled. Wages are clearly not paid from a pre-existent fund of wealth. Indeed if credit were freely available this would be abundantly clear. Yet from this theory has grown the modern view that production is dependent upon investment, and that for a country to prosper it is important to encourage investment. Thus bank credit is controlled, but employers and employees alike are encouraged to save and invest their funds in industry and in government debt.

---

22 Except the cook on a fishing boat who was paid a negotiated daily rate. Why? He provided a service to the fishermen and was not involved in catching the fish.

9.6 Savings

The conventional view is that you have money, which is a claim on wealth that is immediately due to you, because you have worked to obtain it. It is the reward for your efforts. You can say, 'I am not going to spend all of this claim at once. I will save part of it and use it later to go on holiday, or when I am older'. The fiction proceeds: the banks agree to let you save with them. The bank manager takes your immediate claim on wealth and lets someone else use it for the time being. Then later the borrower repays the claim on wealth and the right to exercise it returns to you.[23] The problem is that your future claim on wealth depends on it being recognised by a future generation. If they refuse to acknowledge their debt to you because of inflation or because they can no longer produce as much, your claim will not be recognised. Take the case of someone living in Germany who between 1900 and 1921 managed to save 20 million marks. By the end of the crisis of that year that would quite likely have bought only one egg.

To put it bluntly there is no such thing as savings. Claims on wealth cannot be saved. None of the fruits of the earth is specially marked with your name in perpetuity because you have chosen to take it. The claim is simply not exercised against the generality of production.

The same applies to the man who is said to borrow your claims. In truth all he needs to do is to work. If he works he will have his own claims against production. To get the tools to work he needs credit, which simply means trusting him with the tools to do the job – an entirely different thing to savings.

9.7 Contemporary Banking

In the previous discussion the function of banks was related to the creation of credit and it was said that this was for production. There was no mention of householders. This may seem a little divorced from how we see banks operate today, when the vast majority of the banks' customers are householders and economists argue that household savings are required to provide funds for commercial investment.

Banking has had a chequered career with a number of very serious failures arising from the creation of unsound money, leading in

23 Because such large numbers of people are involved, any individual can withdraw their money whenever they choose.

turn to lack of confidence and a breakdown of the currency.[24] The banking system described above would have been recognisable (in part) during the period after World War II, and perhaps until the late 1970s or early 1980s.[25] This system requires exemplary behaviour by bankers and the trust which arises from personal relationships between bankers and businessmen.

Bankers have gradually forgotten that the banking system creates the money that they advance.[26] Thinking they are lending 'depositors' funds, they look to attract householders as customers[27] to provide the funds they are 'lending', and so have assumed the roles previously played by savings banks, building societies and credit unions. At the same time the banks create money for purchasing homes and consumer goods. This money is not backed by production and so is not extinguished when the production process is completed.[28] It is unsound money.

24 Examples are the financing of Japanese property speculation by Japanese banks in the 1980s, and more recently the situation in Iceland in 2008. Banking does not enjoy a very good reputation today, especially since the excesses that were exposed during the financial crisis of 2008.
25 Some of the tangible changes which occurred at this time include:
  • The collapse of the gold standard and commercial banks becoming directly involved in foreign exchange transactions;
  • The massive increase in funds available for speculation, especially following the oil price rise of the 1970s;
  • Deregulation of the banking system progressively since the 1980s and later in the USA with the Financial Services Modernisation Act of 1999;
  • The introduction of credit cards in the 1970s;
  • Changes in the way that ordinary workers are paid so that every employee is required to have a bank account instead of being paid in cash and, following this, the increased role that banks have in retail transactions.
26 The Reserve Bank of Australia, until August 1990, published tables in its monthly *Bulletin* referred to as the 'money formation tables'. The three major items that changed the volume of money in circulation were bank lending, foreign exchange transactions, and changing levels of government debt. Articles describing this appear in the Reserve Bank of Australia, *Bulletin*, October 1981, and January 1982.
27 Householders (especially those with lower incomes) used to be served by savings banks, credit unions and building societies (savings and loans) for deferring claims on production, and for housing and other non-commercial loans (such as purchasing a motor vehicle). Credit unions originally provided a safety net for the poorly-paid among groups of people known to each other through their workplace or profession. Modern economic theory says households accumulate the funds that are lent to business – see 'Household saving is the main domestic source of funds to finance capital investment', OECD (2011), 'Household saving rate', in OECD, *National Accounts at a Glance 2010*.
28 Although some part of it may be extinguished when a new house is built rather than an existing one changing hands. But even in the case of a new house the loan includes the purchase price of the land. It could also be argued that part of the reason for the increase in housing prices is due to the ready availability of loans from newly-created money.

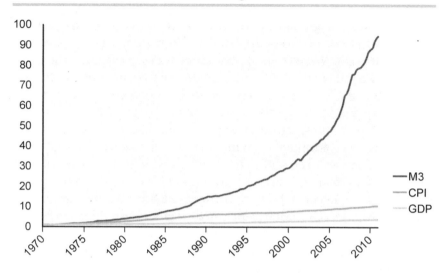

Diagram 29 – Compound Growth in Australia Since 1970[29]

Society has changed too and the expectation has grown that 'credit' can be obtained for the immediate satisfaction of desires that would have taken years to save for in the past.[30] The banks are happy to advance money for this purpose.

Banking has become consolidated to a small number of extremely large institutions, each having millions of customers few of whom ever enter bank premises or even know the name of any of the bank's staff. Servicing millions of customers whom the bank does not know is expensive. It is hardly surprising that banking has become an industrial process bound by rules and procedures instead of a flexible operation that meets the needs of production. Lending is approved based on the collateral provided, and usually the only effective collateral that can be assessed by the system is real estate.[31] The

29 Chart shows compound growth of the Consumer Price Index, Gross Domestic Product at Current Prices, and the money supply (M3). Note that definitions of M3 vary from one country to another. Source Reserve Bank of Australia series D01Hist, G01Hist and G10Hist.
30 One well-known advertisement for credit cards in the United Kingdom in 1976 suggested that the card could 'Take the waiting out of wanting'.
31 In approving a housing loan a banker will consider the market value of the property to be mortgaged as well as the income of the purchaser or, in other words, ability to service the debt (Although especially in the United States until the global financial crisis, both were often overlooked when housing loans were granted). For smaller commercial loans banks will often require a mortgage on the director's home as security. Only for larger commercial loans will the actual business proposition be assessed in its entirety, but collateral will still play an important part.

reputation of a commercial customer is determined by the ratings agencies,[32] instead of from the banker's knowledge of the customer and his business. What is more, banks have encroached on the territories of the merchant banks and insurance companies where they do not traditionally have the experience or the competence to succeed. Treasury operations also form a large part of their profits today.[33]

The effect of these changes is profound. The volume of money created has far outstripped both inflation and the increase in trade (see Diagram 29, page 131), and banks are now so big that, were they to fail, the production and distribution of goods across an entire nation could grind to a halt.[34] To ensure their stability new regulations are coming into effect prescribing that the banks increase their capital and have a greater proportion of AAA-rated securities as part of their reserves. AAA-rated securities are primarily government debt which is likely to become scarce in troubled times.

Banking is not an industry offering products as some would have it. Banks produce nothing but act as catalysts for production and the satisfaction of desires. If the desires they satisfy are merely the accumulation of claims on wealth, these claims will ultimately have to compete with each other for a diminishing amount of production.

32 The most widely known of these are Moody's Investors Service, Standard & Poor's and Fitch Ratings. Ratings agencies assign debt and borrowers into categories beginning with AAA which is the most secure. They are intended to be completely impartial but severe doubt was cast on this during the global financial crisis.
33 Treasury operations manage the bank's reserves, which is of course essential for a prudent banker. A large part of this, however, involves speculation on interest rates, exchange rates and other financial instruments.
34 A situation narrowly avoided in the United States in 2008 and a constant threat in the European Union at present.

AN AFTERWORD ON CONTEMPORARY BANKING

There are two movements in contemporary thought which should also be mentioned here.

In the year 2000 the Peruvian Economist Hernando De Soto published his book *The Mystery of Capital: Why Capitalism Triumphs in the West and Fails Everywhere Else*. His thesis was that the poor in many countries have the enterprise to start new business initiatives. They often have homes, sometimes in shanty towns, but not the land rights required to raise a mortgage. Hence they cannot borrow the funds to start a business. De Soto's work has been highly regarded and, with the assistance of the World Bank, some programmes have been initiated to create land registries or to establish ownership of land to follow through on his observations.

Academics have examined some of the results. *The Economist*, in an article called 'The Mystery of Capital Deepens' (26 August 2006) reported on a situation in Argentina where land rights were granted but although appreciable improvements were made to the occupants' houses, there was no demonstrable increase in lending applied to business ventures. There are anecdotal reports from other countries of problems associated with land titles arising from this move. In Thai villages where the duck pond was common property there is now one person owning it and the rest of the village is excluded; in Cambodia unscrupulous property developers have forced land holders off the land; and reports from Sri Lanka tell of landless peasants flocking to the cities looking for work. There are yet to be any academic or anecdotal reports of the success of this theory.

On the other hand there is the work of micro-credit by Nobel Prize winner Muhammad Yunus, who established the Grameen Bank in the village of Jobra in Bangladesh in 1983. His observation was that with loans of very small sums of money the poor could be more productive and were freed from the grip of oppressive money-lenders. He discovered that in Bangladesh he could lend to women, and that small groups of village women could be bound together to take responsibility for the loan. His bank does not create money in the way we have been speaking of here (in fact he initially had a great deal of trouble raising the money required to operate), but the system he has established is based on trust and is well adapted to the customs and values of his native country.

There are many reports of individual success as a result of micro-lending. Academic analysis of whether this has had any wholesale effect on poverty levels is mixed, but by October 2007 Grameen bank had 7.34 million borrowers and loan recovery rates of some 96.67 per cent – higher than those of most western banks.

The Grameen Bank has been emulated in many other countries, sometimes with noble objectives and sometimes as purely profit-making ventures. The system appears to succeed wherever joint responsibility can be established or where, in other words, there is a sense of community and members feel a mutual responsibility towards each other.

CHAPTER 10

Inflation

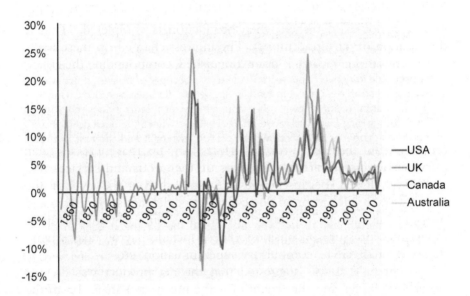

Diagram 30 – Inflation Over the Last 150 Years[1]

INFLATION is generally defined as the tendency for the overall level of prices in monetary terms to rise over time. Inflation then is a monetary problem. In practice it means money buys less or, in terms of our discussion above, that our claims on production represented by money are not fully recognised. When inflation increases to become hyperinflation,[2] the currency may be destroyed, and with it all the claims on production that it represents.

1 Sources: Reserve Bank of Australia, Statistics Canada, UK Office of National Statistics, Federal Reserve Minneapolis.
2 There is no accepted definition of hyperinflation. It is variously accepted to mean a ruinously high rate of inflation, or a rate of inflation that is out of control of the monetary authorities.

10.1 The Causes of Inflation

There are a variety of causes for inflation, three of which are considered below:

Creation of Unsound Credit

The simplest cause of inflation is that created by the trading banks when customers are given advances for purposes other than to facilitate production and trade. These may include consumer loans, loans for speculative purposes and loans for acquisition of land.[3] Such loans increase the money supply without increasing production, and the money is not extinguished when production is completed.[4] That is the creation of unsound money. The interest charged on these loans also creates money which is not extinguished, compounding the effect.

Taxation

Taxation is a little more complex. Any new tax on retail prices (sales tax, VAT or GST, excise tax on fuel, and so on) has an immediate effect on prices. But these have further effects. Any tax that increases retail prices also reduces earnings in terms of the goods and services that can be purchased. Because wages are established at the level of the least a worker will accept, in due course wage demands will follow and pressure will subsequently be felt by business. Similarly, any tax on its inputs puts pressure on business. These include payroll taxes, stamp duties, VAT or GST,[5] compulsory superannuation, etc.

In Chapter 2 it was suggested that the net product was divided between earnings and the tenant's (or the business's) share. From the tenant's share must come the secondary claims on production of rent, interest, insurance and taxation. Although rent, interest and insurance are usually fixed by contract, it was noted that for almost every business, when the lease was signed rent would be fixed at the maximum the tenant was prepared to pay, leaving the business with what was

3 Here we are speaking of the trading banks where lending creates money and not the savings banks and other lending institutions. Nor is it being suggested that all consumer lending is inflationary: for instance, a loan for a car is extinguished more or less over the life of a car. Loans for speculative purposes occur particularly towards the height of an economic cycle.
4 The extra money will be extinguished in due course if the loan is repaid, but the time frames are quite different. Loans for production are usually quite short (months or just a few years), while at the other extreme loans for the purchase of housing can be for twenty or thirty years and are extinguished gradually over that period.
5 VAT and GST because they increase the prices of inputs to the business even if they are offset to some extent later.

perceived as an acceptable margin of profit. All of the above, including direct taxation on profits, erode that margin of profit and, if what remains is insufficient, the business will either increase prices or be forced to close – with the resulting unemployment.

All taxation is therefore inflationary except that levied on the landlord's claim. When prices rise, monetary wages tend to drop below the least that workers are prepared to accept. Workers then demand more and the business in turn increases prices to pay for the new demands, and so the cycle continues.

Debasement of the Money Supply

To raise sufficient taxation to meet the expenses of running a country is a constant struggle – one that has lasted for over eight hundred years in the English-speaking world.

Early English monarchs discovered that by clipping the coin[6] of the realm they could accumulate enough silver to mint more coins and so supplement their resources. The effect of this was to cause inflation in its true meaning. More coins with no increase in production can only mean rising prices. The king gained a one-off advantage to tide him over a difficult period, then rising money prices absorbed the effect of the new coinage in circulation. Eventually the coinage would no longer be trusted and would have to be called in and reissued at proper weight.

In 1542 Henry VIII started a new form of inflation. Instead of clipping the coins he reduced their silver content below the standard of 925 parts per 1,000.[7] By 1560 coins were being struck with a silver content of only 250 parts per 1,000. This debasing of the coinage led to a very sharp increase in prices and it seems probable that they doubled over a period of two decades, which was unprecedented. Eventually there was a new issue of coins at the full silver content and the debased money was called in.[8]

---

6 Clipping was a practice whereby a small (perhaps normally unnoticeable) amount of metal was cut out of the edge of a coin. The accumulated bits were amalgamated and sold for the bullion value. This practice was not confined to kings.

7 A standard which had been in place since the issuance of the Tealby Penny by Henry II in 1158.

8 Of which Shakespeare said:

> Indeed, the French may lay twenty French crowns to one
> they will beat us, for they bear them on their shoulders; but it
> is no English treason to cut French crowns, and to-morrow the
> King himself will be a clipper.

A clever pun that combines crown-of-the-king with crown-as-coin, and makes Henry himself the 'clipper' of both. William Shakespeare *Henry V* (Act 4, Scene 1).

There have been many similar examples of deliberate inflation by rulers and governments to provide revenue. In each case the effect has been the same: more money but no increase in production with the inevitable result of an increase in money prices.

With the introduction of paper money based on indebtedness, the position was made still easier: kings and governments could now finance their expenditure by simply printing additional notes. This practice is very dangerous if taken too far, for people easily lose confidence in a paper currency. This defeats the whole object with disastrous effects upon the economy. The classic example is Germany in 1923 when prices rose astronomically and many billion paper marks could be obtained for a single gold mark.[9] The dangers of excessive inflation are generally well appreciated today. To print money to meet government expenditure is considered irresponsible. It is too blatant, but there are more discreet and subtle ways of achieving the same end.

In order to finance excess expenditure, governments issue treasury bonds. Bonds are long-term debt with periodic interest payments and, being issued by the government, they are usually regarded as very secure. The bonds are sold to banks and other financial institutions including overseas banks. It is commonly argued that banks are merely transferring one asset (the bank's deposits at the central bank) for another (the treasury bonds), therefore no new money is created.

A closer examination reveals that at the central bank the balance in the government's account has increased, and as the government spends this money, it trickles into the accounts of the clearings banks increasing the money in circulation. This money is not backed by current production.

During World War II British government's expenditure was enormous. A certain amount came from increased taxation but since production fell sharply with the conscription of men into the armed forces, there was a limit to the possible increase in revenue. A levy on the whole community would have been the honest way to deal with the situation but instead, as governments have done before, the Chancellor budgeted for a deficit. He borrowed a part of the shortfall by way of war bonds, savings certificates, etc., and issued large numbers of treasury bonds to make up the balance. The effect of creating so much bad money would have been a sharp increase in prices, but this

---

9 In January 1923 one gold mark could buy 709,000,000 paper marks. The exchange rate to one $US was quoted at 840 billion on 13th November 1923, 1260 billion on the 14th, 2,520 billion on the 15th and 4,200 billion on the 20th.

was prevented by price control and rationing although the natural tendency of prices showed in the black market. When government controls were eventually removed prices increased very sharply.

In money terms there was a big increase in revenue from taxation. This enabled the amount of outstanding treasury bonds to be reduced and also eased the payment of borrowed money, for repayment was in terms of money and not of the real wealth that it represented.

In order to avoid the unpopularity of taxation, the government has only to borrow heavily and create large amounts of new money by means of treasury bonds. The new money will lead to inflation and rising prices, and when the loans are eventually repaid the repayments will only be worth a fraction, in real terms, of what was borrowed. Even if the amount of outstanding treasury bonds is then reduced, inflation will have done its work. The effect is that of a tax levied arbitrarily throughout the community and the burden is felt most severely by those living on fixed incomes and savings.

It is all remarkably like clipping the coinage – but so much more subtle and discreet. It is hardly surprising that, despite all that is claimed, governments in fact encourage a degree of currency depreciation.

10.2 The Consequences of Inflation

Three sources of inflation have been considered so far: the creation of money not backed by current production, the debasement of the currency by either the banking system or the government, and taxation. A distinction is often made between the last two. At first this appears a legitimate distinction but on reflection there is little to choose between them. Both are directly attributable to trying to raise revenue without taxing rent. Both cause hardship and disturb the economy. Both are equally unjust. Arising from a combination of these causes, prices in terms of money have been increasing at a steady pace throughout several centuries and at specific periods they have moved very rapidly indeed.

Despite all that is said, rising prices are welcomed in some sectors of the community. Producers, other than those working on contract, find that in times of rising prices, when they come to market their goods, they can raise the prices above what they had expected and thus increase their profit margin. Wages will have been paid and raw materials bought while prices were lower; secondary claims are already fixed by contract at lower prices. As a result the profit margin will increase not only in terms of money but also in real terms.

Such a situation keeps trade booming and encourages greater production. There may be constant claims for higher wages but in fact earnings tend always to lag behind prices so the producer's gain is his employees' loss. Encouraged by the boom, producers will commit themselves to further interest charges and landlord's claims which they can only meet on the assumption that prices will continue to increase. As long as this happens all is well. But it is a very vulnerable condition for, if trade begins to decline, prices will quickly stop rising or even fall and many businesses may find they have overstepped the mark.[10] Such failures are cumulative: as businesses fail unemployment rises and demand falls bringing prices down and leading to more failures. Hence the typical pattern of the trade cycle.[11]

Governments also favour gradually rising prices, despite all that is claimed to the contrary. For not only are they seen to encourage trade, which is generally popular, but they boost profits and consequently taxes generally. They also lessen the impact in real terms of the interest on government debt.[12]

10 Such was the situation throughout the English-speaking world from the end of the 1970s until the early 1990s.
11 See Chapter 13.
12 The inflation target for the Reserve Bank of Australia is between 2% and 3%, the Bank of England 2%, the Reserve Bank of New Zealand and the Bank of Canada between 1% and 3%, the US Federal Reserve 1.7%-2%. See websites of these institutions.

CHAPTER 11

The Organisation of Production

What is good for General Motors is good for the country
CHARLES WILSON
CEO General Motors[1]

ODAY THE overwhelming majority of those who work are employed, and employed not by other individuals but by a legal entity called a company or a corporation. Companies are not new – some forms of company are evident at least as far back as Babylonian times. They were originally associations of individuals sharing the management of a business venture as well as the collective rewards. They also shared the responsibility.[2] With the advancement of the capitalist model the legal form of a company has changed substantially.

This chapter will examine the nature of the modern company, how it arose and some of its implications.

11.1 The Rise of Limited Liability

The history of the limited liability company is a series of changes in the law in response to economic conditions as they developed after the great waves of land enclosure in the sixteenth century. The limited liability of shareholders did not become general in England until after 1855. It is significant that this important step was taken soon after the second wave of enclosures from about 1760 to 1820. However, from 1600 onwards a gradual movement towards that form of economic organisation can be seen.

1 From his testimony before the US Armed Forces Committee, 1952.
2 Although this might be delegated to a trusted person, as was the case for the operation of the Medici Bank where branches, especially overseas, were operated by trusted delegates. See, Raymond De Roover, *The Rise and Decline of the Medici Bank*.

After the decline of the mediaeval guilds,[3] production or trade were in loose forms of partnership or in companies created by royal charter. The modern company grew in more respects from the latter type than from the former. Charters were granted by the Crown usually to exploit a monopoly. The East India Company, chartered in 1600, exemplifies this early stage of development. It was granted a monopoly of trade with the East Indies, and at first its members traded independently, although subject to the rules of the company. In 1653 a joint stock-in-trade company was established to which members contributed in return for a share in the profits of the joint enterprise. In 1692 independent trading was prohibited. The East India Company was then an exclusively joint stock company.[4]

By this time, shares in joint stock enterprises were being bought and sold, for in 1696 there was legislation to control the activities of dealers in shares. The first twenty years of the eighteenth century were a period of growing speculation in new companies. All kinds of dubious enterprises sprang up to exploit public gullibility and old charters were bought as an easy way of claiming company status. For example, the charter of a company formed to manufacture hollow sword blades was acquired by a company holding land in Ireland, and then by a banking company. So there is nothing new in takeovers! This bank, the new 'Sword Blade Company', became banker to the notorious South Sea Company,[5] which took over the national debt of £31,000,000 in order to borrow money for other activities, using the national debt as security. The South Sea Bubble burst in 1720 when the price for £100 of the company's share certificates fell from £1000 to £125 within six months. So many people were ruined by this and so much corruption revealed amongst eminent public men, that confidence in joint stock enterprises was seriously weakened for nearly two hundred years.

3 The guilds were associations of merchants or craftsmen of a particular trade, cooperating for mutual benefit. The guilds effectively controlled entry to and practice of their trade; their members were free men practising the trade in their own right. Entry to the guild was usually by invitation and subject to strict guidelines. It was common for all the guilds in a town to act collectively to control commerce and conduct charitable works. They declined in England after the Reformation (late 16th century). The modern chamber of commerce is one of the legacies of the guilds.
4 A joint stock company was the original term applied to what we now call a company, in which the company's resources are held in common and the owners are issued share certificates to represent the proportion of their entitlements.
5 The South Seas Company was established in 1711 with its charter providing a monopoly on trade with South America, predicated on a victorious conclusion to the War of the Spanish Succession.

The Government's Bubble Act of 1720 did little to give joint stock companies a sound legal basis. Indeed after about 1750 even its vague rules restricting the right to transfer shares were ignored and joint stock companies slowly began to reappear. The building of canals in the late eighteenth century stimulated the incorporation of companies by special Act of Parliament. The canal builders needed to be incorporated as statutory companies in order to have the right to acquire land. At the same time banks and insurance companies were also becoming incorporated by statute. In 1773 the London Stock Exchange was opened to facilitate trade in the shares of joint stock companies.

On the western side of the Atlantic many colonialists resented the powers granted to corporations that were intended to serve the interests of British industrial production, but after the revolution new corporations were formed for many of the same purposes as they were in England, such as building canals. Many of the enabling charters required that corporations terminate after a nominated period of time. Early regulation of corporations in the United States was mainly to ensure that corporations complied with the purposes expressed in their charters. Notwithstanding this, a Supreme Court ruling of 1819[6] determined that the corporation as a whole was an 'artificial person' possessing both *individuality* and *immortality*.

After the Napoleonic Wars industrial and commercial activity in England began to expand and in 1824 another share boom occurred. The following year Mr Huskisson, the President of the Board of Trade, repealed the Bubble Act in order to free company growth from some of the confusing and vague rules that governed it. The English Board of Trade thus began its long interest in company legislation with an action typical of its later tendency to favour the relatively free and spontaneous growth of enterprise.

A less fortunate but equally significant event occurred in 1830 when Mr Huskisson was killed by a train when opening the Liverpool and Manchester Railway – the first important public railway company. Railway development in Victorian England now became the great force behind the establishment of clear rules governing joint stock companies. Like the canal builders, the railway contractors needed statutory incorporation in order to buy land, and this form of company was used until 1844 when Gladstone[7] introduced an Act that enabled joint stock companies to be incorporated by registering their

6 Trustees of Dartmouth College vs Woodward.
7 President of the Board of Trade at the time.

particulars with a Register of Companies. This Act did not create limited liability but by then the idea was in the public mind. It gained wider acceptance in the next decade, both because railway companies had grown on such a huge scale, and, paradoxically, in reaction to the share boom of 1844-46 when many railway companies went bankrupt.

It was still widely believed that to restrict liability was to break the moral principle of honouring one's debts, but frightened shareholders began to demand limited liability. It became obvious that under the general economic conditions of Victorian England, economic growth could only be sustained if those with money savings could be induced to lend them to entrepreneurs who would use them to expand industry and commerce. At least that was how the fiction of 'productive savings' grew up.

In 1856 a further Act was passed enabling companies to register with limited liability, provided they published their name as '… Limited' in order to give warning to potential creditors. In fact, by this time the number of shareholders in many companies was so great that the possibility of suing them individually was unrealistic, so the credit of a company was not greatly diminished by the use of the epithet 'limited'. England followed the United States in recognising a company as a distinct legal person in the case of Salomon vs Salomon (1897).

In subsequent years across the entire English-speaking world the use of one form or other of corporation or company with limited liability has become the basis of almost all business activity. More recently the law has allowed individuals to be the sole owners and operators of one of these entities whilst still retaining the concept of limited liability for its operations.

Three other factors have influenced the development of companies in recent years:

Taxation: for most of the 20th century taxation paid by companies has been less than that paid by wealthy individuals, and arrangements have been put in place so that, if companies paid tax, shareholders were not taxed on their returns. Thus, smaller businesses and family businesses have been provided with an incentive to 'incorporate'.

Multinational companies: multinational companies are not new[8] and the size of some of the early companies was vast even by comparison with some of the giants of today. These giants are now

8 The British East India company for instance, and earlier the Medici and other Italian banks.

so numerous[9] that there is widespread concern that they have gained too much power over all aspects of people's lives.

Superannuation: the spread over the last two decades of super-annuation has multiplied the traditionally large shareholdings control-led by financial institutions.[10] These organisations dominate the voting rights in many public companies, and are usually public companies themselves. Thus capitalism controls capitalism.

11.2 The Nature of a Company

The majority of companies are founded by individuals or small groups of individuals, the entrepreneurs. The entrepreneur invariably has a skill or insight that makes the organisation successful in his chosen field.[11] Limited liability was a device used to protect the entrepreneur and his backers from personal ruin if the venture failed. In the course of time the original entrepreneur passes on. Control of the company is then vested in the shareholders who appoint others to run it for them. Some of these have grown into vast concerns like British Petroleum, General Motors, BHP Billiton, the great insurance com-panies and the banks. They are owned by shareholders who also reap the profits by way of dividends[12] although they have no relationship with the company beyond that.[13]

The true entrepreneur is becoming the exception rather than the rule. Most people find themselves working for a legal fiction[14] where even the person who employs the workers is a hired servant of the company. Those who take the profit, that is generally accepted to be the reward for entrepreneurship, are quite unknown, irrespective of whether they are real or artificial people.

In theory the shareholders control the company by appointing a board of directors. This will often include large shareholders, but as often as not the board will consist of professional directors having

9 See Sarah Anderson and John Cavanagh, *Top 200: The Rise of Corporate Global Power*, 2000.
10 See Paulo Alves and Miguel Ferreira, *Who Owns the Largest Firms Around the World*, 2008.
11 Although it is worth noting that the success rate of new ventures is low, see footnote 7, page 66.
12 These days a great proportion of the shares are commonly held by superannuation funds, insurance companies and the 'sovereign wealth funds'.
13 There are, of course, some businesses in which the descendants of the founders have retained a controlling interest: for instance, Ford, News Limited and Roche. It seems to be more a European trend than one found in the English-speaking world.
14 An artificial 'legal person' as created by the law. The closest tangible thing that could be identified as a company are the articles of association, usually retained in a lawyer's safe.

only very small personal shareholdings.[15] The directors may be employees of some other company holding a significant number of shares, or even a company holding shares in trust.[16] Frequently the directors themselves will nominate whom they would like to have on the board and their nominations will usually be accepted. It is only when things go very wrong that the shareholders unite to attempt to unseat the current directors. Apart from the board, much of the running of the company will depend upon its management who are themselves employees of the company. Thus a vast self-perpetuating monster is reared which becomes employer to thousands, or even hundreds of thousands, and exists for the financial benefit of its many shareholders, who themselves are frequently similar concerns.

Unless the company is trying to raise further funds, prospective shareholders purchase shares from their predecessors. They do not *invest* in the company but purchase claims to present and all future profits, as though expecting the company to be immortal.[17] The price they are prepared to pay varies with the outlook for each specific business and the outlook for business generally.

What are these profits?

Profits will include what we have called the entrepreneur's profit – the reward for expertise and initiative, including, in some cases, a legacy from the company's original innovation,[18] and for the risk carried. Some part of this profit may be taken by the directors and senior management in the form of fees, salaries and bonuses. For some companies these can be considerable or even controversial.

Profits will be supplemented by notional interest charges when buildings and equipment have been purchased using company funds instead of borrowings, as well as by interest earned on retained profits.[19]

Finally, profits will be boosted by the potential landlord's claim where the business is operating with freehold title to the land it uses, or has a very old lease. These can be substantial or even the greater part of the total profits.[20]

15 And often acquired only after they become directors.
16 Banks, insurance companies and superannuation companies.
17 In current economic jargon they are purchasing an 'endowment'.
18 This can be in various forms, the most obvious being patents which can produce income for a long time, but also the unique approach and values of the initial entrepreneur which can have a legacy even if the new managers do not practice these, see James C. Collins and Jerry I. Porras, *Built to Last: Successful Habits of Visionary Companies*.
19 The airline industry for example.
20 Especially for older businesses, such as railways and department stores in capital city locations.

Profits become the greater part of the tenant's share when an undertaking owns its own land and has plenty of working capital to buy equipment. Then only rates and taxes have to be deducted. The rest is available for distribution among the shareholders[21] and is truly unearned income, being in part the fruits of other men's labour, and in part rent due to the community but not paid. This is frequently the case with a mature business.[22]

With such a disconnection between the owners and the employees it is remarkable that undertakings work as efficiently as they do. That the employees put little value on their contribution to industry is hardly surprising.

It is easy for reformers to criticise this complex system of big business that has become known collectively as capitalism. But to attack it as being the cause of all ills is quite useless. It has arisen as the inevitable effect of a combination of industrial progress and total land enclosure. Even Karl Marx eventually recognised this. Near the end of his monumental work *Das Kapital* in which he castigates the capitalist system, he states:

> The starting-point of the development that gave rise to the wage-labourer as well as to the capitalist was the servitude of the labourer…
> The expropriation of the agricultural producer, of the peasant, from the soil, is the basis of the whole process.[23]

Karl Marx saw the real cause of poverty, and yet he preferred for the rest of his work to blame it onto capitalism as such. His followers seldom read far enough to find that paragraph and, in any event, would probably rather have not known about it.

In the capitalist system wages are spoken of as being a cost of production and labour is likened to raw materials or machines. This is an inhumane view. But it is strange how many people will agree that the trouble today is that wages are too high. The irony is that, where mass production is so prevalent, wages are low as a proportion of

21 Note that there are various types of shares. What has been described are 'ordinary shares' which may carry voting rights. In addition there are 'preference shares' which carry a fixed percentage return and take preference over ordinary shares when the dividend is paid. Also, although not strictly shares, there are 'debentures' which are loans carrying a fixed rate of interest and secured on the assets of the company. These take precedence over all shares, both for payment of dividends and in the case of liquidation of the company's assets.
22 Although in the case of a mature business where the land is held on a freehold basis the site is often not used to its full potential even when the bulk of the profit is the landlord's claim.
23 Marx, *Das Kapital*, Part 8, Chapter 26.

GDP, so the worker cannot afford the product of his labour, and unemployment is inevitable.

When it is remembered that Economics is primarily about people and communities, this viewpoint changes. Wages are then seen to be a primary claim on production – a claim arising from one of the two basic factors of all production – labour. Wages are not a cost of production to be kept as low as possible, they are the first claim in the division of wealth, which itself arises from labour on land. What is left of the net product goes to the tenant (the business) by virtue of the control of the land – land which belongs to no one but is for the benefit of all (see Diagram 5, page 34).

Consider what a different attitude to wages arises from these two viewpoints – that of the limited liability company and that of the community as a whole.

Most of us work for limited liability companies[24] and although the term has become unfashionable, we are 'servants' of the company. Those who work elsewhere most certainly come across these companies every day, either in business or at least when they go shopping. Large companies spend a great deal on trying to project a corporate personality, which we seldom recognise, for it is people we are dealing with. These people are serving an 'immortal' legal fiction which of its nature has no body, no heart and no soul.

11.3 Corporations and Ethics

Before moving on, something should be said about ethics and companies.

In 1970 the renowned economist Milton Friedman published an essay in which he argued that the only duty of a company was to return profits to its shareholders.[25] The essay was in response to concerns being expressed about what duties a corporation owed its customers, suppliers, employees and the community around it. The essay excited and still does excite extensive controversy. Companies these days often promote themselves as good 'corporate citizens', socially aware, and environmentally conscious.

---

24 In the US in 2010 self-employment represented 10.9% of the workforce. Approximately one third of these workers were 'incorporated'. Of the remainder it is safe to assume the vast majority work for 'incorporated' businesses. See Steven Hipple, *Monthly Labour Review Online*.
25 Milton Friedman, 1970, 'The Social Responsibility of Business is to Increase its Profits', *New York Time Magazine*, 13 September 1970.

The law which created 'limited liability' removed the responsibility of the owners of the company for the actions of their servants – directors and employees – acting on their behalf. Much subsequent law has attempted to redress as far as possible the imbalance that this creates.

Although a company has been accepted as an 'artificial person' at law, it cannot reasonably be expected to have either duties or a conscience. Ethics and duties are a matter for the living even when acting as servants of a company. Only individuals can make ethical choices, and to try to ascribe these to the company is often an avoidance of personal responsibility.

11.4 Financial Markets

There is a very strong tendency to regard government bonds and stocks and shares as wealth – but they are not – and this can lead to much confusion. Shares are a claim on the production of wealth, both now and in the future. Government loans on the other hand arise largely from the national debt and, far from representing wealth, represent debt. Though usually regarded as very secure because of the standing of the government, which theoretically can always raise taxes to pay the interest, they are certainly not backed by any tangible assets and are of limited duration.

Rises and falls in the quoted prices of shares give the impression of great wealth being created and lost. This is, of course, quite untrue. As production rises and profits increase more wealth is available for distribution, and this is reflected in the general level of share prices. But over and above this the rise and fall is purely internal to the stock exchange. What one person makes by buying when prices are low and selling when they are high is at the expense of less fortunate investors. Fluctuations on the stock exchange do not affect the amount of wealth in the community, nor do they affect the quantity of money, for what one person may receive by selling his shares another has to find to buy them. Nor do fluctuations on the stock exchange affect the level of production. However, the fact that business regards the stock exchange as a bellwether for economic activity does have an effect on confidence.

Even in a system where land is freely available there would still be a need for banks and for the great commodity markets, but not for the stock exchange. Although it is an essential part of our present economic system, it has no place in natural law. To put it quite bluntly, it is a market for dealing in stolen property – in land – and the debts of past generations.

Capitalism then is the view of production as seen by the shareholder. It is a heartless view based only on present and future profits. When the stock exchange is given such prominence in the general picture of the economy, it is not surprising that wages are regarded as a cost of production and that the cost of labour is grouped with those of raw materials and machinery. The proper status of earnings as a primary claim on production becomes completely obscured.

This attitude has arisen and is maintained with the consent of the community. It will continue as long as the community chooses.

11.5 Capital and Interest

As has been said, capital is wealth that is not consumed immediately but used to produce more wealth. Tools and machinery are capital; so are buildings, railways and harbours.

When starting a new venture, a tenant needs the equipment and machinery before production can commence. The tenant will obtain as much credit as possible from the banks but beyond that, as things are now, must either sell a share of the business or borrow the necessary funds. Generally speaking these funds can only come out of the tenant's share of other undertakings.[26] In other words, the tenant will borrow from those who have had a claim on other undertakings, either by way of interest, landlord's claim, or profits.

What will the tenant borrow? A claim on present wealth – usually in the form of money. In return the tenant will eventually give a similar claim on future wealth and will in addition make a regular payment for this facility. This payment is called interest. A business may borrow in this same way to buy a piece of land or to pay off its debts. In such cases no capital is involved but interest is paid on the loan. Interest then arises from the relationship of debtor and creditor and is in no way connected with capital as such.

It is as well to be clear on this point for the two are inextricably mixed in most people's thinking, leading to much unnecessary

---

26 In the English-speaking world, banks tend only to provide short-term advances. This may satisfy some capital needs (where the equipment is paid for rapidly), but it can rarely satisfy the needs for buildings, and major items of equipment, or the acquisition of land. Banks in some cases do purchase commercial bonds if the credit rating of a company is sufficently strong, but rarely for a completely new initiative for which no credit rating has been established.

confusion. Capital is wealth not consumed immediately but used to create more wealth: it is a tangible product of someone's work. The use of the word 'capital' in financial markets refers to *claims* on wealth.

As stated previously, lending money at interest, or 'usury', as it used to be called, was forbidden in Judaic law. The early Christians also frowned upon usury. The Jews were not forbidden, however, from lending to gentiles and so tended to become the money-lenders in society. In this role they were despised, and redress against their debtors could be somewhat precarious. But slowly as land enclosure took its toll it was realised that conditions had been created whereby usury was an inevitable part of economic life. Wages dropped and labourers could not supply their own tools,[27] and so they had to be equipped by entrepreneurs who in turn had to borrow money from those holding claims on wealth – at that time mainly landowners and merchants.

We have seen that over time the view completely changed: usury became first 'money-lending' and is now called 'investment', in which guise it is highly respectable and indeed is regarded as a service to the nation in that it provides work for the masses of landless citizens! Perhaps Judaic law was right in its condemnation of usury.

Rates of interest vary considerably from time to time, and also according to the risk involved in each particular case. Over the years 5% per annum has become recognised as a more-or-less standard rate for highly secure debt,[28] fluctuating with the rise and fall of trade, irrespective of interference in rates by governments and monetary authorities. The rate will increase enormously as the risk increases so that wage-earners borrowing on no security at all may easily find themselves paying twenty-five per cent or more.[29] Generally the interest rate will be determined by the least that money-lenders are willing to accept for lending their money – that is lending their claim to present wealth.

Broadly speaking, the prices of shares on the stock exchange and the prices that people will pay for fixed interest securities move in opposite directions. When trade is booming and share prices rising, demand for investments which give a fixed return is limited.

---

27 It was traditional that craftsmen would own the tools of their trade even when employed by another, a practice which continued in some trades until well after the Second World War. In the capitalist system the expense associated with providing tools to each worker has increased substantially.
28 The average Bank of England rate from 1694 to 2008 is 4.85%. The higher rates between the late 1960s and the turn of the 21st century are historically an aberration. See Bank of England, *Official Bank Rate History*.
29 In the most extreme case, pay-day lending.

Consequently the prices of bonds fall and the yield (the effective return) tends to rise. Conversely, if markets are depressed the move is away from ordinary shares with their risks to gilt-edged and a safe income. The price of fixed-interest investments will rise as the rate of interest is falling. In both cases, however, there is an opportunity to profit from capital gain. An investor may purchase or sell shares or fixed-interest securities with the intention of selling or buying when the price changes. At times the majority of trade may be for such purposes making the financial markets little more than a casino.

The stock exchange is notorious for its capricious rises and falls, being vulnerable to almost any change of outside circumstances. The death of a foreign president, or a change of government will have an appreciable effect, as will some international crisis. It is all highly emotional and quite unreasonable.

The amount of effort that goes into maintaining this whole structure and marketing of investments is seen, in the light of our argument, to be quite shocking. Look at the daily papers and see the amount of space devoted to this subject; consider the hours that shareholders spend checking up on their investments, trying to decide whether to switch to this or that. And it is all devoted to getting something for nothing. Is it any wonder that society places so little value on people's contributions and so much on their attainments and wealth?

CHAPTER 12

International Trade and Finance

TRADE AND production are not ends in themselves. Their aim is consumption which is itself only the means to the satisfaction of people's desires. This is so obvious that it is often overlooked.[1]

International trade is merely an extension of this principle. There probably never was a time when international trade was not practised.[2] However, since the second half of the 20th century, with the advent of cheap transport and communications, the extent of international trade has grown enormously.

Much attention has been given in recent years to the domination of trade internationally by a few very large players or even by one dominant company, and the impact that this has on the lives of smaller, less powerful companies and countries. In this chapter we shall consider international trade and finance from first principles.

12.1 International Trade

In the example on page 81, it was said that I would only exchange my computer for your television if I valued the television more highly, and that you would only accept the exchange if you valued the computer more. If these conditions exist, so that we exchange computer for television, then we both value what we now hold more than what we

---

1 Naturally people have desires for other than material things. They may value production for their contribution to it and this may enable them to develop their talents to the full. But it is not economic to produce something people neither want nor can afford. Hence the end of trade and production is consumption.

2 For example, during the Dark Ages pigments required for some of the inks used in the illuminated manuscripts produced in the islands on the west coast of Britain were mined in Afghanistan; and during Roman times minerals mined in Wales were shipped to the Mediterranean.

held before. To this extent both parties' desires have been satisfied and both feel richer. This is an example of the very essence of trade. To encourage trade is to work towards providing what people want; conversely, to discourage trade is to leave wants unsatisfied.

By means of production natural resources are transformed into wealth. That is, they are made available for consumption as food, clothes, housing, etc., or are made available to assist further production in the shape of tools, machinery, factories and offices. In due course further production leads to goods or services to satisfy desires. Therefore as with trade, anything that encourages production works towards satisfying people's desires, and anything that discourages it has the opposite effect.[3]

If trade between individuals is to be encouraged so as to satisfy desires then what about trade between nations? There is in fact very little trade between nations. Trade is almost always between individuals living in different countries. This must equally be to the general advantage.[4]

Trade encourages production. The purchaser and the producer are inevitably bonded together. Although it is sometimes helpful to think of them separately, almost all trade is a part of production and almost all production would be unable even to start without trade. All but the simplest forms of production depend on specialisation, and specialisation is impossible without trade. To borrow from Adam Smith, it is natural that the butcher should buy his beer from the brewer, that the brewer should buy his bread from the baker, and that the baker should buy his meat from the butcher.[5] It would be impractical for everyone to have to make their own bread – that is not the way in which desires are fully satisfied.[6]

The same must apply when the producers are of different nations. It is more natural for some nations to specialise in one form of production and some in another rather than that all should try to be self-supporting. Left to themselves both individuals and nations are capable of specialising to the full to ensure that desires are satisfied as economically as possible. Each will use their peculiar advantages to best effect, and all must gain.

---

3 This is assuming that people want what is being produced. If they do not, the venture soon fails. Left to itself the economy will produce whatever will satisfy people's desires.
4 Traders and merchants are often corporations rather than individuals but for this purpose the difference is quite immaterial.
5 Adam Smith, *The Wealth of Nations* Book 1, Chapter II.
6 Notwithstanding current trends towards home baking and home brewing.

A very little observation shows that this is certainly not the current situation. Trade and production within and between nations are fettered almost everywhere with restrictions imposed by both commercial interests and government. The international restrictions from commercial interests are the result of attempts to secure an advantage, often an unfair advantage, over either competitors or customers or both. The shipping conferences that maintain high shipping prices exist for this reason.

Why should governments wish to interfere with the natural working of international trade and production? Clearly it is not done wilfully but under the impression that it is for the good of the nation. There appear to be two main causes for government interference. One is to foster the wealth of the nation, and the other is to mitigate the inevitable effects of land enclosure.

This interference has been going on for many centuries in all the more advanced countries of the world. In early days it took the form of heavy taxes to discourage imports, and sometimes bounties to encourage exports – a pattern which may seem all too familiar.[7] The root cause of these policies was the mercantilist theory, the idea that a wealthy nation was the one which held most gold and silver, and this became an end in itself. Since imports were paid for in gold and silver they were considered bad; exports, since they brought more gold and silver into the country, were good.

Clearly this view was held by government and not by the merchants. Trade is carried out by individuals, singly or collectively, and individuals will only trade if they find it profitable. International trade will only be profitable if the citizens of each country prefer what is imported to what is exported. Import tariffs fulfil their purpose not so much by preventing other nations from exporting, but rather by preventing the citizens of the protected country from being able to obtain what they want – in other words, their effect is to prevent the satisfaction of desires.

The obsession with gold and silver blinded nations to the fact that the wealthy nation is the one where production and trade are most abundant, not the one with most gold in its treasuries. Who is the

7 The best known case being the English 'Corn Laws' (corn being the collective noun for grain). The export and import of grain has been regulated at different times since the 12th century. In 1673 an act was passed to provide a bounty on corn exports. In 1773 the export of grain was prohibited, except when the domestic price fell below a nominated amount. In 1815 the importation of grain into England was prohibited, leading to serious rioting in London.

wealthy one? The merchant who lives in a comfortable house, eats and dresses well and carries on a profitable business with his fellows; or the miser who lives on bread and water in a garret and spends his time counting his gold and silver? This is a deep-rooted fallacy and arises from the confusion between the real wealth of goods and services, and gold (or other money) which is simply a medium of exchange.[8]

Adam Smith was well aware of this fallacy and writes of it at great length in *The Wealth of Nations*:

> A rich country, in the same manner as a rich man, is supposed to be a country abounding in money; and to heap up gold and silver in any country is supposed to be the readiest way to enrich it. For some time after the discovery of America, the first inquiry of the Spaniards, when they arrived upon any unknown coast, used to be, if there was any gold or silver to be found in the neighbourhood. By the information which they received, they judged whether it was worthwhile to make a settlement there, or if the country was worth the conquering. Plano Carpino, a monk sent as ambassador from the King of France to one of the sons of the famous Genghis Khan, says that the Tartars used frequently to ask him if there were plenty of sheep and oxen in the kingdom of France? Their inquiry had the same object as that of the Spaniards. They wanted to know if the country was rich enough to be worth the conquering. Among the Tartars, as among all other nations of shepherds, who are generally ignorant of the use of money, cattle are the instruments of commerce and the measures of value. Wealth, therefore, according to them, consisted in cattle, as according to the Spaniards it consisted in gold and silver. Of the two, the Tartar nation, perhaps, was the nearest to the truth.[9]

In order to accumulate gold and silver in a country that had no natural deposits and could not produce for itself, it was clearly necessary to acquire them by trading. If exports exceeded imports then merchants would be creditors to their foreign customers and to settle the debts gold and silver would flow in. During the 1660s various Acts were passed to prohibit the export of gold and silver from England, but that was clearly neither practical nor desirable. This policy was replaced by one of heavy duties or absolute prohibition on certain

---

8 The Mercantilist Theory dominated economic policy in Europe from the 16th century to the end of the 18th century. It was particularly advocated by Jean-Baptiste Colbert, the French Minister of Finance from 1665-1683, who introduced the 'dirigiste' policy of government intervention and direction of economic affairs still prevalent in France today.
9 Adam Smith, *The Wealth of Nations*, Book IV, Chapter I.

imports combined with the giving of bounties on exports.[10] The whole policy was directed toward a favourable balance of trade so that gold would flow in and the country grow rich. What seems to have been disregarded was the fact that not all countries could have a favourable balance of trade: what one gained, another must lose. Nor does it seem to have been appreciated that restrictions on trade must restrict the satisfaction of desires.

At first these restrictions in the form of tariffs or duties were generally unpopular, but then home industries began to gain an advantage as they were 'protected' from competition from abroad. It became apparent that the restrictive tariffs were working in their favour, giving them a monopoly position in their own country, and that if they were removed foreign competition would force prices down. Thus the tariffs imposed by kings and governments to bring gold to the country acquired the support of manufacturers and merchants as being of great advantage to their businesses.

Initially it seemed that the only people to suffer were the citizens – the population at large – for they lost the inevitable benefits which come from freedom of trade. Slowly, however, the emphasis shifted from the mercantilist theory to the theory that a nation should protect its home industry.[11] This found support from all quarters based on the simple observation that production meant employment, that employment meant wages, and wages meant a living for the people. It was argued that foreign competition could put home industries out of business, leading to unemployment. For this reason heavy tariffs must be imposed on all imports to encourage production at home and ensure as much employment as possible. It is easy to see how such a theory gains ground where there is full land enclosure, for people are prevented from working on their own account and must work for another or starve. Employment becomes an end in itself and to this end other nations' produce must be kept at bay.

Henry George was a great exponent of free trade. In his book, *Protection and Free Trade*,[12] he set out to destroy the arguments of the Protectionists and did so very soundly. He reduces these arguments to absurdity by taking them to their logical conclusion. He asks us to consider a community of one – Robinson Crusoe, living on his

10 Bounties on grain exports were introduced in 1673. A bounty is a sum paid to exporters to encourage trade enterprise, on a per unit basis.
11 Widespread, for instance, during the Great Depression when trade barriers were erected all over the world to protect home industries.
12 Henry George, *Protection or Free Trade*, Chapter 12.

island. He suggests that an American Protectionist is the first to break his solitude but that Crusoe decides to stay on his island. The Protectionist warns him of the risks he will now be exposed to since his island has been discovered and is likely to be visited by passing ships. He will be exposed to a deluge of cheap goods that they will seek to exchange for his fruit and goats. The Protectionist goes on to warn Crusoe that unless he makes it difficult to bring these goods ashore his industry will be entirely ruined. 'So cheaply can all the things you require be produced abroad that unless you make it hard to land, then I do not see how you will be able to employ your own industry at all.'

> 'Will they give me all these things?' Robinson Crusoe exclaims. 'Do you mean that I shall get all these things for nothing and have no work at all to do? That will suit me completely…'
>
> 'No, I don't quite mean that.' the Protectionist would be forced to explain. 'They will not give you such things for nothing. They will, of course, want something in return. But they will bring you so much and will take away so little that your imports will vastly exceed your exports, and it will soon be difficult for you to find (full) employment for your labour.'
>
> 'But I don't want to find employment for my labour.' Crusoe would naturally reply. 'I did not spend months in digging out my canoe … because I wanted employment for my labour, but because I wanted the canoe. If I can get what I want with less labour, so much the better, and the more I get and the less I give in the trade you tell me I am to carry on – or, as you phrase it, the more my imports exceed my exports – the easier I can live and the richer I shall be.'

And so the two might part.

Yet these arguments for protection are no less absurd when addressed to one man living on an island than when addressed to millions living on a continent. For all its appearance of being unduly simple, Henry George's argument is irrefutable. When the complications are all taken away the essentials are just as he describes.

While the advantages of free trade are accepted today in theory, it is only being slowly and incompletely achieved. A host of justifications are put forward to show that it will be devastating to various specific interests which are often presented as the national interest. A favourite popular theory is that freely admitted imports would lead to a flood of goods from 'low wage' countries, throwing many out of work since local goods could not compete. This can only happen for a limited period. Eventually these countries will want something back for all the effort they have expended and exchange rates will adjust to balance the apparent advantage.

The truth is that due to a number of different factors from climate to the native genius of a nation, people naturally specialise in what they and the land around them are best suited to, internationally as well as nationally.[13]

Another argument in favour of protection, no longer accepted by governments but sometimes put forward, is that for defence reasons nations should be self-sufficient. This is not possible; no nation has all the raw materials necessary to meet the needs of its population. These are so distributed as to make one think that we were intended to trade. We are all interdependent whether we like it or not.

The only valid argument in favour of interfering with trade is based on the system of land enclosure and the consequent fear of unemployment. Due to full land enclosure, employment is regarded as a boon bestowed on men by a capitalist or a firm. The closing of a factory here, because people elsewhere are willing to sell us cheap cotton shirts at a price we would like to pay, is regarded as a disaster – and so it probably is for the workers concerned. But it is a disaster because of full land enclosure; if it were not for that it would be clearly seen to be beneficial all round.

This examination of trade and production started by going back to first principles, from which it can clearly be seen that both are by their very nature of advantage to all parties concerned. People will only trade with one another if the exchange is of advantage to both sides – that is if each values what is received more than what is given.

In the world today it is generally agreed that free trade should be encouraged as far as possible. But on the other hand, each nation jealously guards against the immediate economic consequences that are claimed to spring from abolishing tariffs. Through the World Trade Organisation politicians are caught up in a web of measures and counter-measures which has been woven over the years. They are trying to unravel it thread by thread but this is a very slow and painful process and can easily lead to even greater confusion. Not the least is the confusion of trade in goods with trade in property rights.

The right to own and profit from the ownership of the natural resources, infrastructure and productive capacity of another country is an aspect of land enclosure in our capitalist economy. It is a means

13 Expressed in Economics as the 'law of comparative advantage', originally enunciated by David Ricardo, *On the Principles of Political Economy and Taxation*.

of extracting a secondary claim from one country and delivering it to another. In third-world countries the effect is broadly to place further burdens on the marginal site, often displacing people from their traditional means of support and reducing wages.

The detail of all of this can be quite bewildering. It is very simple if we keep as a touchstone the plain fact that people will only trade with one another because it is to the advantage of both. Anything that prevents trade must work against the satisfaction of desires however expedient these restrictions may seem. We will only exchange my computer for your television if we both want to, and in that case we both benefit by the exchange. Anyone who prevents us is acting against our mutual advantage. It is as simple as that.

12.2 International Finance

As with internal trade so with international finance: the key is credit, the trust and confidence that others will fulfil their economic obligations. With that trust it is all so simple; without it we may wonder that any trade at all takes place except perhaps by simple barter.

The basic difference between internal trade and international trade is that the former in practice involves only one form of money or currency whilst the latter may involve a large number of different currencies.

To help us see this, let us recall what was said earlier about money. We saw that it had taken many forms through the ages: cattle, cloth, salt, corn, precious and base metals, cowrie shells and cigarettes were a few that were mentioned. If we visualise a community in which several of these forms of money were simultaneously in use, we see that a scale of rates of exchange between different currencies would soon emerge. A hundred cowrie shells might be equal to ten pounds of salt or one hundredweight of corn. Once the exchange rate was established trade would be very simple. But clearly from time to time there would be variations in the exchange rate – a sudden demand for cowrie shells and one might only get eighty to the hundredweight of corn instead of the hundred as before. This would prompt all those holding cowrie shells to spend them while the rate was favourable, or to exchange them for other forms of currency, and the rate would rise again to find a new balance at, say, ninety shells to the hundredweight of corn.

The situation in the world today is very similar. Trade is no longer financed in gold or other commodities but in terms of indebtedness.

Each nation in the world community expresses its indebtedness in its own terms; thus there are pounds, dollars, rupees, euros and so on. A scale of exchange rates between the different currencies inevitably accompanies this. Thus it may be that 100 American dollars are equal to 62.20 British pounds, or 72.30 euros.

As merchants trade they will want to be able to exchange their own currency with that of other nations. If their total purchases and sales (their imports and exports) are in balance then exchange will carry on at the established rate. But if the merchants of, say, Great Britain carry on importing more than they export, after a little while other nations will have more sterling than they want. This will tend to reduce the exchange rate – in other words one will get less of other currencies for £1. The effect of this will be to make British goods cheaper to foreign merchants. Consequently exports will increase, sterling will be in greater demand and the rate of exchange will rise again to find its new level. Where exchange rates are fixed these adjustments still occur but with devastating consequences. Businesses plan and equip themselves based on anticipated prices, and can commit themselves to long term contracts on that basis. If these contracts are international and exchange rates change suddenly, significant losses can be incurred.

This is the essence of international monetary exchange. It is designed to be a self-balancing mechanism and works beautifully if left to operate freely. This is the basis of international finance – all the rest is superimposed. It is necessary to consider the complexities that have been added but only in their barest outline. By getting involved in the detail the real point is lost.

Exchange of foreign currencies takes place between all the clearing banks, reserve banks and a number of other specialist institutions, and is referred to as the International Currency Market. There is no market as such – all business is conducted by telephone and computer systems.

As we have seen, indebtedness is the ideal form of money, provided it is properly controlled. It can be created and extinguished in line with trade and production unlike gold and other forms of currency. But it can also be abused. If governments create indebtedness without commensurate trade and production, the money is available for movement from one country to another beyond the requirements of trade. This pool of money is consolidated in the banking system and is available for an international trade in secondary claims to production, which is now significantly larger than the trade in goods and services. It is extremely liquid and readily available for speculation.[14]

If a currency is not stable and exchange rates fluctuate unduly, merchants lose confidence that they can secure a return for their trade. Loss of confidence handicaps trade and production. Many attempts were made to reduce fluctuations in exchange rates and in 1944 an international agreement was reached at the Bretton Woods Conference. Instead of going back to fundamental principles by avoiding policies which would lead to changes in the worth of their currencies, the nations of the world agreed to fix their exchange rates in relation to one another. As a result, the changes which did eventually and inevitably occur tended to be sudden, large and disruptive to trade.

The Bretton Woods system collapsed in 1971 and progressively since then many countries have allowed their currencies to float freely. Some governments intervene to ensure relative stability; a few still attempt to fix their currencies, primarily against the American dollar.

When the currency is fixed the reserve banks can temporarily act using their own reserves to maintain stability for a time, and other reserve banks may cooperate to provide some degree of support. If the trend does not correct itself then the only alternatives are to change the official exchange rate, that is to devalue, or to cut imports.[15] To devalue undermines confidence and is therefore an unpopular move. So the government is forced to intervene by discouraging imports and encouraging exports to attract gold and dollars. It is all remarkably like a return to the mercantile theory.

Those countries that allow their currency to float freely tend to be more concerned with managing inflation and perceive that the principle way to do this is by adjusting interest rates. When inflation is high the monetary authorities attempt to discourage production by increasing interest rates. Increasing interest rates tends to make that country's government bonds more attractive to overseas financial interests. Money then floods into the country and the exchange rate increases, making imports more attractive and exports more difficult. Such changes can be devastating for marginal businesses, leading to further reductions in trade so that desires cannot be satisfied.

14 The Bank of International Settlements' *Triennial Central Bank Survey* (April 2010) reports average daily turnover in the global foreign exchange market was $4 trillion per day. The WTO report that world merchandise trade for the entire year 2011 was $18.2 trillion – WTO press release (12 April 2012).
15 Take, for instance, the 1997 Asian financial crisis. Since that time the affected countries have accumulated substantial reserves so they are better prepared if the situation arises again.

CHAPTER 13

Economic Cycles

IMAGINE a mayfly with a very short span of life, just twenty-four hours. Imagine a spring day from its viewpoint: dark and cold to start with. Gradually the sun rises and it begins to get warmer, lighter. As the morning continues the insect finds food, and as the day goes on the world gets better and better, warmer and brighter. By midday it is a really beautiful, wonderful world. About three o'clock in the afternoon it gets slightly chilly, by four o'clock cooler still, by six o'clock the sky is darkening, at seven o'clock it is quite dark and cold again, there is nowhere to go, no food, life is miserable. There is nothing left but to die.

This is rather a different view of the day from the one we are used to. When we wake in the morning in the dark we do not doubt that soon it will be broad daylight. When the sun begins to set we have no fear. And what about the seasons of the year? We all know the joy when spring comes and the slight nostalgia of the autumn. But we do not expect summer or winter to last for ever; we have seen them come and pass many times.

From experience we expect the days, months and years to move in cycles. Fruit growers can accept slightly longer cycles; if the crop is not so good one year they do not worry but wait for the following year. In this sort of familiar field everyone knows things move in cycles. The cycle of a human life is accepted; no one expects to live for ever. Cycles of peace and war, cycles in fashion and morality are also easily recognisable. In architecture too the cycles are plain to see; there are periods of great architecture, the styles of which are repeated in slightly varied form centuries later.[1]

1 The neo-classical revival of Greek and Roman architectural styles in the 18th century, for instance.

162

In order to understand the causes that affect the economic organism a much vaster viewpoint is required. Although like the mayfly we cannot rely on personal experience, the mind is capable of considering cycles on a very large scale. We all know from our education at school that there have been many civilisations in the course of history. We read how the Greek civilisation arose, flowered and declined; as did the Roman, the Egyptian, and the civilisations of South America. The same thing happens with cultures. The mediaeval and Florentine cultures arose under the inspiration of the Christian civilisation. The great Chinese civilisation has given rise to many distinctive cultures, each with its own flowering.

When considering nations, one has only to look at an atlas published before 1914 to see how empires have fallen since then; half the nations of that world have disappeared and many new ones have appeared. France has been fairly constant over the centuries. Italy, Germany and Belgium are relatively new nations formed out of a number of independent states during the 19th century. The Middle East and Africa are unrecognisable.

Nothing remains the same, things are moving all the time – in creation there is always movement. On a still broader scale, astronomers tell of the birth and destruction of stars, the appearance and disappearance of galaxies. All is constantly changing.

13.1 Cycles

Everything moves in cycles. The question is what causes the cycle to turn?

Look at it from the point of view of a year starting from the winter solstice. First there is a period of growth, hidden growth often below the ground, but a great upthrust of life. Then comes a tremendous surge of visible activity when all the trees and plants burst into leaf and bloom and eventually bear fruit. All this activity is followed by a period of contraction, leaves fall, plants die; everything reverts to seeming sleep and deadness. Year after year the cycle of seasons turns.

These cycles may be thought of as being governed by universal powers: the powers of 'growth', 'activity' and 'contraction'. These are the powers behind all phenomena. All three are always present. If they were to be exactly in balance nothing would happen at all but when one of the three is dominant there is movement. This can be likened to the movement in an internal combustion engine. There is the force of the explosion, the resistance from whatever is being driven by the

163

motor, and the impetus which carries forward into the next movement. These three forces, working one against the other, turn the engine. If we think in terms of a circle (see Diagram 31), there is the upward sweep which we have spoken of as growth, activity across the top, and contraction as it falls away.

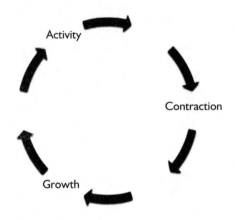

Diagram 31 – The Cycle of Nature

The change from the dominance of one power to another takes place before it becomes apparent. This is clearly to be seen with the seasons of the year. The northern spring does not start in March but at latest in January, summer in April or May, autumn not in October but in August. This pattern can be seen in all cycles.

Similar patterns are to be found everywhere. The genesis of the Renaissance culture was in Florentine Italy where it lay virtually hidden from the remainder of Europe. Under its inspiration came a great flowering of music, literature, arts and sciences across Europe one or two hundred years later. The influence of this is still present in the sciences but it is beginning to fade out, and so far as the arts are concerned it has already gone.

The Roman civilisation in its early days had enormous potential; then came the period of great activity, the conquest of the known world, followed by slow decadence, the hidden decline and the fall. This is a universal pattern. It applies at every level; perhaps even the human race will rise and fall.

In the English-speaking world we live in a Christian civilisation during the course of which the power of the church has waxed and waned in cycles. There have been many phases to it. The early church, backed by the power of Rome, grew, then declined, and subsequently flowered, declined and flowered again. After the Reformation, the Protestant church emerged as a dominant influence. There have been other phases within this civilisation.

When time is introduced to the cycle it appears as a succession of waves each with its own period of growth, activity and contraction.[2]

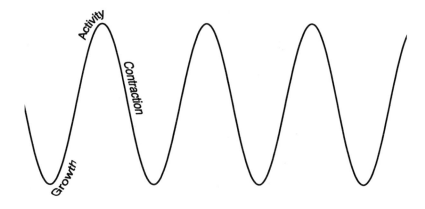

Diagram 32 – Cycles over Time

These cycles or waves can also be seen to depend on larger waves with correspondingly longer periods of growth, activity and contraction.

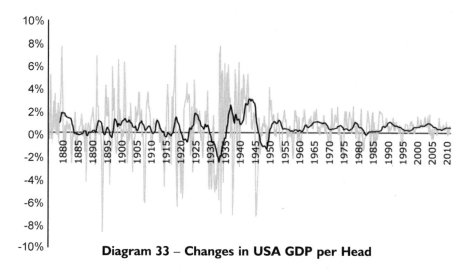

Diagram 33 – Changes in USA GDP per Head

2 Diagrams 32 and 33 show relative changes in economic activity from one point in time to another. If it could be viewed continuously it would appear as a wave.

Before World War I a number of different economic cycles had been observed. First a long cycle of about sixty years which culminates in a recession. Superimposed on this long cycle is a cycle of approximately nine years and a shorter cycle of about four years. None of these cycles are exactly fixed in length; the shorter ones tend to be shorter while trade is booming and longer when it is falling.[3] In the economic literature the long cycle is sometimes referred to as a Kondratiev Wave, the medium length cycle as a Juglar cycle and the short cycle as a business cycle.[4]

13.2 Description of the Long Economic Cycle

To understand the nature of the economic cycle we need to take two views of an economy. The first view, as the economy would appear without land enclosure, must be based on reason. The second view, looking at the cycle under capitalism, can be based on observation and a little history.

The Cycle with Free Land

Cyclical movements are natural and occur irrespective of whether land is enclosed or not. We can imagine a community where land is freely available and the situation that would arise there. Following a period of activity there may come a slight depression (see Diagram 34 on the next page) and for the sake of simplicity let us assume that it results in an even contraction of production on all sites. Because production on the marginal site decreases, earnings reduce somewhat on all sites.[5] As trade grows again profits on the marginal site increase and there is more to share in the form of earnings. The rent remains constant across the whole cycle, being based on a mean level of production. If there were an uplift earnings would rise, and if there were a decline earnings would fall a little. But the effects would not be very serious. A small wave motion in this state of economic justice would make very little impression. There would not be unemployment. People would just take it in their stride.

3 From observation, the long cycle appears to fluctuate between 40 and 60 years. Some suggest it has a natural duration of 54 years. The middle length cycle fluctuates between 7 and 11 years, and the shorter cycle from 3 to 5 years, although it appeared longer in recent times.
4 Named after the early observers, Nikolai Kondratiev (1892-1938), Clement Juglar (1819-1905).
5 Refer to Diagram 6 on page 36.

The Cycle under Capitalism
Under capitalism the cycle is exaggerated. The natural cycle might be something like the solid line in the diagram below and the cycle under capitalism as the broken line.

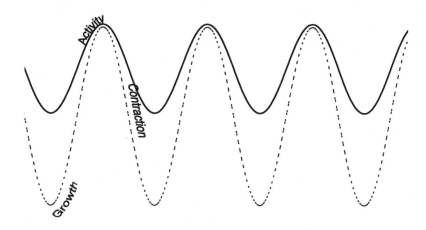

Diagram 34 – Different Patterns of Cycles

Emerging from a low period into a period of growth, trade picks up and activity takes over. Then, as production rises, there is a tendency for landlords' claims in the form of rent to increase to absorb the rise in actual profit margin as well as anticipated future profits. Tenants accept the fact that there will be very little profit in the early period of a new lease, but as production increases with rents fixed for a period they expect in future years to recoup any loss out of increasing revenues.

Earnings also tend to rise. Employees are no longer worried by the fear of unemployment; the trades unions get stronger and the pressure is quite severe. So there is pressure on the entrepreneur from earnings and from landlord's claim. That is fine as long as trade keeps improving, and indeed such conditions encourage production to rise faster than it would naturally because an increase in wages means increased spending. Interest rates also tend to rise.

After a period of growth things begin to flatten a little. Production remains static rather than increasing. Credit suffers and the entrepreneur who has over-estimated his revenue starts getting into trouble. Landlords are forced to ease up on their claims for rent, although in the expectation of greater production later it is a long time before they actually lower their rents.[6] If they cannot get the rent that has become customary they leave premises vacant expecting to get it the following year.

On a site where the secondary claims are equal to or greater than the profit, the tenant shows a loss. The only option available to reduce outgoings is usually to lay off staff, because rent and repayment of borrowings are fixed and interest is fixed or subject to variation only at the whim of the financier.

One or two large firms get into financial difficulties, the banks get cold feet and curtail their credit and these firms fail. Unemployment rises and confidence is shaken. Contraction then increases, with repercussions throughout the economic organism. The failing firms leave behind debts. When firms begin to totter, the banks withdraw their loans, the local authorities press for their rates and the government presses for taxes. Firms come under pressure at the time they can least bear it. What the firm needs is extended credit and that it cannot get. The pressures from those trying to enforce their claims, in fact provoke the crash which will deprive them of their monies. This is the situation that arises quite automatically in a society under full land enclosure.

The firm's creditors are not paid, which puts them in difficulties, the employees worst of all when they lose their jobs. Bad debts are followed by loss of orders, loss of demand. People cannot afford to buy consumer goods. The downturn snowballs and then there is a real crash.

Unemployment increases but it only goes so far. People have to live and there is a certain amount of stability in any economy. Unemployment may rise to twenty per cent of the working population, but there comes a time when those businesses still operating must carry on. There is a levelling-out and production goes on at this very depressed rate. Little changes but in due course by the very nature of things a period of growth starts and production begins to increase. Then very slowly the growth takes over. By this time the landlords are accepting lower rents, wages are relatively low, interest rates are low, so everything is conducive to production, if entrepreneurs have the courage to start new businesses. Once confidence begins to rise as a few people start up, trade improves and starts to flourish. The cycle is back at the beginning but far below the natural curve; the cycle has become grossly

6 It is common for landlords in this situation to offer an initial rent holiday or to pay for fitting out the premises rather than reducing the rent.

exaggerated in shape and never rises to the levels which would compare to the natural state.[7]

13.3 An Historical Perspective

Observations of these cycles are available continuously since the late 18th century, especially the long cycles.

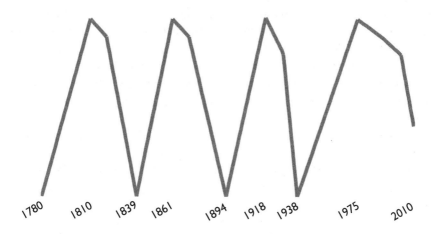

1780   1810   1839   1861   1894   1918   1938   1975   2010

Diagram 35 – Long Term Cycles[8]

Describing the beginning of a cycle, the American researcher, Edward Dewey, wrote:

> In the beginning of the wave's upward sweep … the economy is poised for expansion. The economy is just ending a time of depression when, as in winter, few things grew. Storms have stripped down the decayed trees and weak limbs that could not stand the testing of tempests. In such an economy many debts have been wiped out and others greatly reduced; excesses of many sorts have been paid for; surpluses have been largely distributed; people finally begin to sense in the air a kind of burgeoning opportunity, like the faint smell of spring when there is no change yet visible to the eye.[9]

That was the sense in America and Britain around 1790; again in 1845; around 1898 and again shortly after World War II in about 1950.

7 Not least because of the prevalence of unemployment in the situation where land is enclosed.
8 Indicative only.
9 Edward Dewey (1895-1978) as quoted in *The Debt Delusion* by Will Slatyer.

At these times venture capital started coming forth: industries that had started in a small way towards the autumn of the last cycle began to find growing opportunities – even the most casual scatterings of seed sprang up into a lush growth. In this early phase the innovations that characterize each new cycle began to spring up in full force. The canals that facilitated the industrial revolution existed in small numbers in the early 18th century but became widespread after 1790; the railway was on the scene in primitive form before 1845 but waited until after that impulse for its real development; electricity came into being before 1898 but developed as a great economic force only in the 1900s; and the transistor, discovered before World War II, began to permeate all electronic goods in the second half of the 20th century. The great industrial innovations that arise in such a springtime have usually been planted in the previous cycle. Their really great and characteristic work – a work that ends in transforming the economic scene – begins in each new spring as the new industries rise to majestic adult proportions.

A multitude of other contributory industries rose simultaneously, some great, some small, and as they thrived, so did older industries dotting the scene. Employment grew, money started flowing, credit expanded. When midsummer arrived, when the peak of the growing cycle was reached, there seemed a million evidences around of a new era, a florid age of growth beyond the memory of living man. Speculation regarding the boundless future was rife. That was so in 1929 and again in a different form in 2007.

1837 was a year of serious unrest and depression in Britain following the second great wave of land enclosures, and also in America. Then in Victorian times there was a period of prosperity which had slumped again by the end of the Queen's reign in 1901. Trade began to improve slowly until World War I set it rising quickly; growth continued through the twenties until the great collapse in 1931. The doldrums of the thirties were just beginning to run out when in 1939 the Second World War set trade booming again. After 1945 there was a slight set-back but in the early 1950s trade began to flourish and, spurred on by scientific progress and fierce land speculation, the boom continued through to the late 1960s, with only the occasional flattening-out in line with the shorter cycles. The oil crisis of 1973 provided the first indication that growth would not be continuous. Despite this, with the exception of a contraction at the end of the 1980s and again at the turn of the century, growth continued until the crash of 2008.

Apart from the two world wars, the cycle has been as expected and, although it might have appeared until recently that the boom following World War II would go on for ever, the cycle may have run its course. It is very easy to think all progress is something that goes on continuously. It is not like that at all. The cycle is in constant fluctuation. Despite this, people are always swayed by the appearances of the moment. When there is a sense of optimism around everyone thinks everything will always be all right. In the depth of a depression they think things will never get better. This is the mayfly's view of the world. In reality it is the three powers at work: growth carries optimism, activity carries excitement, decline carries pessimism, and they take society with them.

Consider the stock exchange: if there is a boom on the stock exchange, share prices go up, and everybody starts buying. You might think it would be better to wait until prices came down again, but that is not what happens, and so prices rise faster and faster. When something occurs to bring the prices down, investors start selling shares and prices fall further, leading to more sales. The majority of people always go with this tendency. Even the institutions follow the market. It takes considerable courage to stand against popular opinion.

13.4 Impact of the Cycle

As they manifest today the short-term cycles[10] relate to Levels 1 and 2 of our hierarchy of society.[11] Those working at Level 1 are the hardest hit. At Level 2 trade is badly affected but for the most part it can weather the storm. Level 3 rides out these waves and tends to be able to take a long-term view of the situation.

At the end of the longer cycle Level 3 can also be affected. Many banks failed after the great crash of the 1930s.[12] But when stock exchange prices collapse or depositors cannot get their money from the banks it tends to be the small investors and individuals who suffer most.[13]

With these cycles there also arise waves of company acquisitions and mergers. Acquisitions and mergers mean that production is being merged in the hope of increased profits or other advantages for the

10 The four year cycle and the nine year cycle.
11 See Diagram 3, page 23.
12 Over 9,000 banks failed in America during the 1930s.
13 These days it would be those with superannuation savings, but not the superannuation funds or the fund managers.

shareholders – generally without consideration for the good of the business, the customers, the staff or even the management. More often than not, the decision as to whether or not to let a firm be taken over rests on shareholders, who have no real appreciation of the issues and are only influenced by the size of the bid and the glorious future prospects that the directors prophesy for their threatened business. Bids are usually in terms of the shares of the bidding company, sometimes linked to a cash offer.

Apart from the expectation of increased profits resulting from economies of scale, the bidder may well have other major considerations in mind. Often the attraction lies in land and buildings, which have increased greatly in value over the years but are not being fully utilised and do not appear at their market price in the balance sheet. Such hidden assets are very attractive to a bidder hungry for funds, whose interest in the company taken over is to sell off the property. Under such conditions the takeover is hardly likely to be welcomed by the staff.

Again, the capital structure of the company to be taken over may be of advantage to the bidder: foreign investments, share holdings in another possible takeover victim, useful tax advantages such as allowances for a loss in a year when the bidder's profits have been high. The personal prestige of an owner may be a factor rather than purely economic gain. There are many pretexts for such alliances and great opposition may be offered by the boards and managements of threatened companies.

It is a strange fact that once an economic tendency has become established, government tends to promote it as policy. Despite the general objection in government circles to monopolies, active encouragement may be given to merger and takeover proposals. The assumption is that in certain cases such alliances can lead to a desirable integration of production with economies of scale and avoidance of duplication.[14] This should result in reduced prices and improved competitiveness – often to reduce the impact of foreign competitors. As yet there is little indication as to the real practical advantages but plenty as to the disadvantages, of which staff redundancy, the costs of retraining the retained staff, the capital costs of integration and the advertising costs, are but a few.

---

14 The airline industry is an example of this, despite the introduction of many new 'low cost carriers'. Manufacting large commercial aircraft is another example, with the world dominated by only two manufacturers.

Concentration of companies by merger and acquisition continues as a preliminary to the phase of contraction of the cycle.[15] Meanwhile more and more manufacture is passed over to the mass production methods that are the inevitable accompaniment of concentration in today's conditions. Care and skill are sacrificed to the machine, the computer or the procedures manual in the cause of progress. In one form or another it has all happened before and will happen again.

And through all this what about Level 4? It depends in which direction it is looking. Politics are volatile at the end of a cycle and governments may fall. Over the last few centuries many governments have come and gone in the English-speaking world and so have man-made laws and statutes, but the institutions of parliamentary democracy remain. They weather the storms. It does not matter whether there is a right- or left-wing government, the form is recognisably the same. The law may outlast these cycles, as also may the church and universities. These institutions rise and fall on the much greater cycles of cultures and civilisations.

13.5 Managing the Cycle

The cycles are distorted even more by governments. In the 1930s John Maynard Keynes proposed a way out of the malaise and apathy. His theory was very simply this: he saw that trade went in cycles which were obviously highly undesirable and that therefore the thing to do was to iron them out. When trade was beginning to increase, he advocated high rates of interest to slow down production; when trade dropped, he proposed low rates of interest and high public spending to encourage production again, thus flattening out the cycles. Keynes's theory came into favour when things were at the lowest point and since production increased afterwards it is generally assumed that he was right.[16] His theories have played a very large part on the economic scene since.

One of the devices governments employ to flatten out rises in production is called fiscal policy. The idea is that if taxation is increased a certain amount of money is taken out of the economy, preventing spending, and the rise in production is halted. In theory

15 See *Merger Movements in American History 1895-1956*, by Ralph L. Nelson, which includes a chapter with data on mergers and the business cycle.
16 Similarly it has been argued that since inflation subsided after the 1980s the high interest rate regime intended to curb inflation must have worked.

the government should not spend it either but should budget for a surplus to bring the economy off the boil. One effect of increasing taxation is that wages in terms of money rise because real wages are always the least employees will accept in terms of goods and services.

If there is a general increase in wages, the businesses in any particular trade can all put up their prices together, whereas if wages are steady one firm cannot do it alone.[17] This results in an inflationary tendency which normally encourages production. Manufacturers buy raw materials, apply labour and by the time they sell them the goods are worth much more. It is thoroughly encouraging. Mortgage repayments, interest and rent are less proportionately in times of inflation. Profits therefore rise followed by taxation, making the economy boil faster. At times governments try to institute a policy of pay freezes to limit inflation.[18] The great economic powers are inexorable: no government policy can hold them down though it may distort their natural working.

The other device to flatten the cycle is to increase interest rates (monetary policy). This is normally a function delegated to the central bank so that elected governments are not influenced by political expediency in these matters. The idea is that if interest rates are high new investment will not be profitable and will not proceed. For the most part the community assumes that the central bank can control the interest rates offered to business and the public. In times of stress, however, it becomes obvious that rates are set by what the lenders are prepared to accept.[19]

Do increases in interest rates flatten the cycle? Historical observations show that interest rates rose and fell consistent with the cycles before the idea arose that they could be manipulated. Perhaps it is just what would happen naturally anyway.

17 No collusion is required here because every firm will take up the opportunity as soon as one has moved.
18 In Australia in the mid-1980s, for instance, governments negotiated with the trades unions to have them limit pay claims in exchange for reductions in income tax.
19 There are many examples of this in recent times. For instance, the Federal Reserve in the United States sets the rate at which it will buy treasury bonds. This rate is expected to flow through to the rates at which banks will lend to each other. During the crisis in New York in 2007, however, interbank rates rose significantly despite a very low rate being targetted by the Federal Reserve. In recent years in Australia banks have only selectively followed the reserve bank's targets.

13.6 A Wider View

All discussion in newspapers and legislatures is simply based on the effects of superimposition of land enclosure on the natural cycle. It is only by going back to the basic shapes arising from the nature of things that there can be any real understanding. If we look at the cost of land, the price of shares, the level of wages, there is no hope of seeing any order. The secondary claims resulting from land enclosure disguise the facts beyond all recognition.

The latter part of the current cycle has been dominated by computer technology, especially the internet. One can expect seeds being sown at the present time to bear fruit as the qualities of the next cycle. It is too early to know what these will be. The scale is vast and without appreciating that our view must be four-dimensional we cannot hope to understand Economics.

At present many countries have probably the highest degree of material welfare ever known, but are their societies healthy? One does not have to look very far to find deep unrest, discontent and even violence. Change in the powers we have been discussing is manifesting as unrest throughout the world, not as a chain reaction but simultaneously.[20] These natural powers keep the cycles moving so that similar things happen throughout the world. Just as 1848 was the year of revolutions, 1968 was a year of violence, and so was 2011. The reasons seem to be different − but are they? This upsurge of energy takes different forms in different parts of the world apparently on a repetitive basis. Consider the question of racism: it has one form in America, another in the United Kingdom, another in South Africa. The problem is the same. Racism arises from slavery. Perhaps there is something in the Biblical saying that the sins of the father shall be visited on the children to the third and fourth generations.[21]

In Britain racism arose from empire building. A few generations ago there was slavery in America as there had been in the British Empire. Both were exploitation of one race by another, expressed in different forms but arising at the same time − manifestations of these same powers.

20 Most obvious with the Arab Spring of 2011, where a fatal incident in Tunisia sparked unrest throughout the entire Arab world. Note also the Occupy Wall Street movement which was echoed in many capital cities, the London riots of August 2011, and the ongoing unrest in rural China.
21 *Book of Common Prayer*, Holy Communion, Second Commandment: 'For I the Lord thy God am a jealous God, and visit the sins of the fathers upon the children unto the third and fourth generation of them that hate me …'

All this has happened before. Current society has not achieved the peak of human progress as is often claimed. It is just part of a large-scale picture. At the time of the Florentine Renaissance there were magnificent art and workmanship alongside abject poverty. This was also part of the picture, the interplay of the cycles. There are periods of great material wellbeing and periods of great uplift of spirit and of the arts; but unfortunately they do not all come together. In the English-speaking world today there is the extraordinary situation of a very high degree of civil liberty yet no economic freedom. This is the state of affairs when people's attention is focused above all else on material welfare.

We have been looking at the fifty to sixty year economic cycles, which go on and on in a mechanical process and are readily observable over the last two hundred years. They in turn are part of a bigger cycle. What has sustained this Christian civilisation over the centuries is the strength of the cultures that have grown up within it.

Cathedrals, literature, art, architecture, science, music are symbols of culture, manifestations of successive renaissances. In the 9th century in Anglo-Saxon England before the Norman Conquest there was a high peak of culture.[22] In the 12th century there was the great Gothic Renaissance with its cathedral builders,[23] and in the 15th century the Florentine Renaissance. There is a great difference between the influence of this sort of cycle and the lesser economic ones we have been discussing. It is the spiritual revival generated every few centuries during these great cultural cycles which keeps the whole system of shorter economic cycles from disintegrating.

22 Even during the Viking incursions, the North of England was known as a location for scholarship. Many classic philosophic and religious books were brought to England in this period and were both copied and translated. The scholars provided education and guidance to kings and other leaders, including Alfred the Great and Charlemagne.
23 Apart from the learning required to design and build them, the cathedrals became centres of learning and the beginnings of the universities in Europe.

CHAPTER 14

Taxation

*In the market-place, if goods are exempted when premises
are taxed, and premises are exempted when the ground is
taxed, then traders throughout the Empire will only be too
pleased to store their goods in your market place ...*

MENCIUS 372–289 BCE
Chinese Philosopher[1]

IN CHAPTER 4 taxation was briefly examined as one of the secondary claims on production. In this chapter it will be considered in
more detail.

14.1 The Need for Taxation

When William I conquered England in 1066 his system of government
was very simple. He divided the country among his favourites and left
it to them to keep the peace. In return he demanded that his lords
provide so many men annually to make up an army, the size of which
varied according to his needs from year to year. In addition they were
to fill the royal coffers as required in order to support the court.

Since the days of feudalism government has become progressively
more expensive. For one thing, an increase in population results in a
more than proportionate increase in costs of government. For another,
scientific advance brings new weapons, and the costs of war and
defence increase greatly until today the defence budget even in peace-
time is quite enormous. One of the most important factors resulting
from population increase has been the growth of towns and cities.
That this has tended to happen in all civilisations is evident from the

1 *Mencius*, Book 1, Part A

many sites of ancient cities long extinct.[2] A similar movement can be seen throughout the world due partly to population increase and partly to the constant move from rural areas towards the towns, as is most evident in China at present.

The cost of maintaining a population in a large city is very much greater than when that population is widespread. There are the costs of providing water and sanitation, refuse removal and public health, the maintenance of streets, public squares, parks and meeting places, schools and care of the aged. In large communities there is an inevitable increase in crime requiring some form of police service together with law courts and gaols. To provide communications between the towns and cities, roads and bridges must be built, improved and maintained, new tunnels bored and ferries operated. With each extension of public service the costs of administration increase.

Gradually and at enormous expense an ever-increasing proportion of the community is employed in the service of local and national government. Such expenditure can only be met from taxation, for apart from any land or shares in production which may be nationally owned, a government has no other income.

	1955	1960	1965	1970	1975	1980	1985	1990	1995	2000	2005
Australia	21.7	22.4	21	21.5	25.9	26.7	28.3	28.5	28.8	31.1	30.8
Canada	21.4	23.8	25.7	30.9	32	31	32.5	35.9	35.6	35.6	33.4
New Zealand	26.7	27.3	24.1	26.1	28.7	30.8	31.3	37.4	36.6	33.6	37.4
UK	29.7	28.5	30.4	36.7	34.9	34.8	37	35.5	34	36.4	35.8
USA	23.6	26.5	24.7	27	25.6	26.4	25.6	27.3	27.9	29.9	27.5

Table 2 – Taxation as a percentage of GDP 1955-2005[3]

What is the proper basis for taxation? This question has perplexed governments over the ages and countless forms of taxation have been used: arbitrary taxation assessed on overlords to be collected from their tenants as best they may; taxes on property; taxes on goods, imports, services; taxes on incomes, roads, windows, sale of land, gambling, dogs, dead men's estates, transfer of land; on necessities which no one could avoid; on luxuries such as the old licences to employ domestic servants, to own a coach or to hold silver or gold plate; taxes by way

2 A process well documented by the Arab writer Ibn Khaldun (1332-1406) in his book *The Muqaddimah*.
3 OECD (2010), *OECD Factbook 2010*: Economic, Environmental and Social Statistics.

of stamp duty on cheques and receipts, on transfer of shares and most legal documents; licences for radio and television receivers,[4] for owning and driving cars, for marriage – the list is endless and the expenses of administration are huge. Taxes are invariably inequitable and have unintended side-effects. Having found one year a basis for taxation that works after a fashion and is just about tolerated by the community, the next year shows that even more expenditure is required and another tax must be invented or an old one increased.

14.2 Principles of Taxation

Perhaps it is best to start by considering Adam Smith's famous Canons of Taxation.[5] Although formulated two hundred years ago, they are still accepted as the principles on which taxation should be based. They may be briefly summarised as follows:

1 The burden of taxation should be spread as fairly as possible having regard to the ability to pay.
2 Taxes should be certain and not arbitrary. The form of payment, the manner of payment and the quantity to be paid ought to be clear and plain to the contributor and every other person.
3 Taxes should be levied at the time or in the manner which is least inconvenient to the tax-payer.
4 Taxes should be easy and inexpensive to administer, and should not discourage production.

It will quickly be seen that modern taxation meets few of these criteria. For example, in most modern economies income tax is deducted from employees' pay by the employer. For the majority this tax meets the second requirement as to certainty and it also meets the third requirement. But a tax on income is inevitably unfair with regard to the ability to pay, since it does not distinguish between income derived from earnings and income derived from the tenant's share, and the more refinements that are made to try and make the tax more equitable, the greater the difficulties and costs of administration become.[6]

4 Originally quite a widespread idea used to fund the national broadcaster, these days only the UK still uses this form of taxation.
5 Adam Smith, *An Enquiry into the Nature and Causes of the Wealth of Nations*, Book V, Chapter II.
6 There are two further points to note here. First, this form of taxation discriminates against a business where the costs, in the way they are ordinarily seen, are primarily labour. It encourages the substitution of capital for labour. Second, the reason that many businesses in the developed world are not competitive is that they are required to pay high taxes on wages, whereas those in the developing world are not.

As to the tax being clear and plain to the contributor and every other person, anyone who has completed a tax return, even on a simple basic salary, will agree that simplicity is hardly the keynote in almost any of the countries under consideration.

14.3 Contemporary Taxation

It is common practice to differentiate between direct and indirect taxation. It is said that taxes are direct when the person taxed makes the payment directly to the government, such as income tax, estate duty and local rates. Taxation is said to be indirect when the taxes are not paid directly to the government by the tax-payer but through importers, manufacturers, retailers and other intermediaries. Indirect taxes include excise duties, taxes on goods sold and customs duties.

Generally speaking, direct taxes are levied on income and accumulated wealth whilst indirect taxes are levied on outlay. Table 3 below gives a broad indication of how much money is raised from each source. The principal distinction made between the two forms of tax is that direct taxes cannot be avoided whilst, it is claimed, that payment of indirect taxes is to some extent under the control of the tax-payer. The tax-payer must, it is true, pay tax on necessities but can avoid the tax by not purchasing luxuries. The argument is that taxes on alcohol and tobacco are only paid if people drink or smoke, and there they have the choice. High indirect taxation is even justified on the argument that it promotes savings and hence investment.

Much is made of this distinction but it has little real significance, for as is shown later the real effect of taxes is seldom felt entirely where they are levied. What is more important is that by spreading the burden of taxation as widely as possible its full extent is obscured and people do not realise how much tax they are paying.

	Total Tax Revenue as % GDP	Taxes on Incomes and Profits as % GDP	Taxes on Goods and Services as % GDP	Other as % GDP
Australia	30.8	18.4	8.2	4.2
Canada	32.2	15.9	7.5	8.8
New Zealand	34.5	20.6	11.8	2.1
UK	35.7	14.2	10.3	11.2
USA	26.9	12.6	4.6	9.7

Table 3 – Sources of Taxation (2008)[7]

7 OECD (2010), *OECD Factbook 2010*: Economic, Environmental and Social Statistics.

14.4 Particular Taxes

Changes in the sources of taxation are subject to fashion as well as to pragmatic issues. It is intended here to review briefly just some of the major taxes that are, or have been, popular.

Income Tax

Income tax was first introduced in Britain in 1799 to help meet the cost of the war against France.[8] The standard rate was 10% of a resident's gross income, no tax being paid on incomes less than £80 a year, and a graduated scale applying up to £200 a year. The tax was withdrawn in 1802 when the war ended but was reimposed in 1803 when war broke out again and continued until after the Battle of Waterloo in 1815.

The tax was revived in 1842 by Sir Robert Peel with the intention that it should run for a period of three years only; the rate was approximately 3% on incomes over £100 a year. But unpopular though the tax was, it had to be extended until in 1853 Mr Gladstone enforced it for a further period of seven years with a view to abolishing it at the end of that time. However, only two years later the Crimean War led to the rate being increased to 17.5% of income. In 1860, with the removal of tariff duties under the impulse of the Free Trade Movement, the tax rate was fixed at approximately 4% with no further mention of repeal. The rate had risen to just over 6% by 1902 to meet the cost of the Boer War, and to over 25% by 1918 to pay for the First World War. This tax rate reached its peak during the Second World War at 50% of income.

Income tax is now with us permanently although, as a result of all the allowances and a variable rate, many of the inequities are mitigated. The burden falls most heavily on the higher incomes and these are largely unearned. This is commonly referred to as a progressive tax system.

Income is an arbitrary basis for taxation – a rough sort of justice. But taking the population as a whole, income tax achieves its immediate objects despite being far from fair in many individual cases. However, income tax has other far-reaching effects which are not at first

8 New Zealand inherited the English income tax legislation in 1843; in the United States income tax was first introduced in 1861 at a rate of 3% for income greater than $800 per annum to finance the Civil War; it was introduced in Australia on a state by state basis commencing with Tasmania in 1880; Canada introduced income tax as a temporary measure to finance its expenditure towards the end of World War I.

Australia		Canada		New Zealand		United Kingdom		United States	
6001-		0-		0-		7475-		0-	
37000	15%	42707	15%	14000	11%	35000	20%	8500	10%
37001-		42708-		14001-		35001-		8501-	
80000	30%	85414	22%	48000	17.5%	150000	40%	34500	15%
80001-		85415-		48001-		>		34501-	
180000	37%	132406	26%	70000	30%	150000	50%	83600	25%
>		>		>				83601-	
180000	45%	132407	29%	70000	33%			174400	28%
								174401-	
								379150	33%
								>	
								379150	35%

Table 4 – Headline Income Tax Rates[9]

obvious. Because earnings are set at the lowest acceptable, level all taxation on wages is paid by the employer. Income tax calculated on wages is a tax on employment. On the one hand, it encourages the replacement of workers with machines and, on the other, encourages production to move to countries where tax on employment is less.

Purchase Taxes

Purchase or sales tax – its variations in some countries are called value added tax (VAT) or goods and services tax (GST) – is a major contribution to government revenue. As we know it today it is a relatively new invention. Purchase taxes previously were levied on a product-by-product basis with different rates for different types of products or services. VAT and GST are intended to be the same rate for all goods and services, but in most countries this has been found to be unacceptable. Some purchase taxes are levied as a form of social engineering and it is particularly easy to get increases in tax rates of this kind through the legislature. They include taxes on tobacco, alcohol and gambling. Others with the effect of discouraging consumption are taxes on petroleum products,[10] which raise huge amounts of revenue. In principle purchase or sales tax is paid by the end-consumer, but the collection processes vary enormously.

9 Income tax rates expressed in local currency for 2011/12 as charged by the national government. Rates are not comparable without consideration of the inclusions and exclusions associated with each regime. In some cases states or provinces also charge additional income tax.

10 Not so much in the United States where taxes on petroleum products are relatively light.

The effect of all this taxation on the price of manufacturing is very difficult to trace. It is picked up at varying stages in the processes of production. There may be customs and excise duties payable on raw materials, on tools and machinery, and on component parts, while transport costs are severely increased, not only by these self-same taxes, but also by the very heavy tax on petrol.[11] Finished goods may also attract purchase tax. But that is not the sum total of the effect on prices: manufacture of any item may involve a considerable number of undertakings each requiring a profit margin on its contribution. In order to maintain this margin, each undertaking adds its percentage of profit to the taxes which have been accumulated and so their effect is exaggerated.

VAT and GST especially bring with them a considerable burden of administration both for government and business. The tax is charged on whatever goods are sold and the business is entitled to a rebate for similar taxes paid on its inputs, provided it keeps records to justify the rebates.

Purchase taxes are a tax on trade and hence on any form of specialisation.

Customs Duties

Customs duties are a very old source of revenue. In English history they appear to have been considered originally as taxes upon the profits of merchants, who were generally looked down on by the nobility and were thus fair game for taxation. Duties were assessed both on exports and imports and the resulting revenue was awarded by Parliament to the sovereign. Over the years customs duties on exports have mostly died out[12] but on imports they have been much favoured, not so much as a form of revenue but as protection for home industries against foreign competitors. Import tariffs were dropped during the short period of free trade but returned during the Great Depression.[13] Now with the world-wide emphasis on free trade they have again been reduced substantially.

Insofar as they discourage trade, tariff duties are clearly undesirable. Trade between nations like trade between individuals only takes place

11 Although there is no taxation on aviation fuel, largely because commercial aircraft can fly to low tax countries to refuel. This sort of variation tends to give air transport an advantage over other forms of transport.
12 In fact exports are often subsidised at least by the alleviation of taxation on exports, including taxation paid on inputs to the manufacturing process.
13 Trade in the United Kingdom was progressively liberalised in the second half of the 19th century until the world-wide movement to protectionism in the 1930s.

if it is to mutual advantage. To interfere with it in any way is to the disadvantage of the public at large although it may be helpful to particular industries. Tariff duties fall equally on those who depend on wages for their incomes and on those living on the tenant's share. For many years taxes were levied on what were at the time basic necessities.[14] The theory was that being necessities an increase in their price would not stop people from buying them; this proved to be the case but the taxes caused much hardship when they could not be passed on in claims for extra wages.

Tax on Stock

A common form of taxation was that levied on stock – a man's livestock and equipment. This was the origin of the *Domesday Book*.[15] If heavy, such a tax discouraged the improvement of farms and also led to men hiding what wealth they had and trying to appear poorer than they were. This form of taxation reached the extremes in eighteenth century France with the personal *taille*, as it was called. This tax was paid by the lower ranks, whilst the nobility and upper classes paid a capitation tax based on their social rank.[16] The amount of tax to be raised by personal *taille* throughout the country was decided and then apportioned between twenty regions known as 'generalities' or 'counties of election'. Each generality was sub-divided into 'elections' and each election into 'parishes', the tax being apportioned down to each. The assessors of the parish then apportioned the tax between the lower ranks of the people largely on the basis of their stock. If anyone failed to pay the other members of the parish were further assessed. This whole system was vicious and arbitrary and grew more and more severe with the increasing extravagance of the French kings. It culminated in the French Revolution, for a time eventually comes when tax-payers will bear no more. For this reason, when taxes are high it is necessary to disguise them heavily so that people do not notice how much they are being charged.

General consideration of a tax of this kind reappears from time to time, usually referred to as a wealth tax.

14 See Adam Smith, *The Wealth of Nations*, Book I, Chapter III.
15 The *Domesday Book* was compiled by William the Conqueror in 1086 as a complete survey of all the productive resources of England so that a tax assessment could be made. It goes without saying that there was a strong inclination to hide some of these resources from the assessors – tax avoidance is not new.
16 The *taille* was orginally a tax to meet exceptional situations that became permanent in 1439. In 1680 the rights to collect this tax on behalf of the king were sold to private individuals. Some writers refer to this as a land tax, which is not the case.

Poll Tax

A poll tax,[17] as its name suggests, is assessed on heads of population. In one form it is a tax on the number of slaves or bondsmen and is paid by their masters.[18] In another it is a personal tax payable by free men. In the reign of William III (1689-1702) a very complicated system was devised with a tariff of taxes according to rank: so much for a duke, rather less for a marquis, and so on through earls, viscounts, barons, esquires, gentlemen, eldest and younger sons of peers, and on to a fixed sum for all tradesmen and shopkeepers worth more than £300.

In its various forms a poll tax has been very common throughout history. It is relatively easy to collect and certain in amount but bears little relation to equity. In some countries it has been used for discriminatory purposes: in the United States to prevent the poor (black and white) from voting, in Canada to discourage the immigration of poor Chinese workers. These days it is deeply unpopular, as Margaret Thatcher discovered when she introduced such a tax at the end of the 1980s.

Capital Gains Tax

As a means of blocking a gap in the present taxation system a capital gains tax has much to recommend it. For whereas high incomes are severely taxed, any gains by way of capital, as for example rises in value of land or stocks and shares, can escape tax-free. Generally the tax applies only when the gain is realised. As long as the assets are not sold, the higher income can be enjoyed[19] without paying any capital gains tax.

The method of implementation varies enormously from one country to another and there is contention, as it is argued, that a capital gains tax may discourage investment, which in turn is said to create jobs. The devil is in the detail.

Taxes on Land

Finally taxes levied on land. This is a very old source of taxation and one to be welcomed as coming nearest to matching the ability to pay.

---

17 Also known as a head tax or a capitation tax.
18 In the United States at one stage slave owners were taxed on the number of slaves they owned. Adam Smith, *The Wealth of Nations*, Book V, Chapter II cites examples of this form of taxation being imposed in various European countries.
19 That is, higher rents or higher dividends on stocks and shares.

But it has seldom if ever been levied as a tax on the full economic rent. Usually it has been levied at a part only of the full annual worth and has often included improvements. A tax on improvements is inequitable and discourages the full use of land. A proportionate tax is also inequitable as it gives greater advantage to the person holding the better land.[20] It should be remembered that if other forms of taxation are being levied as well, these reduce the amount that can be paid by way of landlord's claim and thus the annual worth of the land is less than it would otherwise be.

In England the land tax was last assessed in the reign of William and Mary (1689-1694); it was calculated to include improvements and was never very evenly distributed. It was a fixed tax that did not adjust to increasing rent over the years or to changes in money prices. Consequently in modern times the amount of the tax had become quite derisory – often only a few pence a year on one person's holding.[21] Parallel to the land tax was the tithe that was effectively a tax payable to the church. This was originally a tenth share of the actual produce, but in England for convenience it was converted to an annual sum, which again over the years was not adjusted with increases in rent and changes in money prices, so that it also became of little more than nuisance value and is now largely redeemed.

Local rating still reflects the annual worth of land but includes the value of improvements and is subject to important exemptions, including all agricultural land. Even so it comes nearer to a tax on economic rent than any other.

Some countries have forms of site value rating and taxation in varying degrees; these include Australia, New Zealand, Denmark, Hong Kong, Taiwan and parts of Canada and the United States. In all cases the tax is only on a part of the annual worth and is accompanied by other forms of taxation. But so far as they go they have proved to be very satisfactory, especially in Hong Kong, where it has been possible to keep all other taxes very low.

14.5 Taxation and Equity

Over the years many refinements have been added in an attempt to meet the requirement that the burden of taxation should be spread as fairly as possible, having regard to the ability to pay. Income tax rates

20 That is to say, where earnings are a higher proportion of total production, more tax is levied on earnings. Refer to Diagram 9, page 39.
21 The act was finally repealed in 1963.

increase as incomes increase, whilst tax-free allowances are made according to the tax-payer's personal circumstances. Despite this, most governments assess income tax on income levels that are below the poverty line.[22]

How should the burden be spread fairly? Should a single person pay more than a colleague earning the same wages but supporting a family? Should someone earning $40,000 pay twice as much as someone earning $20,000? Or should they pay something less than twice as much? Or something more? Amongst any group of people, whether laymen, politicians or learned economists, the answers will be different, clearly indicating that there is no sound principle on which to base such judgements.

Today income tax is taken for granted. Even though people complain bitterly of the burden especially on any increases in income, it is accepted in principle. But consider a moment: for practical purposes it may be said that the total production of the community is divided between its members by way of income. Thus the basis of taxation is the claim upon total production enjoyed by each individual. It was proposed earlier that the primary division of production was between earnings and tenant's share (see Diagram 5, page 34). Income tax is assessed upon incomes irrespective of whether they derive from earnings or tenant's share. Admittedly in most countries a minimum income is allowed before any tax is paid, but otherwise no distinction is made. Does this mean that the burden is spread as fairly as possible having regard to the ability to pay?

All production of wealth is the result of work on land. Earnings are claimed by virtue of work, tenant's share by virtue of control of land. The two claims are thus fundamentally different. The right to work derives from natural law. The right to control land derives from the consent of the community, from the duty of each individual not to interfere with another's enjoyment of land. But coupled with this is the duty of each individual to pay the full rent for the land they occupy.[23] This also is natural law.

It is impossible to answer the question of how taxation of income should be fairly shared. The measure of a person's income is an utterly unsound basis for taxation. There is no justification for taxation of earnings whilst anyone is enjoying an unearned income, for an

22 The poverty line in the United States is estimated to be $22,314 for a family of four, and $11,139 for a single person (Source: U.S. Census Bureau; *Social, Economic and Housing Statistics Division: Poverty*, September 13, 2011). See Table 4 page 182 for headline income tax rates.
23 This is expanded in Chapter 18 below.

unearned income can only derive from holding land without paying the full rent to the community.[24]

14.6 Government Expenditure

Economists typically classify government expenditure into three major groupings:

- Transfer payments: allocations made for social services, pensions, unemployment benefits, and subsidies for the poor;
- Government final consumption expenditure: government running costs, including the salaries of public servants; and
- Government gross fixed capital formation: expenditure on buildings and infrastructure which will be of value over a number of years.

To these should be added the expenses of servicing the government debt and of defence and public order. The following table suggests that the first grouping above absorbs the largest part of government expenditure.

	Health	Social Expenditure	Public Pensions	Total	Defence, Law and Order
Australia	5.6	16.1	3.3	25.0	n/a
Canada	7.0	16.9	4.2	28.1	n/a
New Zealand	7.1	19.0	4.3	30.4	n/a
United Kingdom	6.9	20.4	5.3	32.6	2.5
United States	8.7	10.2	6.0	24.9	4.2

Table 5 – Government Expenditure as Percentage of GDP[25]

These figures do not include grants and subsidies to industries and regions. We pay an enormous amount of taxation – around 30% of the gross national product – in order that the state may provide for what should largely be the responsibility of the individual. In other words, all this vast burden of taxation is incurred not for the true

24 Which is not to say, for instance, that a pension is an unearned income. Pensions can be considered a deferred claim.
25 OECD (2010), *OECD Factbook 2010: Economic, Environmental and Social Statistic*, OECD Publishing.

purposes of government but in order to bring about a redistribution of national wealth. And still there is poverty!

14.7 Effects of Taxation

Lets us now look at the different effects of taxation levied on earnings or levied on the tenant's share.

Taxes Levied on Earnings

We will look first at taxes on wages and salaries. Suppose that the tax system is adjusted tomorrow so that every wage-earner is charged an additional 10% in income tax. After the outcry had died down (and assuming that the new tax was not expended on increased social services) what would be the effect? Clearly wage-earners would begin to press for an increase in their wages to a level which would leave them in a comparable position after taxation to that before the tax was increased.

Whatever appearances may suggest, it is the employer, that is the tenant, who ends up paying the increase in tax once conditions have readjusted themselves. All taxes on wages are eventually paid out of tenant's share, as are compulsory health insurance contributions, compulsory unemployment contributions, and compulsory pension contributions, all of which are in fact taxes on employment. The employer pays the taxes, and the employees receive their net wages. These are shown on Diagram 36 as 'Direct Tax' and 'Mandatory Social Service Contributions'.

It is true that as a result of tax allowances the net wages of a single worker may be less than those of an equivalent worker supporting a family, and at first glance this difference in net wages appears to be directly related to the taxation 'deducted'. Such factors reflect in the least that men and women will accept[26] – not only as individuals but also in large numbers. This is the working of statistical law.

What then of indirect taxation? In *The Wealth of Nations* Adam Smith pointed out that in 1775 the principal taxes on the necessaries of life were those upon salt, leather, soap and candles[27] and he demonstrated how these taxes must raise wages correspondingly.[28] Today taxation in

26 Before World War II it was a common practice that when a man married he approached his employer and asked for extra wages. The modern tax regimes reflect both this and the operation of the lowest acceptable level of earnings.
27 Adam Smith, *The Wealth of Nations*, Book I, Chapter VIII.
28 *Ibid.*

the form of purchase tax touches many commodities that are regarded as necessities by our present society. Taxes levied on all such commodities increase prices. Any substantial increase in taxation on commodities in general use will result in a demand for increased wages. Although it is difficult[29] to analyse personal expenditure and determine the actual amount attributable to indirect taxes, it can be seen that here again the burden of such taxes is eventually shifted onto tenant's share. This is shown on Diagram 36 as 'Indirect Tax'.

Rates on domestic housing are a further expense for workers and become an additional burden for the tenant in the same way as indirect taxation. This also is shown on Diagram 36.

In reality a person's earnings are what can be purchased with his or her wages, and the least workers are willing to accept is established in terms of housing, bread, meat, clothes, beer, cigarettes, television etc. Diagram 36 illustrates that these two are not the same. The least a worker is willing to accept is reduced because of what is provided by way of social services and subsidies. If these were abolished the lowest wage would jump by a very considerable proportion.

If an employer has to pay more wages to meet increased taxes on commodities, the increase in wages must be sufficient **after payment of income tax** to make up the deficit. The burden of taxes is cumulative.

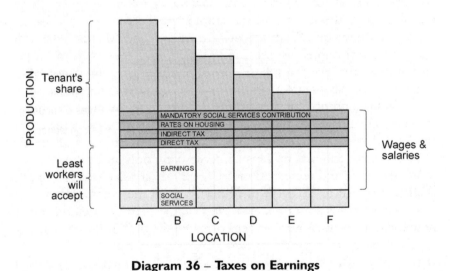

Diagram 36 – Taxes on Earnings

29 There is a large number of informal estimates available on the internet of the total real taxation. The amounts for each person differ according to individual circumstances.

Taxes Levied on the Tenant's Share

In Diagram 37 the employment-related taxes just discussed are shown
with the addition of taxes levied directly on the tenant's share. First
are taxes paid by the money-lender on both income and net profit as
it is spent. Consequently a large proportion of what is paid as interest

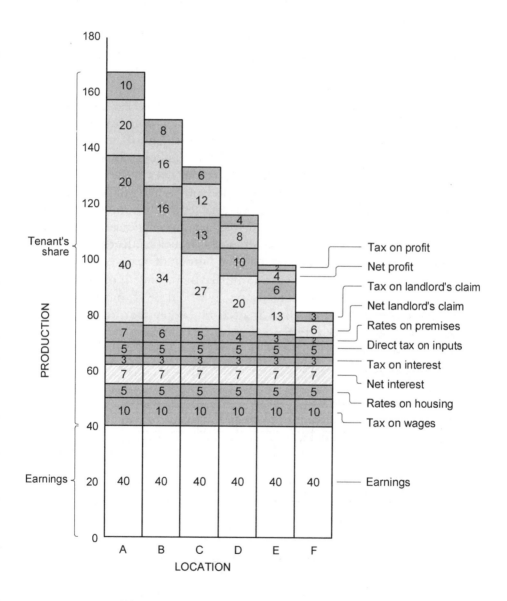

Diagram 37 – Taxes on the Tenant's Share

191

finds its way to the government. Then there are taxes the tenant has to pay directly, such as taxes on petrol, licences required for the undertaking, stamp duties on leases, bills of exchange, etc. These are shown on Diagram 37 as 'Direct Tax on Inputs'.

Leaving rates on premises and landlords' claims aside for the moment, let us consider profit. Due to the competition for sites profit margins are generally reduced to the lowest level at which an entrepreneur is prepared to operate. Naturally an individual undertaking will clear more or less profit according to how successful it is, but there is a general level. The margin of profit is of course subject to tax and, as the profit is spent on goods and services, it also incurs tax.

After removing all these claims what is left is the landlord's claim and rates on the premises of the undertaking. These are related in that the assessment on which rates are levied is supposedly the rent at which the premises would let from year to year, on the assumption that the burden of the rates is met by the tenant. The rates are a tax in themselves whilst the landlord's claim will, like profits, be subject to direct taxes on net income and indirect taxes on the expenditure made. The real pattern is now beginning to emerge: taxation is in fact a claim upon the tenant's share and broadly speaking it is proportionate to the total production of an undertaking.

Looked at in this way, it is extraordinary that a system of such complexity still achieves consistent results. It would be so much easier to tax the tenant's net production at a flat rate equivalent to the current ratio of taxation to GDP[30] and then let the laws governing the division of wealth do the rest. The result would probably be very little different and certainly no less arbitrary.

The Combined Effect

If all the rates and taxes are extracted and put together, the picture appears as in Diagram 38.

It demonstrates that the total of taxation and rates tends to be in proportion to the total of production on each site, and in fact amounts to approximately the general ratio of taxation to GDP. This taxation is evenly spread over production with little variation.

Taking a view of industry as a whole, is total production a sound basis for taxation? At a superficial glance it may appear to be, but look

---

30 Company tax rates in 2011 were 30% in Australia and New Zealand; 16.5% plus provincial taxes (from 1%-16%) in Canada; 26% in the United Kingdom (with some companies paying less); and variable in the United States: from 15-34% plus state taxes, which can be anywhere between 1% and 9%.

a little deeper and the picture changes. When taxation is levied in this way it falls as heavily in proportion on the margin as on the best land available. Earnings are kept down because taxation along with other secondary claims reduces the maximum level to which earnings may rise on the margin. If these earnings fall below the lowest acceptable

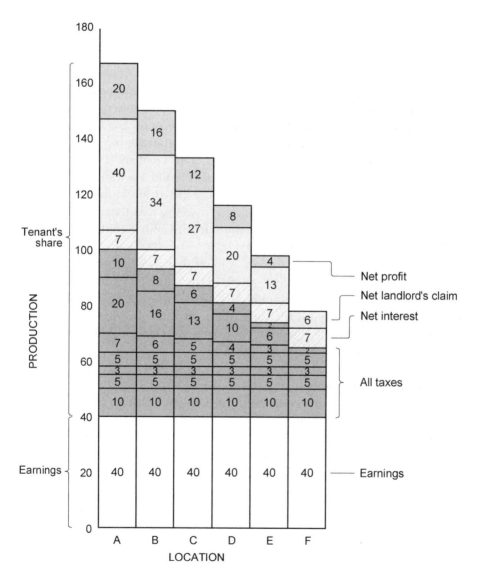

Diagram 38 – The Combined Effect

level marginal sites go out of production. When the margin is put out of production there is unemployment; from this arises competition for jobs and earnings are restricted throughout industry.[31]

Taxation as a proportion of production may be even heavier on the margin than elsewhere. In the case of sites that are remote from their suppliers or from their markets, transport charges are especially important. Increases in taxation by way of vehicle licences and duty on petrol inevitably result in increased transport charges, and these can cripple the margin whilst scarcely touching the better sites.

On a national scale heavy taxation hitting the marginal sites may lead to the appearance of what have come to be called 'depressed areas'. The loss of marginal sites is likely to intensify pressure on the more favoured parts of the country. The North of the United Kingdom has tended to suffer in this way, arising from the fact that it is the marginal region of the country as a whole, as have the so-called 'rust belt' in the United States and the steel-producing cities in Australia. At the same time growth has taken place in other areas such as the South-East of England, the South-West of the United States and the West in Australia. It is natural for one part of the country to be more favoured at one time and less at another. In the 19th century the North of England was enjoying its heyday; now it has declined, with taxation tending to accentuate this decline and to accelerate the drift to the South-East; similarly, the industrial areas of Ohio in the United States have declined in recent years and economic activity has increased in the Southern States.

This effect of taxation is very marked in the Highlands of Scotland where the population is still falling. The move to the towns may lead to increased productivity but at high cost. There is the loss of a local culture; the Highlands can scarcely claim to support as lively a population today as they have done for centuries past, and with the decline in population all services diminish. Taxation can alter the pattern of settlement of a nation, leading to poverty and unrest in one region, whilst increasing the pressures of excessive growth in another, with concomitant distress through housing problems and the overloading of services.

In an attempt to maintain the more vulnerable parts of the marginal industries, a whole system of grants, subsidies and special tax

31 There may be differences in levels of earnings between one region and another. Earnings will be restricted or may fall in regions where there are a lot of marginal sites whilst they may even increase a little in the more prosperous regions. But unemployment generally keeps wages down.

allowances has been built up as well as import tariffs. American farmers receive a great deal of support and protection. The United Kingdom receives farm subsidies from the European Union. The United States provides support for the steel industry and, as recently as 2011, bills were passed by Congress for this. The Australian government is providing support for vehicle manufacture. Subsidies and grants are usually given throughout the industry in order to ensure relief where it is acutely needed – on the margin.[32]

A recent innovation in many countries has been to declare 'development areas', or in some cases 'free trade zones', or 'special economic zones'. In these areas various tax and other laws are suspended as are laws to control minimum wages and working conditions. This is a selective form of subsidy.[33] The key lies in selecting the areas wisely, otherwise it is easy to create even greater hardship around the fringes of these areas where existing industry finds itself suddenly at a disadvantage compared to its neighbours.

What is the effect of all these subsidies on production? The subsidy helps, it is true, but if it is paid to all undertakings within the industry or within the region, it is a free bonus to the better-located firms. This accounts for very high rents and high prices for good land. But in order to raise subsidies and grants and meet the tax allowances, more revenue is required. This means general increases in taxation, which again hit hard on the margin and undo part of the benefit of these subsidies.

Taxation cuts down production and can eliminate certain industries completely. The tin and silver mines of Cornwall and almost the entire English coal industry have been closed because the mines were no longer profitable after paying the taxes on wages. Taxation is seriously affecting the car industry in the United States for the same reason.

This evidence suggests that production is not the proper basis for taxation. There is no room for any taxation on the margin. To be equitable taxation should be levied only on the better sites and then only to the extent that their production is in excess of that on the margin.

---

32 Or even one site at a time because state governments intervene to protect plants in their states.
33 It is also a means of escaping international regulation against subsidy. Jordan and Kenya have especially attracted attention for this practice recently.

IS THE ECONOMIC RENT SUFFICIENT
TO FINANCE GOVERNMENT?

The analysis in this book concludes that all taxation must be derived from the tenant's share. Adam Smith argued that whilst rent was probably the ideal form of revenue, he doubted that the rent of land alone would be sufficient to provide for the day to day needs of government.[34] Many economists since have reached similar conclusions.

An assessment of the economic rent is difficult with the information currently available. In Australia, where land value is assessed and statistics are provided on an annual basis, the true economic rent is still obscured because the land values estimated are deliberately conservative and are subject to speculation and other forces that operate under conditions of full land enclosure.

In 2003, using data covering the period from 1910 to 1999, Dr Terry Dwyer[35] attempted to determine whether the rent would be great enough to finance government in Australia. Dr Dwyer estimated the potential revenue from land by estimating a return of 5% on the official valuation figures, adding rights which are dealt with on a separate basis – water rights, fishing rights, mineral rights, and rights to use radio spectrum – and including the 'capital gain' arising from the change in land values from one year to the next.[36]

His figures suggest that since the decade from 1990 the revenue from land could fund more than 70% of all taxation in Australia. Given the extremely conservative nature of the valuations and the fact that a substantial amount of government revenue in the form of land tax and mineral royalties is already collected at present, the prospect of funding all government expenditure from the economic rent is viable.

34 *The Wealth of Nations* Book V, Chapter 2, Part 1.
35 Dr Terry Dwyer, *The Taxable Capacity of Australian Land and Resources,* Australian Tax Forum 2003, Vol. 18, No 1 (January 2003).
36 Land values are assessed on a five-year cyclical basis.

SECTION 3

An Ethical Perspective

No society can surely be flourishing and happy, of which the far greater part of the members are poor and miserable. It is but equity, besides, that they who feed, clothe, and lodge the whole body of the people, should have such a share of the produce of their own labour as to be themselves tolerably well fed, clothed, and lodged.

ADAM SMITH
The Wealth of Nations
Book 1, Chapter 8

CHAPTER 15

The History of Land Tenure

T HE HEART OF the argument so far has been the system of land tenure. It will be useful at this stage to consider how the system of land tenure evolved into what we are familiar with in the English-speaking world today.

15.1 Saxon Land Tenure

Little is known of the detail of land tenure in Saxon England but the principle is clear. Historians show that the land was held to belong to the community and individuals occupied it, not as owners, but as tenants subject to certain duties. There were two recognised forms of land tenancy: folkland and bookland. Folkland was held at the will of the local community and bookland was held by grant of the king and his counsellors. The latter applied largely to the church and to important citizens but still carried particular duties with it. Both folkland and bookland could be transferred and passed on at death, so that the individual tenant could transfer the benefit of improvements, provided the new tenant undertook the duties pertaining to the land.

At that time there was plenty of free land available and anyone who wanted to could take a piece of suitable land, clear and cultivate it to make a living. Anyone could go out into the wilds if they chose, but usually the choice would be to clear land on the outskirts of an existing settlement. In that case, once the land was cleared and the first harvest gathered in, the new settler would be expected to fulfil duties to the village community. In its turn the community had duties to the kingdom. Exactly what these duties were is largely a matter of surmise. Almost half of the village communities appear to have had a lord or thane, whose nature was that of protector. In return for the benefits of protection, the villagers rendered him services, such as cultivating his land, hewing his wood, and so on. The thane was in the nature of a Scottish chieftain and not a landlord, administering the common land of the village[1] as trustee rather than owner.

In those villages which had no thane or lord, the villagers would have made their own arrangements for administering the common lands, securing justice and providing protection against invaders; no doubt each villager had recognised duties in this respect. In addition all would have owed a duty to the king who was considered to be the protector of the whole kingdom.

It was a simple system, perhaps a little crude, but it worked. Records suggest that people generally lived well according to the standards of the time. There may have been hunger when harvests failed but it was shared by all. Some may have been indolent but they were so from choice. The sick and the needy were cared for by the church and there was no hopeless poverty, for all those who chose to could help themselves.

People could live in the wilds away from any community and owe duty to no one. Or they could enjoy the advantages of community life and accept its obligations.

The full rent in these Saxon communities was paid largely by way of services, which met the needs of the village and of the kingdom. There is no evidence to suggest that the Saxon kings had difficulty in meeting the communities' needs in the ordinary way. However, to keep off invasion by the Danes, the Saxon kings had to give them gold as protection money raised by taxation levied arbitrarily – the famous 'danegeld'. This was an exceptional expense arising from an outside cause – the cost of being a relatively civilised community in a relatively uncivilised part of the world.

In Anglo-Saxon England the principle was that the land belonged to the community and tenants held it in accordance with the folk laws. A landless man was a rarity among freemen, so much so that he was declared an outlaw. True, men did not hold land on equal terms due to the feudalism that had grown up over the years, but usually even serfs acquired their own landholdings.

---

1 One of the arguments currently used for private property in land assumes that common land has no owner and is not managed. This was not the case.

15.2 The Norman Changes

Following the Norman Conquest, King William brought in the Frankish approach to land tenure. Although, apart from the ravages of war, there was little apparent change at first, the effect was to be far-reaching. The new king proclaimed himself owner of all the land, not as a trustee of the community, but in his own right by conquest. This was the first open diversion from the principle that the land belonged to no one but was for the benefit of all.

In 1086 a great survey of all the land was recorded in the famous *Domesday Book*, which gave details of all holdings of land and stock. On this were based the services which each occupant should render. The occupation of land was still recognised as the root of duty to the community, but this duty had been extended a little to include an element of levy by the conquerors.

The king handed large tracts of land to his supporters in return for fulfilment of duties or dues. These men were the new lords of the manors – often of a number of manors – and the existing landlords became their tenants in return for fulfilment of their dues. To ordinary people little seemed to have changed. They paid dues to the new lord, who in turn paid his dues to the king. In effect the king claimed to own all land but farmed out the collection of feudal dues to the lords. They collected what they could from their tenants and in turn owed service to the king.

Originally the feudal dues took different forms of service, each providing free tenure of land. These included knight service or military tenure; tenure by sergeantry; socage tenure; and finally frankalmain or spiritual tenure. There was also unfree tenure, or villeinage, which was later called copy-hold.

Under knight service, by which the lords held land from the king, for forty days in every year each had to produce a specified number of fully armed horsemen or knights. For about one hundred years after the Conquest the army was raised by this means to a strength of some 5,000 knights. This was not a very practical way to raise an army, and about the middle of the 12th century the king began to exact from his lords fixed money payments called 'scutage' in lieu of a quota of knights. By the end of the 13th century in the reign of Edward I, these payments of scutage were quite inadequate to provide the size of army required in a more highly populated and flexible society, and knight service had virtually lost its military characteristics. It was, however, of great importance for another reason which we will discuss later.

Tenure by sergeantry was tenure in return for a specific service and usually related to the great officers of the realm. A sergeant might be required to carry the banner of the king, to lead his army, to be his marshal, his butler, or one of his chamberlains. These duties were held to confer honour and, although early on they lost any economic import-ance, some have continued in England to this day. Among them is the performance of certain duties at the coronation. There were lesser duties of personal service to a great lord but these early fell into disuse.

Socage tenure included any other form of lay duties by a freeholder: agricultural service, provision of certain crops or commodities, per-sonal service, and payment of monetary rent.

Tenure by villeinage, or copy-hold, related to the greater proportion of citizens, whose service largely took the form of cultivating the lands held for his own use by the lord of the manor. The great difference between this and tenure by socage was that the copy-holder only had access to the manorial courts and although he had legal rights to the land he occupied, he was very much in the hands of his lord, whereas a freeholder had access to the king's court.

The last form of free tenure was frankalmain or spiritual service whereby a man made provision for the repose of his soul. A tenancy of land was granted to an ecclesiastical corporation and it was under-stood that, in return, prayers and masses would be said for the grantor and his heirs.

But the concept of paying the due rent was not yet lost.

15.3 Early Land Enclosures

The change of attitude to land tenure under the Normans set the scene for the later enclosures.[2] Instead of the lord of the manor being the protector of the community, acting as trustee of the common land and receiving certain services in return, he now regarded himself as the owner of the manor, his holding restricted by tenants claiming troublesome rights which impeded his freedom to use the land as he would. The law was even misrepresented to make it appear that these rights were really grants given at the will of the lord, consistent with ancient custom.

About this time services were slowly being converted into money payments which, although more convenient, emphasised further the

---

2 'Enclosure' is the name applied to the appropriation, literally the enclosing, of land for pri-vate use.

impression that land was held from an owner in return for a periodic payment.

The first important infringement of economic freedom came in 1236 under the Statute of Merton. For some time the lords of the manor had attempted, with varying degrees of success, to enclose part of the common lands, either to provide new freeholds for those to whom they were indebted, or to form sheep-walks for the growing practice of sheep rearing. The Statute of Merton, the first statute law, legalised this, providing only that sufficient land was left to meet the needs of the commoners. The onus of proof was on the commoners if they considered that their rights had been infringed. The common law was being changed to meet the exigencies of the moment and the interests of the powerful.

Thus began the long battle for private ownership of the soil of England. Magna Carta had laid down that no free man should be disseised[3] of his free tenement except by the ordinary process of law.[4]
. The lords of the manor were gradually assuming the role of landowners instead of protectors. Whereas they had held the common and waste land in trust for the commoners, the concept was growing that the lord owned the common and granted rights over it. In proving commoners' rights at law the fiction arose that the right must have been enjoyed by a lost grant, that is, a right that had been granted by the lord and subsequently lost. By the reign of Elizabeth I (1558-1603) it was no longer acceptable for any right over common land to be held by the inhabitants collectively but only by individuals. The emphasis was now on rights of absolute ownership.

The Statute of Merton and this subsequent approach paved the way for the early enclosures. At first there was little effect and the rural population in general remained comparatively prosperous. But gradually as enclosures became more frequent the population began to suffer severely. More and more land was enclosed for pasture and evicted tenants, unable to get employment in the villages, were obliged to turn to the towns. Various Acts were passed to curb the enclosures, but they achieved little, for they were not implemented effectively.

---

3 Disseised meaning dispossessed particularly in relation to land.
4 Both the Magna Carta (1215) and the Statute of Merton (1236) arose from power struggles between the king and his barons. In both cases the king was forced by his nobles to sign the document. Magna Carta is better known as the basis in English law of the freedom of the individual against the arbitrary authority of government. Both documents, however, also include sections regarding the rights of the nobles to land.

Then in 1348 came the Black Death. The consequent fall in population[5] meant that many of the lords' lands were left untended and hired labour was very difficult to obtain – so difficult that wages doubled. With the loss of labour, the lords lost the advantages their lordship gave them. Further land was enclosed as pasture since sheep farming needed far less labour than arable farming. At first they enclosed the uncultivated land. Then they began to turn to the manorial wastelands, depriving the tenants of their ancient rights of pasturage. Sheep farming proved highly profitable, for wool was in great demand and its price was increasing. Enclosures also made possible the sale of holdings of land to the merchants, who were becoming very prosperous and were anxious to set themselves up on the land.

Enclosures continued even after most of the uncultivated common land and the wastelands had disappeared. These further enclosures necessitated actually turning out tenants and destroying their homes, and this was done quite mercilessly. Steps were taken by the king and parliament to prevent the continuance of enclosures but they remained half-hearted, for those in positions of power were often themselves enclosing land.

By the early 16th century the great shortage of manpower after the Black Death had been made good. There was a surplus of labourers, unemployment had appeared for the first time, and the dispossessed were left destitute to beg or steal a living. The lord enjoyed his land unencumbered by tenants. Having paid the meanest of wages to his employees the full fruits of the land were his.

As the years passed the population grew, movement became easier, and the needs of the community became more complex, and more expensive. But the payment of rent by the lords remained fixed at the amount struck when the feudal dues were commuted to money, reflecting neither the changes in monetary prices nor the increased economic rent of the land. Equally the rents paid to the lords were fixed. The position was aggravated still further by land enclosures, when the lords forcibly took occupation of much of the land of the manor and kept all the profits to themselves.

Without collection of the full rent, the royal revenues were insufficient and had to be supplemented from taxation. It had early been established that, apart from certain duties or imposts (tonnage and

5 Approximately 1.5 million people died between 1348 and 1350 from a population of about 4 million.

poundage) made available by custom to the king, taxation could only be levied with the consent of parliament. Thus from very early times the kings fought to build up adequate revenue – a fight which governments continue to face today. If economic rent is not collected, there is little chance that the revenue will ever equal the demands of government.

By the end of the 16th century over half the common lands of England were enclosed. Then the momentum began to die down a little for sheep farming had lost its great attraction and labour was plentiful. A landlord could live quite comfortably with the old common system. A certain amount of enclosure continued ostensibly by agreement in order to improve the layout of the fields, but often the smaller landholders were over-ridden and lost their rights. By 1601 the problem of unemployment among the dispossessed had become so great that the Poor Law Act[6] was passed, putting on the parish the responsibility for supporting their own poor.

15.4 Later Land Enclosures

During the late 18th and early 19th centuries there was another, greater wave of enclosures largely under Enclosure Acts passed by parliament, which finally engulfed virtually all the remaining common land in the country. In theory the enclosures were by consent or for the common good of all concerned. In practice the lord gained and the villagers lost almost everything.[7]

The land, instead of belonging to the community for the benefit of all, had become the private property of the few. The majority were left landless and poverty was rampant. Wages were very low and hours very long as men competed with one another for employment.

Outside the United Kingdom in the 17th, 18th and 19th centuries land became available in the New World,[8] whether by conquest or by declaring it 'terra nullius'.[9] In either case the English custom of private property in land overrode any existing traditional arrangements. The availability of land was a major stimulus for emigration and new land could be held by individuals without obligations being imposed on them as landholders. At first land was abundant and cheap or even

6 See Footnote 20, page 74.
7 For details see John and Barbara Hammond, *The Village Labourer*.
8 For the English-speaking world here we include, the United States, Canada, Australia and New Zealand at least.
9 That is, belonging to no one, although in some situations it had to be fought for.

free for the taking. Unused land generally remained the property of the crown[10] and was often made available to settlers. Today no further land is available and populations have grown so that the situation across the English-speaking world is largely the same.

Clearly the old strip system[11] of Saxon times would not work today. But when the old system failed the law could not devise a new system based on natural justice to take its place. So the powerful usurped the land at the expense of the weak. 'This is my land' became the cry and duties were forgotten. Landowners were only interested in their rights and gradually the law came to support them. Statute law and equity (so-called)[12] cut right across common law with its concept of duties in relation to land.

15.5 Absolute Ownership of Land

The rights of private ownership of land became sacrosanct in the eyes of the law and probably reached their culmination in 1895 in the case of Bradford Corporation v. Pickles.

Mr Pickles wanted to sell his land to Bradford Corporation for a reservoir. They could not agree terms and so the reservoir was built on adjoining land. Pickles said that if they did not buy his land he would direct the underground water in his land so that the reservoir would dry out. Bradford sued Pickles to get an injunction to restrain him and the case went up to the House of Lords. Pickles was held to be acting within his rights and won the day. Part of the judgement reads:

10 In the United States after the revolution crown land (unused land) first became the property of the states and was subsequently ceded to the Federal Government by the Continental Congress. The effect is the same.

11 In the strip system the fields around a village were divided into strips approximately a furlong in length (200 metres). The village collectively would allocate to each family a number of strips for ploughing for the season. Next season they would be re-allocated or left fallow. This permitted each family to partake equally of the varying qualities of the land. The practice still survives in the village of Laxton in Nottinghamshire and one or two other locations in England.

12 In the English legal system 'equity' was a principle, established within the Chancery courts to deal with situations where the common law did not provide outcomes that accorded with conscience. Amongst the areas particularly dealt with were issues related to property in land (including inheritance, trusts and other interests). Such interests became pertinent after the dissolution of the monasteries. The Chancery rulings over time became inconsistent, complex and perhaps even prejudiced, especially given the vast expense associated with these cases. For a wry depiction of the nature of the equity courts see Charles Dickens' *Bleak House*, Chapter 1.

The owner of land containing underground water, which percolates by undefined channels and flows to the land of a neighbour, has the right to divert or appropriate the percolating water within his own land so as to deprive his neighbour of it. And his right is the same whatever his motive may be, whether bona fide to improve his own land, or maliciously to injure his neighbour, or to induce his neighbour to buy him out.

The judges clearly recognised the injustice of the case but could do nothing about it – here was damage but no legal remedy. There is no mention of duties in this case, only the rights of legal ownership.

15.6 The Aftermath

A great branch of the common law is the law of contract, and one of its main principles is the sanctity of contract. When free people make a bargain it is proper that each should be held to what has been agreed, even if circumstances have changed so that one has lost on the bargain to the gain of the other.

How can sanctity of contract properly apply when people are not free? What of the relation between landlord and tenant, employer and employee? When you want a roof over your head, you have to accept the landlord's terms. When you want a job, you have to take what you can get and you are in no position to argue with the employer about the detail of the terms of contract. The common law of the English-speaking world is a law for a free people. It can do little to protect individuals against being forced into unjust leases and employment contracts because of their economic dependence.[13]

At the end of the 19th century the position regarding land law in England had become quite intolerable. The judges tried to interpret the law to help the weak, but that only worsened things by making proceedings cumbersome and slow. Public resentment intensified until the way was open for legal reform. Slowly new statute laws were introduced to try to ease the economic situation. Today across the entire

---

13 In taking a lease a tenant may be forced to agree to put the property into good repair. Over a short lease this could be very severe but at law the tenant can obtain no relief. Or a contract of employment may contain no provision to support the employee or his family in times of illness. If he cannot work his wages may stop immediately regardless of long years of faithful service; there may be no provision for old age either, only a wage just sufficient to live on from day to day. Some employment contracts these days include disability insurance but this is often limited to better-paid jobs.

English-speaking world[14] a vast jungle of statute law has grown up, mainly from genuine attempts to reintroduce justice into an area of law where it was largely missing. Each year the list of statutes grows longer no matter which political party is in power, until at the present time governments can scarcely keep up with their programmes of legislation.

And what is the purpose of it all? It is an attempt to remedy the social injustices which arise when economic freedom is lost. At best such forms of legislation can only mitigate the more flagrant breaches of justice – the causes are not touched. Meanwhile industry is hampered by the resulting deadweight of controls and restrictions, which do nothing to encourage either the growth of the economy or the prosperity of the people.

The concept of paying full rent for occupation of land is foreign to modern minds. It is difficult to imagine a society devoid of private property in land.[15] The other recognised model is state ownership of landed property, with the state replacing the present landowner and becoming landlord of all. This would merely transfer power from one set of hands to another, as happened in Russia. It is not economic freedom.

15.7 Conclusion

A third alternative exists which recognises that land belongs to no one because no one made it. However, improvements[16] to the site and buildings on it belong to those who added them. In order for the owners to enjoy what is theirs, they must have occupation of the land, for the nature of buildings and other improvements is that they become integrated with the land on which they stand. Occupation of land and ownership of land are two quite separate concepts. Enjoyment of improvements made to the land is not possible without security of tenure, but there can be no right to tenure to the exclusion of others unless the due rent, if any, is paid to the community at large.

---

14 Although the social conscience of the nation was moved earlier and legislation to protect workers began to be passed as early as the 1830s.
15 Curiously title to land often comes with conditions. In the United Kingdom the extensive footpaths and rights of way have to be respected. In Australia some agricultural land is subject to the rights of aboriginal peoples for transit, hunting and traditional ceremonies.
16 For instance on agricultural land, dams, drainage ditches, fences and cleared land, as well as fruit trees and vines.

And what is the due rent? It is a measure of what may be enjoyed from exclusive occupation of land, arising from the special advantages bestowed on that particular site by the community, relative to what may be enjoyed by occupation of the least advantageous land in use. Diagram 5, page 34 illustrates these relative advantages.

In what form should the due rent be paid? In whatever form is most suitable for the community and the individual. There is no reason why it should not be paid in crops, goods, services, or money. Nowadays money is the most appropriate means of payment but it has not always been so, and we should avoid thinking only in terms of monetary rent.

All title to land has become effectively freehold, but even so the sovereign (or in America the government) remains technically the ultimate owner. The best title anyone can have to land is to be the tenant in fee simple, absolute in possession. Although in name still a tenant of the sovereign, one is in fact regarded as the absolute owner and pays rent to no one. Yet the duty which the Saxons recognised has neither changed nor lapsed in any way. It is still the duty owed by every citizen to the community. Over the centuries it has been recognised less and less and is now completely ignored. The duty remains.

In tracing the history of the economic duty to pay rent we have seen how a nation may change its mind, how it may deliberately turn its back on what it once knew. It is well to remember that the ideas which seem so foreign to our modern minds were universally accepted a thousand years ago. There is nothing difficult about the fulfilment of economic duties. If only they were recognised, a way to implement these duties according to the needs and conditions of the day could be found.

CHAPTER 16

Property

EALTH IS of the man-made world (see Diagram 1, page 15): it is a result, the fruit of work on land. Land, however, is fundamental, one of the natural elements that belongs to no one but is for the enjoyment of all. That is the great difference. To claim land automatically creates a prior claim to all that is produced on it, both now and in the future, and leaves others to establish what claims they can. A community that consents to claims on wealth not only deprives its own generation but, by consenting to claims on land, the community is also depriving future generations.

To use land for purposes of production, the occupier needs to be able to claim exclusive enjoyment. This is perfectly natural and proper. In recognition of the enjoyment of exclusive rights, the economic duties that go with it should be acknowledged and observed. It is important to be clear on this. Land enclosure does not mean merely putting a fence around a piece of common land: there is much more to it than that.

It should also be borne in mind that all recognised claims have the consent of the community. The very claiming of wealth – apart from the claim of wages – makes poverty and injustice quite inevitable. The claiming of things for oneself arises from fear of poverty, and fosters that fear, so that in due course the land itself must be claimed, ensuring that there will always be poverty.

How does the community come to consent to this claim to the land? Sir William Blackstone, the great English lawyer of the 18th century, in his *Commentaries on the Laws of England,* traces the history of property. Note how the viewpoint changes half way through:

> There is nothing which so generally, strikes the imagination, and engages the affections of mankind, as the right of property; or that sole and despotic dominion which one man claims and exercises over the

external things of the world, in total exclusion of the right of any other individual in the universe. And yet there are very few, that will give themselves the trouble to consider the origin and foundation of this right ... We think it enough that our title is derived by the grant of the former proprietor, by descent from our ancestors, or by the last will and testament of the dying owner; not caring to reflect that (accurately and strictly speaking) there is no foundation in nature or in natural law, why a set of words on parchment should convey the dominion of land; why the son should have a right to exclude his fellow creatures from a determinate spot of ground, because his father had done so before him; or why the occupier of a particular field or of a jewel, when lying on his deathbed and no longer able to maintain possession, should be entitled to tell the rest of the world which of them should enjoy it after him...[1]

In the beginning of the world, we are informed by holy writ, that the all-bountiful creator gave to man 'dominion over all the earth; and over the fish of the sea, and over the fowl of the air, and over every living thing that moveth upon the earth.' This is the only true and solid foundation of man's dominion over external things, whatever airy metaphysical notions may have been started by fanciful writers upon this subject. The earth therefore, and all things therein, are the general property of all mankind, exclusive of other beings, from the immediate gift of the creator. And, while the earth continued bare of inhabitants, it is reasonable to suppose, that all was in common among them, and that every one took from the public stock to his own use such things as his immediate necessities required.

These general notions of property were then sufficient to answer all the purposes of human life; and might perhaps have answered them, had it been possible for mankind to have remained in a state of primeval simplicity: as may be collected from the manners of many American nations when first discovered by the Europeans; and from the ancient method of living amongst the first Europeans themselves... Not that this communion of goods seems ever to have been applicable, even in the earliest ages, to aught but the *substance* of the thing; nor could it be extended to the *use* of it. For, by the law of nature and reason, he who first began to use it, acquired therein a kind of transient property, that lasted so long as he was using it, and no longer: or, to speak with greater precision, the *right* of possession continued for the same time only that the *act* of possession lasted. Thus the ground was in common, and no part of it was the permanent property of any man in particular; yet whoever was in the occupation of any determinate spot of it, for rest, for shade, or the like, acquired for the time a sort of ownership, from

1 See also Plato, *Laws*, Book XI, 923.

which it would have been unjust, and contrary to the law of nature, to have driven him by force; but the instant that he quitted the use or occupation of it, another might seize it without injustice. Thus also a vine or other tree might be said to be in common, as all men were equally entitled to its produce; and yet any private individual might gain the sole property of the fruit, which he had gathered for his own repast...

But when mankind increased in number, craft, and ambition, it became necessary to entertain conceptions of more permanent dominion; and to appropriate to individuals not the immediate *use* only, but the very *substance* of the thing to be used. Otherwise innumerable tumults must have arisen, and the good order of the world been continually broken and disturbed...

As the world by degrees grew more populous, it daily became more difficult to find out new spots to inhabit, without encroaching upon former occupants; and, by constantly occupying the same individual spot, the fruits of the earth were consumed, and its spontaneous produce destroyed, without any provision for a future supply or succession. It therefore became necessary to pursue some regular method of providing a constant subsistence; and this necessity produced, or at least promoted and encouraged, the art of agriculture. And the art of agriculture, by a regular connexion and consequence, introduced and established the idea of a more permanent property in the soil, than had hitherto been received and adopted. It was clear that the earth would not produce her fruits in sufficient quantities, without the assistance of tillage: but who would be at the pains of tilling it, if another might watch an opportunity to seize upon and enjoy the product of his industry, art, and labour? Had not therefore a separate property in lands, as well as moveables, been vested in some individuals, the world must have continued a forest, and men have been mere animals of prey; which, according to some philosophers, is the genuine state of nature. Whereas now (so graciously has providence interwoven our duty and our happiness together) the result of this very necessity has been the ennobling of the human species, by giving it opportunities of improving its rational faculties as well as of exerting its natural. Necessity begat property; and, in order to insure that property, recourse was had to civil society, which brought along with it a long train of inseparable concomitants; states, government, laws, punishments, and the public exercise of religious duties. Thus connected together, it was found that a part only of society was sufficient to provide, by their manual labour, for the necessary subsistence of all; and leisure was given to others to cultivate the human mind, to invent useful arts, and to lay the foundations of science...[2]

2 William Blackstone, *Commentaries on the Laws of England*, Book II, Chapter 1.

The entry of ignorance can be pin-pointed to the fourth paragraph: 'But when mankind increased in number.... ' As so often, expediency is permitted to justify what is known to be contrary to natural law. The ignorance is deliberate. People knew better but they deliberately ignored what they knew.

We can observe this in ourselves. What is our reaction when asked to put money in a parking meter on a public street? We know instinctively there is no property in a public street and consequently think there should be no obligation to pay. We are up against a very basic idea in human nature – this concept of property. We should observe the built-in reluctance to any attack on absolute ownership of land. People who have no hope of ever owning a house will still defend the right to private property.

Here are two simple principles from Henry George, already quoted in Chapter 2, both of which are self-evident:

1 That all have equal rights to the use and enjoyment of the elements provided by nature.

2 That each has an exclusive right to the use and enjoyment of what is produced by their own labour.[3]

Henry George goes on to say:

There is no conflict between these principles. On the contrary they are correlative. To fully secure the individual right of property in the produce of labour we must treat the elements of nature as common property.[4]

There is one other thing that we ought to examine along with private property in land. That is lending with increase, or usury, money-lending. Usury can only arise in a community which recognises absolute ownership of land. This has been examined in Chapter 9 but it is worth a brief recapitulation. As a tenant one receives a claim on wealth. By the nature of things it is not necessarily convenient to exercise that claim immediately, and therefore it is useful to be able to defer the claim. That people can do so, is by virtue of the intelligence in the community. This is a great boon: to be able to defer a claim and take it up years later, to be able to enjoy the fruits of the earth now by virtue of labour years before, or by virtue of having been a tenant.

It has been demonstrated that production is impossible without credit, unless wealth is immediately available to purchase materials and

3 Henry George, *Protection or Free Trade,* Chapter 26.
4 *Ibid.*

213

to sustain employees and their families. Provided there is the necessary trust, credit arises naturally. Yet an extraordinary situation occurs: in a condition of land enclosure, because of the way in which society is organised, credit is not easy to obtain.[5] Therefore some will turn to others to borrow their claim to wealth. In return for the use of that claim, the lender can demand an increase known as interest. It is natural that the banks, which create credit, should demand for their troubles an appropriate service charge. But there is no justification for anyone to charge interest on the use of a claim to wealth which they are in fact only too pleased to be able to defer until another day. There is even less justification for bankers to charge interest on claims they create. A community that recognises and encourages the loan of claims to wealth in return for interest is doing itself great harm. The charging of interest on the use of claims to wealth, and the absolute claim to land are the causes of the economic state of the world today. They are a blight on the community which acknowledges them. It is all too easy to take them for granted but both are equally unnatural. They are not in accordance with the law of nature.

That is the measure of those two mainstays of economic bondage. Theories, opinions and beliefs will rally to protect these two enemies of freedom. It takes a lot of effort to recall and act by the principles of 'no claim to land' and 'no charge for the use of a claim to wealth'. Consider the building societies[6] which grew originally out of the needs of individuals. They were traditionally non-profit-making and arose largely so that those who wanted to defer a claim to wealth might make it available to others who needed a claim in advance to buy a house. Economic conditions have obliged building societies to match the current rates of interest payable by borrowers and to lenders. Yet it is very simple for a community to devise a just system for the granting of credit.

5 For people working in prosperous societies this may seem contrary to general observation. After all, most readers of this book are likely to hold credit cards. But beyond these amounts credit is not so easy to obtain. For the majority of the world population credit cards are not available.
6 Building societies (or savings and loans institutions) are often (but not exclusively) mutually owned by the depositors.

CHAPTER 17

Government

GOVERNMENT arises in response to the needs of society. Even the most primitive societies have some kind of government, whether they are hunters, shepherds roaming with their flocks, or the simplest of agrarian communities. The object of government is to bring together the diverse aims, ambitions and natures of citizens in accordance with a common purpose. As suggested in Chapter 1, this is to enable individuals, through cooperation, to grow in skill, happiness and knowledge, leading to prosperity in every sense. It is important that government should remember its objective. When it is remembered, government is strong. When it is forgotten, government is weak. A bad government abandons the true objective and puts another in its place – for instance, the prosperity of the state or even the prosperity of the individuals in government. From this arise tyranny and corruption.

The history of the world is littered with examples of times when the true objective of government has been abandoned or forgotten. In ancient Sparta the individual was subordinated to the well-being of the state until this became an end in itself. So it was in the communist countries until after 1989. The state took priority over the individual. In the English-speaking world today the true role of government is remembered in some areas; in the economic field it is largely forgotten.

Government pursues its true objective through three lines of action: by securing justice, showing mercy, and protecting the people from all forms of violence.

17.1 Justice

What is justice? This is a very big question and not to be answered lightly. No one can tell us, each must discover it for him- or herself and it may prove specific to each situation.

One of the early Roman lawyers gave the following fine description:

Justice is the constant and perpetual will to render to each their due.[1]

Justinian tells us that justice is only to be achieved by constant endeavour; that once achieved it can be maintained only by unceasing vigilance. Justice is not concerned with rights, but with duties. Only by observance of duties can justice be found. Everyone has their due. The economic and civil duties apply to the benefit of all without exception. This is their due.

Here is another description of justice:

Justice is the sovereign public virtue, peace its child and freedom its constant companion.[2]

This puts justice before freedom and peace. It is useless to pursue freedom or peace if justice is neglected. Only the constant will to render to each their due can bring freedom and peace.

Before justice there must be knowledge. Duty has to be discovered. Although it arises from the nature of things, it is hidden: only once discovered is it seen to be self-evident. In the common law the civil duties have been discovered. The man in the street may not be able to formulate them but knows them in his heart, and when they are contravened is filled with uneasiness. The law upholds the civil duties and is highly respected in the knowledge that freedom is imperilled if the law is disregarded.

Justice is secured by discovering the law, formulating it so that every citizen may clearly know their duties, enforcing it against all transgressors and, by constant vigilance, ensuring that it is not debased to meet the exigencies of the moment.

In those countries which have inherited it, the English common law provides that a person may not wrongfully assault, imprison, or defame another; that once a contract has been entered into, the terms of that

1 'Iustitia est constans et perpetua voluntas ius suum cuique tribuendi', found in Justinian's *Institutes* based on the work of the Roman jurist Ulpian (c.AD 170-223). Emperor from AD 527-565, Justinian was known principally for having restored the Roman law by his systematic treatise on law, *The Institutes*, on which most European law is based.
2 Possibly a variant of 'Truth is [justice's] handmaid, freedom is its child, peace is its companion, safety walks in its steps...', attributed to Sydney Smith (1771-1845).

contract must be fulfilled; that a man must not be negligent – must not so conduct himself as to cause a danger to others. Little of this provision is to be found in any acts of parliament or congress; it is mostly in the common law – that great body of judge-made law that has grown up over the centuries and is growing still. Indeed, statute law tends rather to lay down exceptions than to declare the general law.

That duties in the civil field are intuitively known is hardly surprising, for common law is based upon previous judgements. The judges, hearing the dispute and bearing in mind the whole precedent of previous judgements, seek a just solution to the case before them. In this way the judges give embodiment to natural law, which may then be recognised by the community.

But all this is the civil field only. The common law relating to land and thus to the economic sphere has been sadly debased by the so-called law of equity, (a complete misnomer),[3] and by statute law; so that when, for instance, the English Law of Property Act was passed in 1925, its stated aim was to enable the transfer of land to be as simple as the transfer of chattels. Although at law lip-service is still paid to the principle that a man cannot own land but only an estate[4] in land, in practice today ownership of land is claimed just as completely as that of any chattel.

17.2 Mercy

What does it mean to show mercy? Justice is said to be impartial. The fundamental duties are owed by each to all. What then of the sick, the disabled, the old, the mentally unstable, the widowed, the orphaned? If in one respect or another they were unable to fulfil their duties, especially the economic duties, justice would treat them as transgressors. But in a wisely governed community goodness shines through as mercy. It not only relieves them of these duties but provides for their sustenance and well-being. Good government shows mercy.

If anyone transgresses the law of the community in letter but not in spirit there may be a case for showing mercy; again the circumstances of the offence must always be regarded. But mercy is not to be confused with sentiment. Generally speaking, offenders must pay for their actions. If the law of the community is transgressed justice

3 See footnote 12, page 206.
4 'Estate': Middle English legal term meaning the interest anyone has in lands, tenements or other effects.

demands punishment: but to provide for the dependants in their misfortune – that is to show mercy.

17.3 Protection

The third line of action is to protect the people from violence of all kinds. Government must protect the state from attack by an enemy either from without or from within; it must take all necessary steps to secure the peace. The whole body of criminal law belongs to this realm of government, as do all dealings with governments of other states to ensure the safety of the people.

If citizens offend against the law they must be punished, both to prevent further transgression, and to act as a deterrent to others who might be tempted to do likewise. But punishment must only be for the crime actually committed. No one must be imprisoned merely because they might commit a crime, however serious that crime might be. When politicians are tempted to detain their rivals before any crime has been committed, then the law is debased and justice abandoned. In the short run the needs of the state may seem well served, but in the long run irreparable harm is done, for justice once lost is not easy to re-establish.

Stealing is a violation of a person's right to property. What each earns by his or her labour is his of right. For another to take it by whatever means is stealing. To the extent that the law permits it, it is bad law and to that extent government is weak or bad, or both. We would readily condemn government for permitting anyone's posses-sions to be taken from them. What of government that permits one to live by the labour of another or by the labour of many others? Can we reasonably condemn the one and condone the other?

CHAPTER 18

Economic Duties

ECONOMIC DUTIES were mentioned in the preceding chapters. It was noted that our Anglo-Saxon ancestors acknowledged and observed the economic duties, but as time passed they were forgotten.

What is the situation today? The landowner and the tenant can both enjoy full rights to occupation of land and, with that occupation, can also properly claim the full product, after meeting employees' earnings and any costs of production. But there the similarity ends, for the tenant can lose everything when the lease expires,[1] whereas the landowner's title is in perpetuity. The tenant also has to meet the land-lord's claim. This tends to increase on each renewal of the lease to the highest sum the tenant can bear, leaving just enough profit to make production worthwhile. But the tenant is usually also under obligation to keep the land in good condition and to repair the buildings on it, sometimes even to rebuild them.

The landlord pays nothing, has no employees and is under no oblig-ation to keep the land in good condition. It may even be profitable to let the land lie idle for a while in the expectation of increasing rents. Indeed one of the main planks of a system of total land enclosure is that the landowner should not suffer through holding land out of use. The requisite conditions for this are: no rent, no rates, no taxes, no liability to repair. A tenant under a normal lease cannot afford to hold land out of use and is soon obliged to occupy or surrender it, or to assign his interest.

A system of total land enclosure affects the distribution of wealth by lowering the general level of earnings. But consider the position

---

1 In fact the situation can be worse. Most leases provide that the tenant should return the premises to their original condition at the conclusion of the lease. If this is enforced not only does the tenant lose what has been built on the site but must also pay for its removal.

from the point of view of the community as a whole. Every time a piece of land is held out of use the community is that much the poorer. Imagine a garden rich and fertile at one end and rocky and under-nourished at the other. Only a poor gardener would leave patches of soil untended and weeds growing in the fertile part while spending time trying to raise a plant or two on the stony ground. Inevitably the yield of this garden would be reduced by such poor husbandry. Yet, at a national level this is precisely the effect of holding good land out of use, forcing production to the margin.

Where land has been improved and buildings erected over the ages, they are part of the heritage of the community. Without the work of previous generations society would be very much the poorer. Surely there is a moral obligation on each generation to ensure that land is handed on to posterity in good condition and that buildings are kept in good repair?[2]

Over two hundred years ago the following words were written by the French philosopher, Jean-Jacques Rousseau:

> The first person who enclosed a piece of land and bethought himself to say: 'This is mine', and found people foolish enough to believe him, was the real founder of our social system. What crimes, wars, murders, what miseries and horrors would have been spared to mankind, if some-body had torn down the stakes or filled up the ditch, and had warned his fellows, 'Beware of listening to this impostor; you are lost if you forget that the produce is for all, and the earth for no one.'[3]

The economic ills that spring from full land enclosure are not something that happened years ago and cannot be redeemed. For the fruits of land enclosure to be enjoyed by those in possession of the land, the necessary conditions have to be maintained: *the community must constantly assent to landowners being relieved of the obligation to fulfil their economic duties.*

No tenant under a normal lease will willingly take more land than is required for immediate needs. Even for the tenant to sub-let any land surplus to requirements is not usually a very attractive proposition. The tenant is still responsible to the landowner for paying the rent, fulfilling the repairs, and other covenants of the lease. True, rent may be recouped from a sub-tenant and the liability to repair passed on. But if it is difficult to find a sub-tenant, or if the sub-

---

2 Not to mention the effect failure to keep buildings in good repair has on the surrounding community.
3 Jean-Jacques Rousseau, *Basic Political Writings*. See also Cicero, *The Offices*, Book I, VII.

tenant fails, then the tenant is left with a heavy burden which cannot be transferred.

Would any landowner under similar obligations hold more land than was required?

18.1 Economic Duties of Individuals

A lease almost invariably requires rent to be paid and the land kept in good condition and repair. In return the landlord offers quiet enjoyment of the land.[4] Look at any lease and these covenants will usually be found. The rent, or landlord's claim, will not necessarily be the same as the full economic rent: it will normally be equal to the tenant's share less other secondary claims and, where appropriate, a profit margin. Sometimes it may be less, if a premium or other 'consideration' is given for the lease, but rent is always required, even if it is only nominal such as a peppercorn rent.[5]

What we call private ownership of land is really nothing but a dispensation from these conditions. The community exempts all so-called landowners from the payment of rent and from keeping the land in good condition, while ensuring that everyone else is required to allow them quiet enjoyment of the land.

The fundamental economic duties owed to the community by every individual occupying land are these:

- To pay the full rent;
- To keep the land in good repair;
- Not to interfere with another's quiet enjoyment of land.

The duties are surprisingly simple yet their influence penetrates into every aspect of economic life. No one can change these duties; they stem from the nature of things just as do the civil duties. If they are recognised and observed, one set of conditions will arise. If they are ignored, another set of conditions will follow. Natural law works quite inexorably.

4 'Quiet enjoyment of land' is a term arising from the common law. It simply means that on 'my land' I should be free from interference from others by way of smells, sounds, pollution or any other hazard from neighbouring properties. Equally it means that on 'my land' I should not create any form of pollution that would interfere with another person on their land.

5 In many countries the common form of land tenure is in fact a lease with the lessor being the government. Legally a lease is a contract and a contract requires both parties to provide 'consideration'. Peppercorn leases are a tradition in many countries whereby the consideration given to the lessor is a 'peppercorn', which is to say something of no value. The peppercorns, of course, are not actually delivered.

These duties are known but they are not recognised as applying to all. In most countries the majority of people do not occupy land by owning it. Businesses especially tend not to own the land they occupy. Why should some be exempted from the general practice?

The great majority of people do observe their economic duties and pay rent but it does not reach the community. It is held by the few, who do not observe their duties, either in respect of the land they occupy themselves or the land they lease out. This is the reality behind that time-honoured institution known as private property in land or real estate.[6]

18.2 Duties of Government

By nature human beings are land animals and gregarious. Consequently they live in society with their fellows with whom they must share the surface of the earth.

In the most primitive forms of society people gather in tribes, roaming or settling according to their custom, and live by hunting or by cultivation of the land or by a mixture of the two. Although tribal life is primitive and hard and lacks the refinements associated with culture and civilisation, it enables people to live together and share the land without creating any serious problems or inequalities. The chief and elders may have privileges but they also have responsibilities. The young and the old are cared for by all. When the hunt or harvest is successful all eat well; when it is not all go hungry. A natural balance is found.

As society develops, it would appear that with the advantages of specialisation and scientific progress living conditions should surely improve universally. But, as we look at the world around us now and throughout the ages, this clearly has not been the case. Many have benefitted enormously but many more have not. Slavery and poverty exist amidst plenty, few individuals are able to follow their natural talents, and there is strife within and between nations. In the world at large there is very little real freedom. The potential is there but something is lacking.

Having taken such great care in all other matters, surely nature has made provision for each to develop naturally in society? Does the difficulty not arise from ignorance of the natural laws in accordance with which society should be governed?

6 It is the rent of the land that is due to the community. Anything more which is paid in respect of improvements such as buildings is due to whoever owns them.

How should society be governed? The principal functions of government are these:

- To defend the nation from external enemies and to deal with foreign affairs;
- To secure justice by ensuring civil and economic freedom to the individual whilst maintaining law and order;
- To establish and protect the currency and deal with internal emergencies and tensions as they arise;
- To make provision for public utilities and services insofar as they cannot be provided by private enterprise and by citizens for themselves;
- To raise the necessary revenue to cover government expenditure.

In the civil sphere we have seen how the observance and enforcement of the duties, not to assault, imprison or defame, secure the freedom of the citizen and maintain law and order in the community. The duties having been recognised and accepted by the community, all that is necessary for the government is to enforce them against all dissenters. But there must be no exceptions. The duties must be observed by everyone from the sovereign downwards.

The English-speaking world has gone a very long way in securing civil liberty and maintaining law and order – probably as far as is possible until economic freedom is secured. The law is highly regarded today but it was not always so. Gradually through the centuries, the English-speaking people came to realise how well the judges administered the law, and to what extent the administration of justice under the common law upheld their freedom.

Many parts of the world have yet to learn that internal peace can never be established by force; that law and order is a sham unless accompanied by individual freedom. If it is open to any head of government to execute or imprison his political enemies to forward his own ends, there can be no freedom and no peace.

The effectiveness of government in the civil sphere may best be judged by the degree to which it is successful in ensuring that the civil duties are observed by all citizens. This is the working of natural law. Insofar as the civil duties are observed, to that extent are both aims secured: the individual enjoys freedom, and law and order are maintained. What could be more natural?

18.3 Economic Duties of Government

The economic duties of government run parallel to the economic duties of the citizen. They are:

- To make unused land available to whoever wants it;
- To preserve unused land in good condition;
- To enforce fundamental duties against all, from the prime minister down (including collecting the rent);
- To look after those unable to support themselves.

It is clear that together these provide the foundations for economic freedom. Observance of these duties would eliminate the concept of private ownership of land, but would ensure that each received the fruits of their labour by raising earnings to the full product of the marginal land.

The duties of the individual would ensure that no more land was used than was strictly needed and that there would be a stock of unused land. Some would be good land which would command a rent; some would be poor land which no one would want to retain since it would have to be kept in good condition and would have no speculative value. There would also be marginal land, no better or worse than the least productive land in general use. By definition such land would carry no rent and could thus be offered free to anyone who wanted it – subject to observation of the other duties.

This stock of free land – marginal land available without charge – is very important to economic freedom[7] for it means that anyone who wishes can take a piece of land and use it to earn a livelihood. The mere existence of this possibility ensures that the general level of earnings cannot be forced below what can be earned on such land – the net product of the marginal site. It also ensures that no one can be forced into unsuitable work for lack of alternative employment.

By observing the economic duties, a community ensures economic freedom for its citizens. This is a natural process. If citizens and community observe their duties, a balance is struck at the margin, which ensures that no earnings will be less than what can be produced on the least productive land in use. Occupation of the better sites is by consent of the community; it is therefore quite proper that whatever additional amount results from the advantages of these sites over the

---

7 The importance, for instance, of government making land available is noted in many ancient texts. See, for example, *Mahabharata*, Santi Parva, Section 65.

margin should be returned to the community, whose existence is the source of these advantages.

When these simple duties are observed, natural law ensures economic freedom for all members of the community.

18.4 Government Finance and Expenditure

Apart from ensuring economic freedom for all members of the community and securing justice, the other principal functions of government are to defend the realm against attack and to deal with foreign affairs; to meet and alleviate emergencies and tensions at home; and to make provision for public utilities and services including the building and maintenance of roads and bridges.

Finally, the government has to find the means to finance these functions, the cost of which, together with the necessary administration, can generally only be met from taxation. The scale of services and works required, and the resulting volume of taxation, increase as a society develops in size and as its towns and cities expand. How to raise the necessary taxation is always a vexatious question. But it need not be so.

Since the rent arises from the community it is right that it should be returned to the community.

As the society develops so the need for revenue increases but so also does the economic rent. With an expanding society the advantages of the better sites over the margin tend constantly to increase. From this it is clear that the economic rent is the natural fund to cover public expenditure.

This has all the hallmarks of natural law. Take the economic rent for the benefit of the community and all necessary public expenditure can be met. This very public expenditure increases economic rent and so the fund is also being replenished. It is surprisingly simple and highly intelligent. It is also very natural and has been recognised by some individuals in government, although the opposition has been so great that they have been unable to put it into effect. As former British Prime Minister H.H. Asquith put it:

> The value of land rises as population grows and national necessities increase, not in proportion to the application of capital and labour, but through the development of the community itself. You have a form of value, therefore, which is conveniently called 'site value', entirely independent of buildings and improvements and of other things which non-owners and occupiers have done to increase its value – a source of value

created by the community, which the community is entitled to appropriate to itself ... In almost every aspect of our social and industrial problems you are brought back sooner or later to that fundamental fact.[8]

The duty of the community to look after those unable to support themselves is observed to a high degree in European countries and much public expenditure today is incurred in relief of poverty. In England originally it extended only to the ragged schools, the workhouse and the infirmary.[9] Today this has expanded to include a very expensive system of state schools and higher education, public housing, hospital and medical services, as well as state pensions, unemployment and sickness benefits, family allowances, and many other such payments. Clearly all these matters are primarily the responsibility of the individual and should only be undertaken by the state when individuals are unable to support themselves. Today the welfare state provides these services for all because citizens cannot pay for them out of their earnings. In other words the system has arisen to relieve the poverty caused by the unequal distribution of wealth.

Observation of the economic duties would allow the level of earnings to rise, and government expenditure on mitigation of poverty would no longer necessary.[10] Every family would be able to afford the education of children, payment for medical care, and savings for old age. If they wanted to insure against ill-health or take out an annuity they would be in a position to do so voluntarily and not by compulsion.[11] The problem of unemployment would largely disappear.

A system of taxation levied on rent includes a built-in safeguard against extravagant expenditure. The fund is limited and, unlike other taxes, cannot be increased at the government's whim. Sound expenditure is covered by a corresponding increase in future rent; but uneconomic expenditure is not so covered. If public expenditure tends to outstrip revenue, the government will be quickly called to task for its irresponsible actions.

Bureaucracy is not good government. Interference with the individual should be restricted to a minimum. Provided individuals observe

8 Speech delivered at Paisley, 7th June 1923
9 The ragged schools were a 19th-century charitable movement to provide free education for the urban poor; for work-house see footnote 20, page 74; the infirmaries were the early equivalent of publicly funded hospitals, especially established for the poor during the 18th century.
10 Although there will always be some in genuine need.
11 This has come to be accepted in some countries since World War II, but note the resistance to compulsion in the United States.

their duties they should be left to conduct themselves as they will. With taxation and national expenditure streamlined to their natural form whole ministries could be closed down or become small inspectorates. A government role in education, labour, health, pensions and unemployment insurance would be largely redundant, as would the promotion and regulation of trade, much of public housing, and many other current provisions. Those duties which were still required could be brought together under the remaining authorities. The saving in expenditure would be enormous and the heavy hand of bureaucracy removed.

Having said this, we must beware of trying to conjure up a picture of a society in which the economic duties are recognised, and then passing judgement on our picture. There is room for infinite diversity within a system of free land just as there is within a system of enclosed land. It is all too easy to look from the viewpoint of present society and find that many current institutions do not fit the new conditions. Having become accustomed to the present institutions, it is difficult to envisage a reasonable degree of existence without them. There is a temptation to reject any change, to say it is idealistic and quite impractical.

But consider a moment the situation of someone brought up in a society that relied on slavery – and if we look at history, slavery is the rule rather than the exception. Tell such a man of the civil duties. He will probably agree that they sound just and reasonable but when he thinks about it a little longer he will conclude that a condition of free men would be quite impractical. He will be quite unable to envisage a society without slaves, bearing in mind all the economic and social repercussions. Yet 'free men' is a practical proposition. It works quite naturally. Why should not 'free land' be equally practical even though it may be difficult to foresee exactly how it would operate?

Slavery and land enclosure are very close parallels. After all it is not everyone who can afford slaves. In societies based on slavery only the fortunate elite owned slaves – the rest had to manage without or were themselves the slaves!

Our society believes in 'free men' and yet, economically, slavery is little different from economic servitude. Henry George wrote:

> Place one hundred men on an island from which there is no escape, and whether you make one of these men the absolute owner of the other ninety-nine, or the absolute owner of the soil of the island, will make no difference either to him or to them. In the one case, as the other, the one will be the absolute master of the ninety-nine – his power

extending even to life and death – for simply to refuse them permission to live upon the island would be to force them into the sea.[12]

We can only conclude that man's emancipation is no more than half completed until the economic duties as well as the civil duties are universally recognised. Society did not grind to a standstill with the abolition of slavery and there is no reason why it should do so with the abolition of private ownership of land.

The genius of a people for adapting themselves to their conditions and working within them is a very powerful factor. Anyone living in medieval England before the land enclosures would have been hard-pressed to visualise our modern industrial society. Even if such a person were able to grasp the possibilities arising from the invention of machines, how could they ever hope to dream up the complex structure of our present economy?

Who could have imagined the limited liability company, the stock exchange, the modern banking system, foreign exchange control, income tax, purchase tax, and all the other taxes? It is an economic system which has evolved to meet the conditions of full land enclosure and modern scientific progress. Looking from a distance, one would not see how it could possibly work yet within its limitations it works surprisingly efficiently.

Whatever the degree of civil liberty and the conditions of land tenure of a society, an economic system will evolve suited to the time and place. The native genius and natural character of the community will play a very big part in this. The system will not be static but will be adapted from time to time to meet changing conditions. Set the conditions and society will soon find a way to work within them.

These then are the economic duties. They lie at the root of economic freedom. If the civil duties and the economic duties are recognised by all, the way is open for the enjoyment of freedom by the community and the individuals within it: freedom for the community to fulfil its true purpose of enabling all to develop their natural talents and skills to the full; freedom for individuals to devote their energies to finding and fulfilling their true purposes in the world.

18.5 Economic Justice

At the present time there is unease, not freedom. The economic duties are not upheld by the law. In order to alleviate the worst abuses

12 Henry George, *Progress and Poverty*, Book VII, Chapter II.

countless statutes have been passed to try to bring some relief to the economic hardship, but in this field the law commands less respect. Indeed in many instances the law is enforced not by the courts but by committees, tribunals, commissions and the various ministries.[13] What respect these enjoy does not arise from recognition of their power to uphold justice. It is borrowed from the respect which the law has won for its vigilance and dispensation of justice in the civil field.

It is not that the economic duties have still to be discovered. They have always been known,[14] but communities have preferred to ignore them. Even when they are clearly presented there is resistance to accepting them. The resistance based on habit, opinion, fear, self-interest, is inevitable and blinding.

Until the community as a whole faces up squarely to the facts, until they are prepared to recognise the economic duties, there can be no real justice in the economic field. Without justice there can be no real peace or freedom. It is fine to value freedom and peace highly but charters of freedom and treaties of peace are of no avail of themselves. It is useless to be a champion of freedom without the realisation of how it may be achieved.

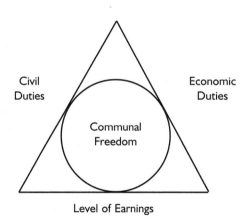

Diagram 39 – Conditions of Communal Freedom

13 Common among these in most countries are provisions to prevent monopoly (especially by merger), and assessment of the national interest when companies are taken over by foreign concerns.
14 The Hebrew law in the Old Testament for example, has numerous expressions of economic duties: the concept that the land may not be owned (*Leviticus* 25: 23), that land acquired should be returned to the community at the end of 50 years (*Leviticus* 27: 21), are just two examples as applied in a specific set of conditions. Babylonian law provided for the collection of the rent.

These three, the level of earnings, the civil duties and the economic duties, together determine the communal conditions of freedom. To the extent that a community observes the civil and the economic duties, it is free. To the extent that these duties are ignored, so far does a community condemn itself and its citizens to bondage and eventual extinction. The process may be slow, but the end is certain: history is littered with examples.[15] If there is to be justice between men, these duties must be recognised. The choice is for the community – it will reap what it sows. Natural law cannot be flouted: whether recognised or ignored, it works inexorably .

15 Failure to pay the full rent leads eventually to massive inequity in the distribution of wealth and very often to revolution – e.g. the French Revolution of 1789. Failure to keep the land in good order leads to land becoming waste land in various forms – e.g. Libya was the food bowl of the Roman empire. Interfering with another's quiet enjoyment of land, taken to extremes, was the destruction caused by Genghis Khan and the Mongol hordes during the 12th century.

SECTION 4

The Nature of Society

T HE CONCEPT of a hierarchy in society was introduced in Chapter 1 where it was stated that this hierarchy, amongst other things, facilitates specialisation. The higher levels have influence over and serve the lower levels. This influence exists in both time and space and has qualitative as well as quantitative dimensions.

Specialisation, as well as permitting greater efficiency, enables each member of the community to find their calling and to express their nature. This enriches the whole of society.

It is clear also that each civilisation, culture and nation has its own nature that determines what is valued, how relationships between individuals in society are governed, as well as the production and distribution of wealth.[1]

It is not intended here to examine particular societies but to trace the common threads which join all of them and from which the economic organism is woven.

---

1 For example, it could be argued that individuals in medieval Europe were worse off than individuals in Europe today. But building the great Gothic cathedrals during that period demonstrates that the values of society were very different, that individual material well-being was valued less highly than the relationship of the community to God. It can also be seen that today's 'banking' began in the culture of the Florentine Renaissance.

CHAPTER 19

Society as a Hierarchy

T HE SIMPLE DIAGRAM from Chapter 1 has been expanded below to help examine society in more detail. The names of these levels have a geographical dimension, reflecting in the lower levels as entities which may with a little observation be seen around us even in this age of rapid communications and the Internet.

Diagram 40 shows a hierarchy which exists irrespective of the specific political and social arrangements. Musicians might recognise this as a musical scale and the qualities applicable to musical notes within the scale are equally applicable here. Like all scales, it is a key to relationships. In this case it shows the different levels of society, each contained within the one above and culminating in the whole human race. Economics is concerned with men and women in society and there is no place for individuals on this scale.[1]

It is important to keep the diagram whole and not try to split the levels nor to employ only what we think we understand whilst dismissing the rest. It is a scale of relationships within the human race. Leave that out of consideration and it becomes pointless and misleading.

19.1 The Elements of the Hierarchy

Village and Labouring Communities

The first level is that of all ordinary labour: manual labour, clerical work, and household work. It can be related to traditional villages associated with rural labour and a lack of sophistication. Irrespective of what sort of work we do, if we are honest we shall find that by far the greater part of all our working time is spent at this level. Add to

---

1 The diagram shows this hierarchy in an Anglo/European context. The names may be slightly different in other civilisations; for example, in the traditional Indian civilisation universities may be replaced by ashrams where the men of learning would be sages.

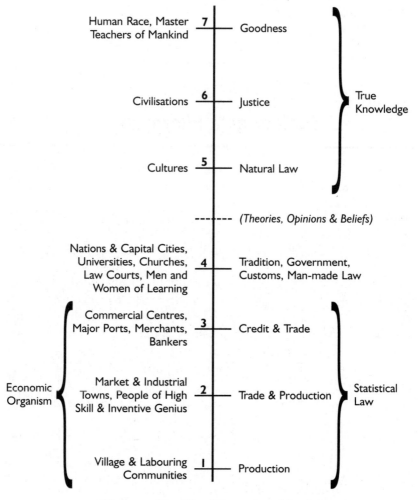

Diagram 40 – The Hierarchy of Society

the work done in offices the tasks in and about our homes, and it is clear that throughout the whole community there is a prodigious amount of ordinary labour. Ordinary or unskilled labour is not to be underestimated; it is the foundation of society.

This is the realm of large numbers. The influence of individuals at this level counts for very little; they may be easily pushed around, their earnings reduced to the least they are prepared to accept. To deal with this weakness unions are often formed in which members band together to find the leadership that allows their voice to be heard at Level 2.

Market and Industrial Towns

The next level is that of the town where villagers come together to exchange goods in a market. The craftsmen and specialists whose work supports and refines village production establish themselves here in the larger community.

In most people there is something of Level 2, the realm of true skill.[2] It is found in the craftsman working at his best; the architect facing a tricky problem of design; the surgeon performing a delicate and dangerous operation; the entrepreneur estimating costs and organising production to ensure maximum efficiency. The craftsmen and the professionals, when acting in these roles, manifest steadiness and confidence.

The retail trade, retail markets and the suppliers of tools and materials to trade and industry belong at Level 2. Leadership too belongs at this level – the ability to arouse in people devotion, respect, endeavour, patience, and all the finer qualities. The relationship between the leader and those being led is one of service. This is the great difference between leading and driving. In driving people there is little care for them. To lead requires service and has an emotional quality. This quality manifests also in true skill and craftsmanship and, for example, through love of the materials being worked with.[3]

At Level 2 the influence of the individual is far greater; one man can direct the work of many at Level 1. An architect in charge of a building contract may direct the efforts of hundreds; an engineer may devise a mechanical process affecting the work of thousands at Level 1.[4] Similarly errors at Level 1 are numerous but generally of small consequence, but at Level 2 they are more serious: lives may be lost through faulty design, or a business brought to bankruptcy through maladministration.

To be a town is not just a question of size. Throughout the world there are many communities which undoubtedly are towns although

2 An aspect of skill observed by Leon MacLaren is contained in his book, *Nature of Society*: 'The man who is in love with his work will not degrade it for his customer, but while satisfying his customer will honour himself. Thus his desires will be ordered so that he puts working towards finding and following his calling first, and pleasing his customers, second. By this his customers will gain, for he will give of his best; but he will gain more, for he will be laying the foundation of a full life'. This requires great confidence.
3 Consider, for example, the relationship between a master craftsman and his apprentice, although this has become sadly debased today. Note also Plato's observation that a craftsman works for the love of the craft, not for the reward that may arise from it (*Republic*, Book 1).
4 Consider, for instance, the effect that James Watt had on the nature of work at Level 1 with his invention of the steam engine and its application to spinning and weaving in the 18th century.

they may be very small: as markets or centres of industry their influence may be widespread despite lack of size. On the other hand there are mining villages with populations of tens of thousands but there is no doubt that they are still not towns.[5] Many suburbs of huge cities cannot claim to be anything more than sprawling villages.[6]

Commercial Centres and Major Ports

Level 3 is the realm of the merchants with their special role in the economy. Do we ever ask ourselves how it is that we can buy sugar, wheat, tea, coffee, copper, timber, cotton and so on whenever we want them? How is it that the supply of these materials, often produced at the other end of the earth, is so accurately balanced to the demand? All this is the work of the merchants, whose efforts ensure that the basic commodities, and many finished goods also, are available throughout the world in the right quantities, at the right price, at the right time. Without ever handling the goods, merchants link buyer and seller across nations and discover the price which will keep the two in balance, avoiding gluts and shortages.[7] This enables producers to be sure of prices in advance of their needs, so that they can estimate costs and quote prices for finished goods.

The merchants at Level 3 rarely handle any actual goods or materials but only claims to them.

Alongside the work of the merchants is that of the bankers and shippers.[8] Banking essentially oils the wheels of trade by bridging the gap between payment for labour, and raw materials and receipt of purchase price from the final consumer. Shipping must be understood to include all worldwide transport by sea, land and air.

To those employed in this area it is evident that only a fraction of working time is spent in true trading or banking, a little more at the level of skilled work, and by far the greater part in unskilled labour. Each of these levels contains the level below.

Level 3 depends upon a very broad view in which time and timing are all-important. It requires intellectual powers, foresight and a deep understanding of statistical law.

5 The 'city' of Broken Hill in Australia, used in the example of land prices on page 28, is in this analysis merely a large mining village with a population of around 20,000.
6 Found mostly in what are commonly known as dormitory suburbs.
7 The cargo of an oil tanker, for instance, can be sold while it is at sea, and its destination changed to meet the needs of the market.
8 At different times and places these functions have been variously combined into a specific business but it is the function that we are interested in here not the business.

Markets at Level 3 can be fickle and the degree of confidence may change very rapidly. Their operation tends to be quite discreet. For example until the late 1960s the world centre for trading wool was Bradford in Yorkshire. The surrounding area was heavily engaged in rearing sheep and producing woollen cloth (Levels 1 and 2). The wool exchange operated in a grand but shabby building hidden by old shops and offices, behind a door with a notice saying: 'Members Only'. The London Metal Exchange or the Chicago Board of Trade may not be quite so hidden but generally attract little attention. In business the real entrepreneur – not the person in charge of the business as a result of heredity or academic training – belongs to Level 2. Their names are often household words – Anita Roddick, Richard Branson, Bill Gates or Laura Ashley. Those who work at Level 3 – have you ever heard of them? Scandals aside, could the man in the street name the CEOs of the various banking houses (Citi Bank, HSBC or Morgan Stanley)?[9]

The influence of individuals here is greater than at the levels below: the decision of a single individual can affect whole industries. Errors of judgment can prove enormously expensive. Generally very high standards are imposed on people working at this level to prevent abuse of its unique position, for corruption here is a serious matter. An example was the slave trade of the 18th and 19th centuries. Slave traders shipped merchandise to East Africa, exchanging it for negro prisoners who were then shipped to the West Indies and the Southern States of America and sold to buy sugar and cotton. This lucrative practice was the cause of the rapid growth of the city and port of Liverpool, but its effects in terms of human misery are still felt today. In 2008 errors made at Level 3 were the catalyst for the global financial crisis, and consequent damage.

This level has great influence on international trade and through banking on the financing of the whole economy. Extreme examples of the influence of this level were the British East India Company[10] and the Hudson Bay Company,[11] both of which were merchant ventures with immense power.

9 The recent banking crisis has given a certain notoriety to the heads of some banks but this is exceptional.

10 An English trading company with a monopoly on trade between England, India and the Far East, which from the early 17th century to the mid-19th century became so powerful that it had for a period effective rule of India and in places even issued its own coinage.

11 Founded in Canada by British Royal Charter in 1670, the company (which is still operating) grew to dominate trade in northern and western Canada and even the north-western parts of the USA. It was influential enough to issue its own bank notes in the later part of the 19th century.

Level 3 can only work properly with a high degree of trust. 'My word is my bond'.[12] So much depends on a word. Once a bargain is made there is no excuse for getting out.

These first three levels constitute the economic organism and usually the study of Economics is limited to the interaction between them. This is where it is so important to remember our scale, to remember that all this must be seen in relation to the whole human race.

Nations and Capital Cities

Level 4 is the dominant level on this scale. Standing halfway between the economic organism and the higher levels of the hierarchy, it is the level of nations, capital cities, governments, laws, traditions and customs, as also of churches and universities. These transcend political boundaries. Level 4 functions as a bridge. Working properly it allows the influence of the higher levels to pass down into the economic organism. If a nation has good laws, well administered, then the whole community is the richer, for it comes under the civilising influence of justice at Level 6. The work of formulating and administering the law belongs to Level 4. Our high degree of civil liberty is assured only by constant vigilance at this level. Its place on Diagram 40 on page 234 demonstrates that this is not the ultimate seat of power as may be imagined by politicians and statesmen. The economic organism cannot be bent to suit political whim.

It is easy to be critical but, if people cut themselves off from the higher levels or do not know of their existence, it is hardly surprising that this leads to bad government. Generally the enemy is ignorance rather than deliberate misuse of power. At Level 4 an individual's influence can make or mar a nation: George Washington founded a great nation; Adolf Hitler brought another to its knees.

This level is not easy to envisage geographically.[13] Its substance is words. Government, law, church, universities, learning – all these act through the spoken and written word. Parliamentary debates are words. Laws and treaties are formulated in words. Lawsuits, trials and judgments are all conducted with words. Religious teachings, doctrines and

12 See footnote 24, page 30.
13 The centres of political power, law, intellectual life and religion are often not in the same location. In the United Kingdom for instance law, political power and the church are seated in London, principal universities at Oxford and Cambridge; in the United States, Washington is the centre for law and political power, Boston for intellectual life, and a specific centre for religious life is difficult to identify.

edicts are all expressed in words. In the universities the work of previous generations is all carefully recorded by the written word: each succeeding generation adds its share of theses and formulae to be handed down in writing to the next. As for learning, the libraries of the world must carry nearly as many printed words as there are grains of sand in the Sahara desert.

Language is an immensely powerful instrument: its influence spreads right through the whole community. Great care is needed to ensure that this influence derives from the higher levels and not from ignorance and lack of understanding.

Cultures

At Level 5 are the men of understanding, those who comprehend natural law, who work through culture, and are able to reorientate it, put it back on its proper course and inject new energy into it. Generally little known, they shun publicity yet act as a leaven in society and save it from deteriorating.

There are surprisingly few statues to anyone at Levels 5 or 6. In Westminster Abbey for instance the memorials are nearly all to those at Level 4. Consider all the controversy about who wrote the works attributed to Shakespeare. How many people know of the contribution to the Florentine Renaissance of Marsilio Ficino?[14]

At this level may be discovered the civil duties and the economic duties owed by all citizens to each other, and the duties owed by the community to its members.[15]

Culture includes all those attributes of our society peculiar to the modern western world. Scientific progress, music, literature, painting and architecture – all have their influence on the economic organism. Culture manifests as the national characteristics of a community, its real historical traditions. In a free society every community would develop according to its own traditions and inherent nature. Individuals would also be free to evolve through the development of their own particular qualities and natures.

14 Marsillio Ficino (1433-1499) was the wise philosopher, doctor and priest who inspired the Florentine Renaissance. He made Platonic thought available to Latin-speaking Europe through his translations and writings in a way that did not oppose the theology of the time but focused on the divinity of man. Writers such as John Vyvyan trace his influence in much English literature from the 1500s, arguing that Shakespeare's plays express Ficino's philosophy and that this would have been recognisable to many of his audience at the time.
15 See Chapters 17 and 18.

Civilisations

The lawgivers,[16] sages and prophets belong to the realm of justice at Level 6. Justice is second only to goodness. It assigns to every level its proper duties and orders all things.[17] Justice will be done. Although it may appear possible to evade justice this is not the case. As a person – or nation – sows, so shall they reap, for justice is impartial.

The economic and civil life of the English-speaking world is founded upon those standards of behaviour which have their origin in Christianity. This 'civilised' behaviour is highly valued even though many may be unaware of its source; indeed it is valued so highly that nations will fight for it if they believe it is threatened.

Human Race

At Level 7 are the master teachers of mankind (Jesus, Krishna, Confucius, Lao Tsu, Buddha, etc.), who, as is evidenced by their teachings, knew the unity behind all things. Their influence lasts through thousands of years. These are the founders of civilisations.

Level 7 is the realm of what we have called goodness, by virtue of which everything exists. Lack of goodness is a disease, which will eventually lead to destruction. If a nation lacks goodness it must surely die. Goodness is perfectly free and knows no bounds. Being free it allows freedom – even the freedom to resist its good influence. Thus individuals and nations are free to turn their back on freedom and goodness, if they so wish, free to ensure their own destruction, if they so please.

Only the master teachers can fully comprehend the power and freedom of goodness. Only lawgivers, sages and prophets can fully comprehend justice, and only the men and women of understanding can fully comprehend natural law. But we can recognise the workings of these forces from the higher levels and, in this recognition, appreciate why they are so important to the government of a community.

The Lower Levels

Levels 1, 2 and 3 make up the economic organism. The word organism is apt for it is indeed a highly organised entity in which all parts are completely interdependent. Only when properly balanced and

---

16 This title is customarily attributed to those known individuals who gave laws on which nations, cultures and civilisations are based. These include Moses, Zarathustra (the Persian civilisation), Solon (the Athenian law), Lycurgus (the Spartan law).

17 See for instance, Marsilio Ficino, *The Letters of Marsilio Ficino*, Vol 1, Letter 78: '...It is the duty of a citizen to consider the state as a single being formed of its citizens who are the parts; and that the parts should serve the whole, not the whole the parts ...'

controlled from above is the economic organism capable of fulfilling its proper function. It is like the human body which is entirely dependent upon the mind for its control and proper use. If the mind is distorted then however perfectly constructed the body may be, its actions will be unbalanced.

The economic organism is regulated by statistical laws, the laws of large numbers. These laws determine the division of wealth between earnings and tenants' share and set the general level of earnings according to the given conditions. The laws also ensure that the number of people choosing to follow a particular training also match the need. Statistical law is quite indifferent as to which individuals become doctors, bricklayers or road-sweepers, but it ensures that the need to fill these different occupations is met. In the same way it ensures that if there are too many coffee shops in a retail district and not enough shoe shops, then one of the coffee shops will close down and a shoe retailer take over. It cares not which individual business closes down nor whether it sells out at a profit or goes bankrupt.

Statistical laws work quite blindly and inexorably within the economic organism. At first impression they may appear cruel, but one cannot blame the economic organism for that; it is only a machine, albeit a magnificent one. It works within the framework of customs, traditions and human laws laid down at Level 4. If these lack understanding, then cruelty, injustice and inefficiency are inevitable. Statistical law relates to markets where demand and supply are equated, enabling businesses to predict their sales over the coming period and to plan accordingly. Individual bargains may vary greatly but the market will settle a general balance between demand and supply, whether in terms of goods, of foreign currencies, or of titles to land. Without statistical laws business would be chaotic.

In many great cities the workings of the different levels of this hierarchy can be readily observed. For instance, most of London is a huge collection of villages, the homes and workplaces of millions of labourers, but throughout, there is the influence of Level 2. This influence shows itself in the markets and business centres dotted all over London, resembling an agglomeration of small towns – often with an industrial estate, offices, schools, shopping streets in each, and sometimes an open market. This is the area of highly skilled workers and retail trade. Here are the specialists and the professionals; the shops are the final outlets of trade where customers and producers meet. The range of Level 2 is wide, extending to include Petticoat Lane and

Bond Street, or the offices of Barking and Mayfair;[18] even the West End of London is only a specialised town centre.

Permeating both of these lower levels is the influence of merchants and bankers at Level 3. In London this is epitomised in the City where every other building is the home of a commodity market, a trading house, a shipper or a banker.[19] It is the work of this level that makes London the financial centre of the world.

Above all London is a capital city. One of the few real capitals in the world, it is a centre of government and law and more than that, a city where culture and civilisation flourish. For all the crime and stupidity that abound, this is clearly still one of the great centres of society that have prospered throughout history. In London are represented Levels 1 to 4, each level containing and permeating the levels below and combining to provide an instrument capable of transmitting knowledge from higher levels still.

The Higher Levels

The geographic aspects of the higher levels are not as clearcut as those levels below. The renaissance culture had its geographic centre in Florence from where it reached out to include all of western Europe and many of those lands in which the European nations subsequently settled. But where is the centre today? The same would be true of civilisation. These higher levels are intangible. However, we get a sense of them from extraordinary statements in our literary inheritance. Of Level 7 we can say very little more than: 'The earth is the Lord's and the fullness thereof'.[20]

Pertaining to justice at Level 6 are statements such as, 'Thou shalt not steal';[21] and, 'Render unto Caesar the things that are Caesar's and unto God the things that are God's'.[22] These are the key to justice on Diagram 40.

At Level 5 justice needs to be formulated into law for the guidance of society. And so for instance Justinian[23] writes, 'Justice is the

18 Petticoat Lane is a street market in East London associated with cheap goods. In Bond Street in London's West End are the shops for the highest quality and most expensive clothing, jewellery and footwear. In New York this would be 5th Avenue. Barking in the East End of London is associated with docks and factories, and Mayfair is a major London centre for luxury hotels, restaurants, boutiques and embassies.
19 Many other cities have an equivalent financial centre.
20 *Psalms*, 24, v.1
21 The Ten Commandments, see *Exodus*, 20.
22 *St Matthew*, 22, v.21.
23 See footnote 1, page 216.

constant and perpetual will to render to each their due', and, 'Jurisprudence is the knowledge of things divine and human, the science of the just and the unjust.'[24]

To Level 5 belongs jurisprudence, the handmaiden of justice, the science of what should and should not be rendered to Caesar.

Justinian later continues: 'The precepts of law are these: to live honestly, to injure no one, and to give everyone their due.'[25]

In terms of our civil life the principle at Level 6, 'Thou shalt not steal,' becomes in law, 'You shall not take a man's life, nor his health, nor his good name.' Interpreting in this way the broad principles of law, Level 5 stands below justice to serve government at Level 4. There the laws are formulated and put into effect according to the particular needs of the people and the times.

A civilisation may last thousands of years. Cultures inspired by men of understanding last hundreds of years. Within this span nations come and go. Economic cycles rise and fall in much shorter periods of time. We are living in the Christian civilisation and in the culture which began six hundred years ago with the Florentine Renaissance. These influences are very strong but they need to be sustained through each generation if they are not to be lost. This is the special function of those at Level 5. Such men and women work largely unnoticed. Their praises are seldom sung.

At the highest level, the source of it all, is the human race. Volumes have been written trying to solve the question, 'What is Man's purpose in the universe?' In Economics this is not our concern. We are concerned, however, to study and discover the laws which govern relations in society; in this way the cause of economic slavery and the key to liberation may be discovered. Whatever the great purpose may be, it is more likely to be fulfilled in a state of freedom than slavery.

The dominant level of our scale is Level 4. People want to be able to believe in government. However rude they may be about it, in their hearts they have faith that it knows what it is doing, although the degree of faith varies from time to time. When government is guided by the higher levels, it will have the power and knowledge to carry these all-important influences through the whole community. When the connection from above is missing the power remains but ignorance rules.

24 Justinian, *The Institutes*, I, 1.
25 *Ibid*, I, 3.

19.2 Operation of the Hierarchy

In Chapter 1 the purpose of society was said to be, 'that, by co-operation, individuals may grow in skill, happiness and knowledge, and so may be led to prosperity in every sense'. Why should there be any difficulty in ensuring that tradition, custom and man-made law accord with the principles of justice and natural law, or that happiness, knowledge and prosperity for all automatically follow? It would seem to be the natural thing.

The economic organism is a highly intelligent structure, magnificently designed to meet all needs. It brings together labour and land to produce and distribute wealth. Whether it does so in accordance with the principles of justice and natural law, or whether these are ignored, depends upon the conditions in which labour and land meet at the point of interaction. The outcome will be very different according to whether land and labour meet in conditions where land is free or where it is all enclosed. In either situation the organism will function to maintain society, but the people will prosper only if the conditions are favourable and accord with justice and natural law.

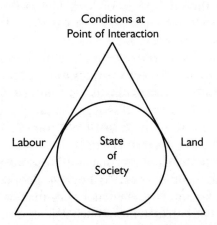

Diagram 41 – The State of Society

The conditions at the point of interaction are not determined by the economic organism alone. They are also influenced by governments, universities, churches, law courts and the acknowledged men of learning.[26] All these together with the lower levels which they serve,

---

26 In the realm of Economics the writings of Adam Smith, Ricardo, Malthus, J.S. Mill and J.M. Keynes, among others, are still highly influential.

constitute a nation. It is at Level 4 that traditions, national customs and man-made laws are crystallised and may be changed – for better or worse – but only with the consent of the people. Any change which antagonises public opinion is doomed to failure, sooner or later, and will have no lasting effect upon the conditions at the point of interaction.

The same pattern applies to the civil aspect of society: traditions, customs and man-made laws will set the limits of both economic and civil freedom.[27]

Diagram 40 on page 234 shows a broken line drawn between Levels 4 and 5 which represents a point of difficulty in the development of the scale. The theories, opinions and beliefs represented by this line are thrown up from below and usurp the place of understanding. Instead of allowing Level 4 to fulfil its roll as a bridge for the passage of influences from the higher levels, theories, opinions and beliefs form a barrier against them. With the entry of ignorance between Levels 4 and 5, the economic organism is subjected to additional laws which, unlike the statistical laws, do not control its operation but restrict it.

An example of one of these laws is the proposition that to set up in business requires money – in other words either the entrepreneur's own claims on wealth, or access to wealth controlled by others. This proposition has no foundation in the natural order of things.[28] It is entirely a restriction arising from conditions of land enclosure which in turn are the results of ignorance in the realm of theories, opinions and beliefs.

So it is that the economic organism becomes cluttered with unnecessary restrictions requiring devious remedies such as the whole structure of investment, limited liability companies and stock exchanges. These limitations arise from ignorance and are self-imposed upon the nation. By denying natural law and justice people expose themselves to all the harshness of statistical law under conditions of

27 Private ownership of land and of slaves, for instance, are subject to tradition, custom and man-made law. These cannot be changed ahead of public opinion.
28 Although credit will undoubtedly be required. See Chapter 7. There are partial examples of this in recent history. In the New England area of the United States during the 18th and 19th centuries there was a practice in farming communities called 'barn raising'. A new farmer would assemble all the materials required for a very large barn and the entire community would voluntarily come together and erect the barn. The practice still continues in some communities. Perhaps some money was required to purchase materials and pay specialist craftsmen, but the practice essentially relied on the fact that the recipient would reciprocate at some future time.

ignorance. They find themselves bound by these additional restrictions and the complexities to which they give rise.

As long as people seek peace and plenty the door is effectively locked, for their interest is in rights and not in duties. The only way to escape this impasse is by a change of mind. When justice in human relations is sought, and sought regardless of cost, then the doorway to freedom may be opened. This is seen in the way in which civil justice is highly valued in the English-speaking world, sometimes more highly than peace and comfort. The civil duties are largely recognised and enforced and a high degree of civil rights follows. But there is little interest in economic justice. The cry is for plenty and for more economic rights: the duties are forgotten. This is ignorance. Society is thus hampered with new and unnecessary bonds and restrictions. The economic organism loses its natural simplicity and resilience and becomes instead a machine of alarming complexity and ruthlessness.

When understanding fills the interval between Levels 4 and 5 the higher influences can flow unchecked through the whole structure. In this condition customs, traditions and human laws at Level 4 will be based on wisdom and will ensure that the fundamental duties in both the economic and the civil spheres are observed in full. The rest of the structure will then quite naturally be ordered aright and the populace may well be unaware of the way in which they are governed.

There is another large gap between Levels 2 and 3. This gap is bridged by trust. We trust the post will arrive just as we trust the sun will rise. We trust in money. Trust is there every time we ride on a train, switch on an electric light, or turn on a tap. We are trusted when we eat a meal in a restaurant and pay afterwards, and when we jump in a taxi and pay on arrival. Trust is working throughout, supporting the whole of society. It is so familiar that it is easy to miss it. It is fundamentally important. Without trust we would be reduced to simple barter and even then each would be afraid to be the first to part with the goods. Trust springs directly from the goodness in everything.

At Levels 1 and 2 only is it possible to get by, taking goods to market and bartering them. But nothing would work without trust at Level 3. The Metal Exchange has been mentioned where huge quantities of metals are purchased on the spot. The dealers do not need to carry them home. It is all done on trust, no goods change hands.

At Level 3 no goods or wealth are manifest, only services. We think of bankers as trading in wealth[29] but in fact they trade in credit,

---

29 It is not uncommon these days for banks to advertise themselves as 'wealth managers'.

demonstrating again the importance of trust at this level. A bargain is made, there is no written word. 'My word is my bond.' It would never work if everything had to be documented on the spot. If a dealer goes back on his word, he is out.[30] The slightest deflection from the rules is looked upon as an inexcusable offence.

When the whole hierarchy is present in its perfection there is the condition which may be called virtue. When the interval between Levels 6 and 7 is not filled so that the society is not ruled by goodness but by justice, then something has been lost. This is still a very fine condition; we may call it righteousness. When the understanding is lost, so that the higher influences no longer run untrammelled through the whole society but trust remains and society is able to function, this is the condition we call propriety – good manners. This condition has been recognised in the world for many centuries. When trust is missing there is disorder and society is in great trouble.

With the three special links in place there is a movement from disorder to propriety, to righteousness, to virtue. These are the four conditions possible for society.

---

30 Until recently all money market transactions were conducted by telephone. Now they are recorded but the recording is only used when one or other party has made an error. For an extensive description of how this operated before these technological changes see *The City* by Paul Ferris.

CHAPTER 20

Government in the Hierarchy

20.1 Society and Government

IN TERMS of society as a whole, the level of government is something of an anomaly, belonging neither to the field of true knowledge nor to that of statistical law. Level 4 is more than just government: it includes the whole realm of universities, church, law, and so on. These institutions are contrivances by which true knowledge can be carried through to the whole sphere of economic activity. In this way the courts of law have brought knowledge into the lives of the people, maintaining their civil rights in the English-speaking world over the centuries.

Here is another view on government expressed by Emerson in his essay 'Politics', written in the early 19th century:

> In dealing with the State, we ought to remember that its institutions are not aboriginal, though they existed before we were born: that they are not superior to the citizen: that every one of them was once the act of a single man: every law and usage was a man's expedient to meet a particular case: that they all are imitable, all alterable; we may make as good: we may make better. Society is an illusion to the young citizen. It lies before him in rigid repose, with certain names, men, and institutions, rooted like oak trees to the centre, round which all arrange themselves the best they can. But the old statesman knows that society is fluid; there are no such roots and centres; but any particle may suddenly become the centre of the movement, and compel the system to gyrate round it, as every man of strong will, like Pisistratus,[1] or Cromwell,[2] does for a time, and every man of truth, like Plato, or

---

1 Popular tyrant of Athens 546-527 BCE.
2 1599-1658 Military and political leader who temporarily overthrew the Stuart monarchy. Ruled as Lord Protector of the Commonwealth of England from 1653 until his death.

Paul,[3] does for ever. But politics rest on necessary foundations, and cannot be treated with levity. Republics abound in young civilians, who believe that the laws made the city; that grave modifications of the policy and modes of living, and employments of the population; that commerce, education, and religion, may be voted in or out; and that any measure though it were absurd, may be imposed on a people, if only you can get sufficient voices to make it a law. But the wise know that foolish legislation is a rope of sand which perishes in the twisting; that the State must follow, and not lead the character and progress of the citizen; the strongest usurper is quickly got rid of; and they only who build on Ideas, build on eternity: and that the form of government which prevails, is the expression of what cultivation exists in the population which permits it. The law is only a memorandum. We are superstitious, and esteem the statute somewhat: so much life as it has in the character of living men, is its force. The statute stands there to say, yesterday we agreed so and so, but how feel ye this article today? Our statute is a currency, which we stamp with our own portrait: it soon becomes unrecognisable, and in process of time will return to the mint. Nature is not democratic, nor limited-monarchical, but despotic, and will not be fooled or abated of any jot of her authority, by the pertest of her sons...[4]

Later he writes:

Every man's nature is a sufficient advertisement to him of the character of his fellows. My right and my wrong, is their right and their wrong. Whilst I do what is fit for me, and abstain from what is unfit, my neighbour and I shall often agree in our means, and work together for a time to one end. But whenever I find my dominion over myself not sufficient for me, and undertake the direction of him also, I overstep the truth, and come into false relations to him. I may have so much more skill or strength than he, that he cannot express adequately his sense of wrong, but it is a lie, and hurts like a lie both him and me. Love and nature cannot maintain the assumption: it must be executed by a practical lie, namely, by force. This undertaking for another, is the blunder which stands in colossal ugliness in the governments of the world. It is the same thing in numbers, as in a pair, only not quite so intelligible. I can see well enough a great difference between my setting myself down to a self-control, and my going to make somebody else act after my views; but when a quarter of the human race assume to tell me what I must do, I may be too much disturbed by the circumstances to see so clearly the absurdity of their command. Therefore, all

3 Saint Paul, or Paul the Apostle, whose writings, including the *Acts of the Apostles*, form a considerable part of the New Testament.
4 Emerson, *Essays*, Second Series, Essay 7, 'Politics'.

public ends look vague and quixotic beside private ones. For, any laws but those which men make for themselves, are laughable. If I put myself in the place of my child, and we stand in one thought, and see what things are thus or thus, that perception is law for him and me. We are both there, both act. But if, without carrying him into the thought, I look over into his plot and, guessing how it is with him, ordain this or that, he will never obey me. This is the history of governments – one man does something which is to bind another. A man who cannot be acquainted with me, taxes me; looking from afar at me, ordains that a part of my labour shall go to this or that whimsical end, not as I, but as he happens to fancy. Behold the consequence. Of all debts, men are least willing to pay the taxes. What a satire is this on government! Everywhere they think they get their money's worth, except for these.

Hence, the less government we have, the better, the fewer laws, and the less confided power. The antidote to this abuse of formal government is the influence of private character, the growth of individual; the appearance of the principal to supersede the proxy; the appearance of the wise man, to whom the existing government, is, it must be owned, but a shabby imitation. That which all things tend to educe, which freedom, cultivation, intercourse, revolutions, go to form and deliver, is character: that is the end of nature, to reach unto this coronation of her king. To educate the wise man, the State exists; and with the appearance of the wise man, the State expires. The appearance of character makes the State unnecessary. The wise man is the State. He needs no army, fort, or navy, – he loves men too well; no bribe, or feast, or palace, to draw friends to him: no vantage ground, no favourable circumstance. He needs no library, for he has not done thinking; no church, for he is a prophet; no statute book, for he is a law giver; no money, for he is value; no road, for he is at home where he is; no experience, for the life of the creator shoots through him, and looks from his eyes. He has no personal friends, for he who has the spell to draw the prayer and piety of all men unto him, needs not husband and educate a few, to share with him a select and poetic life.[5]

Emerson is saying that men and women may have true self-government; the state, which is Level 4, is only a stand-in until they are ready to govern themselves. Meanwhile the state should properly fill the gap and provide for individuals what they cannot provide for themselves.

The true aim of Level 4 is to render itself unnecessary. It may be a very long objective.

Plato spoke of the ideal government being that of the philosopher king or alternatively of the true aristocracy when the government is

5 *Ibid.*

shared between a number of wise men.[6] This appears very much akin to the reign of justice. Short of self-government, this is Level 4 at its highest. The Saxon kings were not rulers by chance; they were often elected as wise leaders by the *Witan*, an assembly of the highest ecclesiastical and secular officers of the nation.

Plato then describes the four further forms of government. After aristocracy comes timocracy, which he likens to the Spartan state, akin to aristocracy except that it has begun to degenerate. Timarchy is a form of warrior government whose aims are the wellbeing of the community, but subject to a hint of a division in the minds of the rulers between the desire for the best for the nation and self-interest. This is the beginning of the corruption of government. Plato then speaks of oligarchy when the rulers' principal concern is with money, their own wellbeing: government by the rich with a view to their own good.

Plato next describes how this leads to democracy when the down-trodden rise up by force or other means. On the face of it democracy appears to be highly desirable, everybody has their say. But it is weak, there is no clear direction and no one knows where they are going.

Then he comes to the last form of government: tyranny, government by a despot. When democracy breaks down the way is open for a liberator to free the country – and then to set up as a tyrant. There are plenty of recognisable examples in the world today.

In English history Alfred the Great[7] represents the philosopher king; William the Conqueror, the beginning of timocracy;[8] and England in the 17th and 18th centuries, when rich land-owners ruled the country and the poor had no vote, the oligarchy.[9] Today the English-speaking countries are so-called democracies, and many other countries are subject to tyranny. The picture is constantly changing.

---

6 Plato, *Republic*, Book 8.

7 King of Wessex 871-899 AD. Effectively the first king of England and a man of learning who translated amongst other books Boethius' *Consolations of Philosophy*. He promoted learning amongst the people, supported the work of the monasteries, and was responsible for law reform, unifying the laws of England.

8 Where 'honour' is the virtue sought, and wealth (land and houses) and power for the honour attached. These would still be a highly disciplined people but contentious and ambitious, who have the populace bound to them as servants and supporters. See Plato, *Republic*, Book 8.

9 For an examination of an oligarchy over a very long period see John Julius Norwich, *A History of Venice*.

The great weakness of democracy was demonstrated after the Second World War in Italy, which was quite unable to keep a strong government for any length of time. Nazi Germany was clearly the rule of a despot. In Russia and other communist states there was an unusual situation where tyranny was centred sometimes on a party and sometimes on a person. These different forms of government which Plato outlined are still clearly recognisable.

Democracy, though it safeguards freedom, often leads to licence. All that democratic governments seek, as election year approaches, is to gain votes; so they govern largely from Levels 1 and 2. The only thing that can save a democracy from really running into trouble is Level 5, the inbuilt traditions of a nation. Fortunately the higher influence is written in. It gets eroded but it comes back again.

Comparing democracy with our diagram gives a sense of the current position. The great multitude of voters are at Level 1; they are very weak and incapable of putting things into words. Their strength is in saying 'No' but not saying what they want. The voice at Level 2 is very strong. The trades unions, the organisations which speak for particular sectors of the community,[10] and the various trade and industry associations have a powerful influence on government. In fact Level 2 is one of the strongest influences on government especially with the emphasis today on the accountant's viewpoint.[11] Level 3 is discreet, keeping its counsel very much to itself, working in a similar way to Level 1, by its veto. If traders and bankers are upset they will be heard. For instance, it is very clear at the moment that governments in the Euro area have to be careful not to get on the wrong side of the bankers,[12] but the bankers do not lead.

Level 5, in the form of hidden tradition, is also influential and has a very strong effect on civil freedom, though even that is being eroded. In the economic field tradition is missing almost completely; here the lead is very largely from Level 2.

Society may be governed by the wise, at Level 5 or 6, but even they can only anticipate and formulate the wishes of the people, they

10 These vary from one country to another. In addition to industry groups they are likely to include groups concerned with consumer rights, civil liberties, public education, public health (including specific groups around particular diseases and ailments), mental health, support for the elderly, for refugees, ethnic minorities, public housing, and more.
11 Large amounts of government energy are spent allocating money and debating the impact of legislation on particular financial interests.
12 Not least because at the beginning of the 21st century almost all governments are dependent on the banks (worldwide) to finance their debt.

cannot go against them. This happened with Moses. The Mosaic Law has quite a lot of limitations which Moses could certainly have bettered but that was all that the people could take.[13]

Level 4 is so dominant that it rules society and yet its power can come from anywhere on the scale. The one great advantage democracy has over other forms of government is its fluidity. If a nation changes its mind it only has to wait until the next election to vote into power any government it wants; in an extreme situation it will not wait that long.[14]

Service is always downwards. There used to be a beautiful tradition in the British civil service of ending letters with the phrase: 'I remain, your obedient servant'. This may ring hollow today but remember what lies behind those words.

In the last two hundred years there has been a very big general improvement in the prosperity of people especially in England.[15] This has come from a change of mind in the nation, but a change of mind qualified by lack of true knowledge of how to put into effect its wishes. The result is a hotch-potch of legislation to try to ameliorate conditions. Without a fundamental change in the values of society this kind of situation cannot be avoided. The real cause of the great improvements in the standard of living is the fact that people are no longer prepared to tolerate the conditions they accepted two hundred years ago. The English nation as a whole accepted land enclosures, which brought people to a state of poverty and apathy from which they have gradually emerged.[16]

This is not to say that all legislation is useless: in regard to personal relationships it is especially valuable. For example, there are now laws regulating the conditions under which people are allowed to work that workers would have found difficult to bring about by themselves. But when it comes to introducing legislation to improve the standard of living very little can be done.

---

13 For example, see *Leviticus*, 25 on the Jubilee Year. Moses was able to legislate against usury but not against private ownership of land. The pragmatic compromise was that land tenure was for a maximum of 50 years and then a redistribution took place, preventing the gradual monopolisation of land by the fortunate. See also *Isaiah*, 5, 8-10.

14 There are many examples of this: in those countries where the period for elections is not fixed, for example the fall of the Whitlam government in Australia in 1975; and where elections are fixed, the resignation of Richard Nixon as US President in 1974.

15 Conditions have generally improved throughout the English-speaking world over this time, but especially in England where wages and conditions in the 18th and 19th centuries were significantly worse than in the New World.

16 Despite the fact that in the last couple of decades fear of unemployment has seen working hours increase and wages drop across the whole English-speaking world.

Mitigation is directly opposed to freedom. This argument is often used as a justification for *laissez-faire*,[17] but is there much gain in preserving personal freedom in a society where there is no economic freedom, only licence and privilege? It depends whether the objective is privilege for the individual or freedom for everyone. People vote for the party offering the most privileges. But though they may enjoy freedom, privilege for the majority is impossible. This goes back to Plato's objection to democracy. Representation, yes, but Level 1 does not have the wherewithal to govern itself. Is it better for the direction to come from Level 1 or Level 7? Whichever level it is will have its effect on government at Level 4.

20.2 Tradition in Society

Tradition is shown on the diagram at Level 4 but the real root is at Level 5 – not the ritual and forms but the national traits and characteristics which outlast the centuries.

Describing the Saxons before they even occupied England, the Roman historian, Tacitus, wrote that they were:

> Severe in manners, with grave inclinations and a manly dignity. They live solitary, each one near the spring or wood which has taken his fancy.[18]

The French writer, Taine, in his *History of English Literature*, adds that:

> Even in villages the cottages were detached; they must have independence and free air. They had no taste for voluptuousness; love was tardy, education severe, food simple. Violent intoxication and perilous wagers were their weakest points, they sought in preference not mild pleasures but strong excitement. In everything, even in their rude and masculine instincts they were men. Each in his own house, on his land and in his hut, was his own master, upright and free, in no wise restrained or shackled. If he bends, it is because he is quite willing to bend; he is no less capable of self-denial than of independence, self-sacrifice is not uncommon, a man cares not for his blood or his life.[19]

These characteristics are still recognisable even at the beginning of the 21st century. In the English-speaking world people still build their houses as far as they can from their neighbours, and choose the most

---

17 A term used in Economics to mean unregulated by government.
18 H.A. Taine (1873), *History of English Literature*.
19 *Ibid.*

remote seat in the railway carriage, taking an empty compartment if possible. It is all in their nature. How different from those with Latin blood in their veins!

Level 5 does not change; there is something natural, inbuilt, which persists from generation to generation. For example, the tradition of working for others without reward had been largely covered up but now, slowly, is beginning to emerge again. Tradition belongs above this barrier between Levels 4 and 5; it is more powerful than theories, opinions and beliefs and hence, movements such as Clean Up Australia, the Great American Clean Up,[20]Clean Up Britain, Keep New Zealand Beautiful and the Great Canadian Shoreline Cleanup resonate powerfully although they may have only a small impact on the environment.

In the law courts tradition is so strong that lawyers and judges still work in the light of principles established when Henry II's[21] judges were setting down the common law eight hundred years ago. It is worth noting that the common law was not established under a democratic government.

For knowledge to be freely available to serve the lower levels, understanding is needed. But tradition is very powerful and can fill this step through an innate sense of values so that one may come under the influence of the higher levels without understanding the laws by which tradition is governed. This is a great blessing and brings justice and goodness into the lives of ordinary people. Over the ages judges, church, universities and government have served their nations through the power of tradition and in this way, despite great problems and a loss of direction, much good continues to flow.

In the economic sphere today both understanding and tradition are missing and so the government is ruled by theories arising from the lower levels; the methods applicable to running a business or to maintaining credit are being used to govern a nation. The trades unions, industry groups, and bankers, among others, provide the theories and opinions and these are given the backing of law by Level 4.

20.3 Conclusion

Influences from the higher levels manifest lower down as principles. The relevance and application of these principles is often not easily recognised; they need to be interpreted into a form that will guide

20 Under the umbrella of Keep America Beautiful.
21 King of England from 1154-1189.

ordinary behaviour so that each person may act from principle or, as Emerson says, may be 'self governing'.

For instance, almost everyone would acknowledge as a guide for human relationships the Christian principle that says, 'Thou shalt love thy neighbour as thyself.'[22] Few though, if asked, would be able to express what this means for practical life. In 1932 in his speech giving judgement in a famous case in English law,[23] the judge (at Level 4) said: 'The rule that you are to love your neighbour becomes in law, you must not injure your neighbour...' To the question, ' Who is my neighbour?', the judge went on: 'The answer seems to be – persons who are so closely and directly affected by my act that I ought reasonably to have them in contemplation as being so affected...' It is therefore every manufacturer's responsibility to take reasonable care to ensure that no consumer is harmed by the product. This decision is the foundation of legislation on negligence and consumer protection.

Today the institutions of Level 4 have lost much of their influence. The churches are struggling to find a sense of direction; the universities have become workshops and training schools for Level 2. The law courts have preserved much of their influence in the civil field, although they are heavily overburdened and their work retarded by the amount of new statutory legislation especially in the economic sphere. But when there is a need to preserve civil freedom they work very quickly. An injunction to prevent the infringement of a person's recognised legal rights can be speedily obtained from the court. A writ of *habeus corpus*[24] is always readily available to prevent anyone being wrongfully imprisoned.

Whether or not a wise ruler is generally acknowledged matters little; it is important only that his influence prevails. This can only happen when the nation as a whole understands, albeit instinctively, that duties are meant to be observed. For this is the interval between Levels 4 and 5 needs to be filled. Nor need the rulers be at the level of government; they can work from beyond it.[25] Today the high regard

22 *St Mark*, 12, v.31, King James translation.
23 *Donoghue v. Stevenson*, House of Lords 1932, quoted in L.L. Blake, *The Royal Law*, Chapter 1, Shepheard-Walwyn, 2000.
24 Meaning a person must be presented in court, and can only be imprisoned if the court finds it lawful.
25 The Chinese philosopher Lao Tsu (551-479 BCE), *Tao Te Ching*, Chapter 17, put it: 'The highest type of ruler is one of whose existence the people are barely aware. Next comes one whom they love and praise. Next comes one whom they fear. Next comes one whom they despise and defy.'

for civil justice has filled the interval so that at least in that sphere there is a great degree of freedom. The rulers who have made this possible are not the government, the supreme courts, or the law lords. They are the many men of understanding at Level 5 and beyond whose work laid down and has maintained our common law and our judicial system over the centuries. It is true indeed that people do not know their rulers and claim the credit for themselves.

Afterword

THE LAW OF RENT is the expression of natural law which lies at the root of the Science of Economics. It is as fundamental to Economics as the law of gravity is to physics. But the law of rent will never be grasped through learning alone. It requires us to look around and observe. Out of observation grows experience, and out of experience grows understanding. Those very things which are self-evident are the most difficult to discover; they are so obvious that we ignore them. The conclusion of Leon MacLaren's original course material stressed this essential need for observation as follows:

> We will all remember from our schooldays the delightful story of Archimedes, the Greek natural philosopher, whose task it was to test whether a crown was of pure gold or had been debased. The specific gravity of gold was known – all that was needed was to measure the crown's volume. But in view of its intricate design, the question was how to do this without destroying it. It is told that as he stepped into his bath it overflowed – and there was the answer to his question: the volume of an object is equal to the volume of the water it displaces.
>
> Observation, experience, understanding. No wonder Archimedes is said to have run naked through the streets of Athens shouting, 'Eureka!' To this day this simple, self-evident fact is still known as the 'Archimedes Principle' and part of the apparatus used for measuring volume in this way is known as an eureka can!
>
> So it is in Economics. Like Archimedes, what we need to know is all around us and is just as self-evident as the fact that the volume of an object is equal to the volume of the water it displaces. But without training we do not see the self-evident, we are too busy looking for the obscure and complicated. The training we need is to use our eyes and ears, and our other senses, so that we may accurately observe what is all around us. From observation we move to experience. What we have learned is then no longer theory – we feel it in our bones. Then, in time, we can move from experience to understanding – understanding of the natural laws by which society is governed.

258

Many implications of this analysis are obvious even within the current scope of Economics, the most fundamental being that many economic ills could be dealt with by the collection of the economic rent, but it does not stop there. Any shifting of the primary source of taxation from earned to unearned income would, among other things, go a long way towards lifting the burden from the marginal site, encouraging new enterprises and removing some of the factors that cause production to move offshore. An understanding of the nature of secondary claims could lead to much better management of financial markets.[1] When understood, the concept of the lowest acceptable level of earnings could change the way economic modelling is conducted.

The course concluded with the following paragraphs:

Much time has been spent here discussing the natural order of things. Why not concern ourselves merely with the economic situation as it is? Consider for a moment the study of medicine. The first necessity is to study the workings of the body in good health, in its natural state. When that has been mastered, then is time enough to study the diseased body, to diagnose its disorders and prescribe treatment. In so doing, the physician should never lose sight of the healthy state of the body. This should be the constant touchstone for his work.

So it is in Economics. Only by studying the natural state of the body of society can we discover the causes by which it is governed. When these been mastered we can turn our attention to the disorders of society as it is today. But we must not become fascinated and mesmerised by its intricate details and technicalities. We must constantly bear in mind the economic causes from which the present situation has arisen, for only by constant reference to those causes can real understanding grow.'

The study of Economics as we know it began with Adam Smith. His book, *An Enquiry into the Nature and Causes of the Wealth of Nations*, was based on an extraordinary collection of observations – some direct and some acquired through study. Very little in this book contradicts his observations. For Adam Smith, however, the focus was wealth[2] and the command over it. This rapidly leads to a view of the 'economy' as

---

1 Dirk Bezemer identified that only a handful of observers predicted the financial crises of 2008 and of those that did the difference was that their models included the flow of funds into financial assets. 'No One Saw This Coming: Understanding Financial Crisis Through Accounting Models', Munich Personal RePEc Archive, 2009.

2 Note, for instance, the difference in emphasis between Adam Smith's description of the division of labour in *The Wealth of Nations*, Book I, Chapter I, and the description in Chapter 1.4, page 17, above.

an entity served by its workers and consuming the earth's resources for its own ends.

For Leon MacLaren human beings and the natural laws governing their activity are the proper subject of Economics. Men and women naturally work to satisfy their desires for physical, mental, emotional and spiritual wellbeing, and wealth is produced. Distribution of wealth is a function of natural law. If natural law is observed justice and prosperity will prevail. The system of land tenure our community accepts has deprived the great majority of both justice and prosperity. There is a high risk that the situation may soon become very much worse. The collection by the community of the economic rent would provide a basis to redress this danger.

During the 1966 course the question is asked, 'How may a nation change its mind?' No answer is given but one suggestion is that a nation may change its mind when, like the prodigal son,[3] its people's standard of living sinks to the least they are prepared to accept.

Today groups of people around the world are rallying against many forms of injustice in ways that did not occur a generation ago: against unfair global trade, the exploitation of labour in third world countries, excessive executive salaries, patents on naturally occurring phenomena, genetically engineered crops binding farmers to the patent holders, commercial projects which destroy people's traditional livelihoods, and more. Work is being undertaken to ensure the sustainable use of land, water, air and the biosphere. Writers are questioning the morality of the capitalist model; religious influences from the East are beginning to permeate the churches; new approaches to Economics are being explored.

These urgent enquiries are surely signs of desire for change.

The medieval culture developed out of a desire for protection from the turmoil in continental Europe after the decline of the Roman Empire; the scientific culture grew from a desire for spiritual, intellectual and physical freedom. The seeds of the next cycle are being sown now. If the desire for economic justice is strong, that will be what fertilises them.

3 *St Luke*, 15:11-32

Glossary of Terms

Capital – wealth used to produce more wealth. Capital includes tools, buildings and improvements made to the land that contribute to the productive process. Capital is the physical product of labour, not any right to it or its product. Shares and money are not capital as the term is used here.

Claims on wealth – a title to some part of production, usually held in the form of money. Claims on production represent a debt to the holder of the claim.

Company – a legal entity, at law an artificial person, formed for the purpose of conducting business that guarantees its owners limited liability for the actions of the company or its employees.

Corporation – *see* company.

Earnings – that share of production in terms of goods and services which individuals may obtain as a result of their work, irrespective of whether they own the business or work for another. Earnings here includes any subsidy the individual may receive from the government but excludes any taxation paid as a result of the employment.

Economic rent – the measure of the advantage to the tenant of any particular site over the least advantageous site in use. Ultimately the economic rent is measured in terms of goods and services rather than money. In this book it could be either depending on the context.

Economic duties – the set of natural obligations that arise in a community for the support of each individual, and the individual's contribution to the whole community.

Economics – the study of the natural laws which govern the relations between individuals in society.

Interest – the payment made by a person in return for the loan of a claim on wealth, usually, a loan of money. Interest is not related to capital.

Land – the term land is used in two senses in this book. In the first sense, in its natural state, it is the generic raw material for all production. In this sense it includes all natural resources in the universe that we can access:

sunlight, air, water and earth. A self-sown fruit tree is land, a fruit tree deliberately planted is capital; the fish in the ocean are also land, as is the oil under the floor of the ocean. In the second sense it means the space on the dry surface of the earth that is required to produce and/or retain wealth.

Landlord – the person (or company) holding legal or customary title to land, to whom a charge is paid for occupancy. Landlords may choose to occupy the land themselves, in which case they fulfil the roles of both tenant and landlord in this analysis.

Master-man – *see* Introduction, page 6.

Production – the process of turning natural resources into goods and services in order to satisfy human desires.

Rent – generally in this book by rent is meant the monetary payment made by a tenant to a landlord for the occupation of land. In the context of the law of rent, however, it is the measure of advantage to the tenant that any particular site has over the least advantageous site in use.

Secondary claims – charges made on the business by a third party by virtue of the power of that party. Secondary claims include the claims made by the landlord, taxation, interest, and insurance. In this sense they are not a cost of production but a charge on production. Secondary claims are always in monetary terms.

Tenant – the business operator, be it a person or a company, having exclusive access to the site. The tenant may be the owner of the site or may lease it. In the former case the business operator in economic terms fulfils both roles.

Tenant's share – what remains of net production on a site after earnings are paid. Note that the focus is on production and not monetary profit. Out of the tenant's share are paid secondary claims.

Tools – wealth used to aid production. Tools may range from bows and arrows to nuclear power stations. All tools are capital.

Wages – the net payment – made by an employer to an employee in monetary terms.

Wealth – land (natural resources) modified to satisfy human desires, that is, the product of labour applied to land. In this book wealth is not financial assets, nor is it land in any sense.

Select Bibliography

Anderson, Sarah & John Cavanagh, *Top 200: The Rise of Corporate Global Power*, Institute of Policy Studies, 2000.

Alves, Paulo & Miguel Ferreira, 'Who Owns the Largest Firms Around the World', in *International Research Journal of Finance and Economics*, Issue 21, 2008.

Aristotle, *Politics*, translated by B. Jowett, Harvard University Press, Forgotten Books Series, Cambridge, Mass, 1997.

Bible, King James Version.

Blackstone, William, *Commentaries on the Laws of England*, Facsimile Edition, University of Chicago Press, London, 1979.

Blake, L.L., *The Royal Law: Source of our Freedom Today*, Shepheard-Walwyn, 2000.

Carlyle, Thomas, *Sartor Resartus*, Oxford World Classics, 1999.

Collins, James C. & Jerry I. Porras, *Built to Last: The Successful Habits of Visionary Companies*, Random House Business, London, 2000.

De Roover, Raymond, *The Rise and Decline of the Medici Bank*, Beard Books, Washington DC, 1999.

De Soto, Hernando, *The Mystery of Capital: Why Capitalism Triumphs in the West and Fails Everywhere Else*, Basic Books, New York, 2000.

Dewey, Edward (1895-1978), as quoted in Will Slatyer, *The Debt Delusion*, Universal Publisher, Boca Raton, Florida, 2008.

Emerson, Ralph Waldo, *Collected Works of Ralph Waldo Emerson*, Harvard University Press, 1983.

Ferris, Paul, *The City*, Penguin Books, London, 1962.

Ficino, Marsilio, *Letters of Marsilio Ficino*, Volume 1, Shepheard-Walwyn, 1975.

Friedman, Milton, 'The Social Responsibility of Business is to Increase its Profit', in *New York Times Magazine*, 13 September 1970.

George, Henry, *Progress and Poverty*, The Robert Schalkenbach Foundation, New York, 1975 (first published 1879).

– *Protection or Free Trade*, The Robert Schalkenbach Foundation, New York, 1935 (first published 1886)

Gillett Brothers Discount Co. Ltd, *The Bill on London*, Chapman & Hall, 1976.

Hammond, John & Barbara, *The Town Labourer*, Fraser Stewart Book Wholesale Ltd, Abingdon, Oxford, 1995.

Hammond, John & Barbara, *The Village Labourer*, Fraser Stewart Book Wholesale Ltd, Abingdon, Oxford, 1995.

Hipple, Steven, *Monthly Labour Review Online*, September 2010, Vol. 1, 133, 9.

Hobson, Oscar, *How the City Works*, The Dickens Press, 1966.

Hodgkinson, Brian, *In Search of Truth*, Shepheard-Walwyn, 2010.

Justinian, *The Institutes*, quoted in Roscoe Pound, *Readings in Roman Law* ..., Harvard University Press, 1914.

Khaldun, *The Muqaddimah: An Introduction to History*, translated by Franz Rosenthal & N.J. Dawood, Princeton University Press, 1967.

Lao Tsu, *Tao Te Ching*, translated by John C.H. Wu, Shambhala Publications, Boston, 1961.

MacLaren, Leon, *Justice*, The School of Economic Science, London, 2001 (first published 1951).

– *Nature of Society*, School of Economic Science, London, 1947.

Marco Polo, *Travels of Marco Polo* (*c*.1280), translated by Ronald Lathem, Penguin, London, 1958.

Marx, Karl, *Capital*, translated by Samuel Moore & Edward Aveling, Charles H. Kerr & Co., Chicago, 1909.

Mencius, *Mencius*, translated by C.D. Lau, Penguin Classics, London, 1970.

More, Sir Thomas, *Utopia* (1556), translated by Ralph Robinson, Wordsworth Editions, 1997.

Nelson, Ralph L., *Merger Movements in American Industry 1895-1956*, National Bureau of Economic Research, Washington, 1959.

Norwich, John Julius, *The History of Venice*, Vintage Books, New York, 1989.

OECD, *OECD Factbook*, Organisation of Economic Co-operation and Development, 2010.

Peddle, Francis K., *Cities and Greed: Taxes, Inflation and Land Speculation*, Canadian Research Committee on Taxation, 1994.

Plato, *Laws*, translated by Benjamin Jowett;

– *Republic*, translated by Benjamin Jowett, W.J. Black, New York, 1942.

Reserve Bank of Australia, *Bulletin*, Reserve Bank of Australia, Sydney.

Ricardo, David, *On the Principles of Political Economy and Taxation*, G. Bell & Sons, London, 1927.

Rousseau, Jean-Jacques, *Basic Political Writings*, translated by Donald A. Cress, Hackett Publishing Company, Indianapolis, Indiana, 1987.

Schumacher, E.F., in Folkert Wilken, *The Liberation of Work*, Routledge & Kegan Paul, London, 1969.

Smith, Adam, *An Enquiry into the Nature and Causes of the Wealth of Nations*, Liberty Classics, 1981.

Stewart, John, *Standing for Justice*, Shepheard-Walwyn, London, 2001.

Taine H.A. *History of English Literature*, translated by H. van Laun, Chatto, London, 1920.

US Census Bureau, *Income, Poverty, and Health Insurance Coverage in the United States: 2009*, US Census Bureau, Washington, 2010.

US Census Bureau, *Business Dynamics Statistics*, 2009.

Vyvyan, John, *Shakespeare and Platonic Beauty*, Barnes & Noble, Inc, New York, 1961.

Wakefield, Gibbon, *England and America: A Comparison of the Political and Social State of Both Nations*, Volume 1, Richard Bentley, London, 1833.

Wakefield, Gibbon, *The Collected Works of Gibbon Wakefield*, Harper Collins, New York, 1968.

Yunus, Muhammad, *Banker to the Poor*, Aurum Press, London, 1998.

Index

Access to natural resources: controlled by landowner, 21; stages of production, 18

Advances, 120

Advertising: and price, 92; two types, 93

Airlines: monopolies after WWII, 91

Alfred the Great, 176, 251

Aristotle: Slavery, 60

Asquith, Prime Minister, 225

Auctions: price, 88

Bailment, 119

Banking, 116; AAA securities, 131; advances, 120; central bank, 122; collateral, 131; contemporary, 129; deposits, 119; evolution, 116; fees & interest, 121; hierarchy of society, 236; land enclosure increases risks, 124; micro-credit, 133; needs double entry accounts, 117; other business activities, 131; payment system, 121; ratings agencies, 131; requires trust, 116; usually short term finance, 125

Bill of exchange: private money, 110

Black death, 204

Blackstone, 210

Borrowing: claims on wealth, 72

Bradford Corporation v. Pickles, 206

Bretton Woods Agreement, 161

Bubble Act of 1720, 142

Building Societies, 130, 214; don't create money, 116

Buyer: and price, 86

Canals: industrial revolution, 66; needed limited liability, 142

Capital: accumulation of, 125; and interest, 149; defined, 261; *see also* Tools

Capital cities: and community, 238; examples, 24

Capital gains tax – *see* Taxation

Capitalism: cause of, 146; earnings low, 70; rise of, 63; vs socialism, 70

Common law – *see* Law

Central bank, 122

Cheques: private money, 112

Chicago Board of Trade, 237

Civil duties, 56

Civil freedom: set by traditions, customs and man made law, 245

Civil rights, 57, 60, 248, 252; and earnings, 56; England 13th century, 55; freedom, 56; required for economic development, 57

Civilisation: and community, 22, 240; bring advantage to business, 30; Christian & Roman, 164; influence of, 13

Claims on wealth: defined, 261

Clearings banks, 116

Clipping coins: Inflation, 136

Common land, 202, 203, 204, 205, 210; administration, 200; enclosed, 52; Saxon England, 51

Common law, 59, 61, 203, 207, 216-17, 255

Community, 22; facilitates specialisation, 17

Companies, 140; a legal person, 142, 143; boards controlled by institutions, 144; ethics, 147; multi-national, 143; nature of, 144; no relation of owner to company, 144; origins in UK, 140; origins in USA, 142; shareholder involvement, 145; started by entrepreneurs, 144; tax less than income tax, 143

Company: defined, 261

Cooperation, 46

Corporations – *see* Companies

Cotton mills: Lancashire, 25

Credit, 97, 101; bridges time gaps, 109; definition, 101; limitations of credit, 123

Credit cards: not money, 115

Credit unions – *see* Building societies

Culture, 242

266

Ecclesiastical history of England
Bede, Penguin Classics

Afterword